The Thracian Maid and
the Professional Thinker

SUNY Series in Contemporary
Continental Philosophy

Dennis J. Schmidt, Editor

THE THRACIAN MAID
AND THE
PROFESSIONAL THINKER

Arendt and Heidegger

(La fille de Thrace et le penseur professionel: Arendt et Heidegger)

by
Jacques Taminiaux

translated and edited by
Michael Gendre

State University of New York Press

Originally published in France under the title
La fille de Thrace et le penseur professionel: Arendt et Heidegger
by Jacques Taminiaux. Copyright © Editions Payot, 1992

Published by
State University of New York Press, Albany
© 1997 State University of New York

For information, address State University of New York Press,
State University Plaza, Albany, N.Y. 12246

Production by Marilyn P. Semerad
Marketing by Dana E. Yanulavich

Library of Congress Cataloging-in-Publication Data
Taminiaux, Jacques, 1928–
     [Fille de Thrace et le penseur professionel. English]
     The Thracian maid and the professional thinker : Arendt and
Heidegger / by Jacques Taminiaux ; translated and edited by Michael
Gendre.
         p.   cm. — (SUNY series in contemporary continental
philosophy)
     Includes bibliographical references.
     ISBN 0-7914-3861-9 (hardcover : alk. paper). — ISBN 0-7914-3862-7
(pbk : alk. paper)
     1. Arendt, Hannah.   2. Heidegger, Martin, 1889–1976.   I. Gendre,
Michael.   II. Title.   III. Series.
B945.A694T35   1997
320.5'092—dc21
[B]   97-30557
                                                                                  CIP

10 9 8 7 6 5 4 3 2 1

Contents

Preface

Since this book was written and came out in French, the corpus of Arendt's texts liable to shed some light upon the theoretical debate with Heidegger has been augmented, first, by the posthumous collection of a number of articles unpublished or difficult to find, *Essays in Understanding 1930–1954* (ed. Jerome Kohn, New York: Harcourt Brace, 1994), and, second, by the publication of *Qu'est-ce que la politique? (What Is Politics?)* (ed. Ursula Ludz, French trans. Sylvie Courtine-Denamy, Paris: Le Seuil, 1995), a collection of seven manuscripts conceived as materials for an "Introduction to Politics" that the German publisher Klaus Piper had suggested to Arendt in 1955 but which was never completed.

Although those publications might warrant a nuance here and there in the reading approach I followed in this book, I do not think that they invalidate it in any way.

By contrast, concerning the intellectual relation under analysis in this book, some readers will not fail to object against my approach the results of an inquiry by Elzbieta Ettinger, whose small book, *Hannah Arendt/Martin Heidegger* (New Haven: Yale University Press, 1995), immediately gave rise in the press of the United States to a number of reactions voicing outrage and easily summarized under the motto that "love is blind." Its author relies upon the totality of the still unpublished correspondence between Arendt and Heidegger and also makes mention of letters sent by Arendt to her husband, Heinrich Blücher, as well as to Karl Jaspers, inasmuch as those letters evoke Heidegger. Limiting herself exclusively to a psychological level of inquiry, Ms. Ettinger claims to prove—drawing heavily on carefully selected quotations from Arendt's letters and summaries of those by Heidegger—that Arendt, who supposedly never recovered from the early death of her father, always remained with respect to Heidegger in a state of dependent infatuation and that Heidegger, who supposedly was above all mindful to preserve the mental peace secured for him by his wife

vii

and home, was nothing more than a manipulator in his dealings with Hannah Arendt. He allegedly was so during their secret love affair in the 1920s. He allegedly reassumed that position again after they came into contact in 1950, as he allegedly relished his ascendancy over his former student in the hopes of rehabilitating himself on the international scene, while hiding as long as possible his long years of compromising with the Nazi regime. Without ever bothering to consider the works of the two protagonists, upon whose relation she claims to shed some light, Ms. Ettinger attempts to reconstruct this relation by means of a somewhat hackneyed explanation: the former mistress was for ever in awe of her former lover, she received the support of too generous a husband, she was deadly jealous of the devoted wife, as much as the wife was of this former, immensely bright muse—and all three were under the spell of a cheater, who was nothing more than your average Nazi, yet gifted with a strange power of fascination. According to that account, everything happens as though Arendt—from the time she renewed her connection with Heidegger in 1950—had deliberately renounced any capacity to think for herself and to judge matters dealing with him. Only to her discharge would be the fact that Karl Jaspers also allegedly had lost that capacity in dealing with Heidegger.

Such a laborious psychologism would hardly deserve mention if it did not give the impression to a hurried reader that, on the one hand, Heidegger's work is merely the epiphenomenon of some visceral Nazism and that, on the other hand, the intellectual relationship of Arendt to the master who had seduced her can be summarized in three phases: the initial seduction of the 1920s, the bitter rejection in the years 1933–50, and the subsequent return to the dependent infatuation of a youth. In order to give any credit to this impression one must keep one's eyes tightly closed on the texts of either protagonist. For Ms. Ettinger's exorbitant claim that National Socialism was "Heidegger's ideology" (87) is tantamount to her refusal to grant any attention whatsoever to the works and written lecture courses of Heidegger from 1933 until the end of the war—in which, undoubtedly, expressions of homage to the "National Socialist Revolution" abound, but *always* in the name of the thought of Being and the pre-Socratics or Plato's *Republic* and *never* in the language of the official "ideology" of the regime, which is explicitly held at a distance. In addition, the claim Ms. Ettinger makes that, after their reunion in 1950, Arendt discharged her former lover of any responsibility because, in her eyes, he stood as "the personification of the *Geist*" (88) is tantamount to her refusal to ask whether the very notion of "personification of the *Geist*" has any meaning whatsoever for someone who centered her reflection on plurality. Likewise, we see Ms. Ettinger underscoring—without in any way questioning—that "a refrain in her letters to him was that her thinking would not have evolved as it had 'without what I learned from you in my youth'" (7, which quotes a letter of 8 May 1954) and she adds immediately—as though this were a total evidence that needed no further ado—"he inspired her thought." And it is indeed in the register of unquestioned evidence that the following sentence is sounded: "Apart from her personal feelings, studying under Heidegger was an enormously serious matter for her, as is evident in *The Human Condition* (1958), which, as she wrote to him, 'owes you, in every regard, almost everything'" (21, which quotes a letter of 28 October 1960). From such a claim it takes only one step to conclude that her dependency was not merely affective, but in addition intellectual.

Now, it is such a step that some level of attention to, and scruple in front of, the texts prevented me from taking. Already, Arendt's expression "almost everything" should give food for thought. What does the reservation hide? In addition, there should be food for thought in the fact that Heidegger's name is nowhere to be found in *The Human Condition*.

It is, then, a specific attention, a specific scruple that guided me in this study now in this English translation. The quotations and letter records alleged by Ms. Ettinger seem to confirm after the fact the legitimacy of my reading. They confirm, first of all, that this intellectual relationship was one way: he talked, she listened.

They confirm, in addition, that Arendt's two major philosophical works, *The Human Condition* and *The Life of the Mind,* reveal at every page not at all a dependency upon Heidegger, as Ms. Ettinger suggests, but rather a constant, and increasingly ironic, debate with him.

At the time when I wrote this book, I was unaware of the letter sent to Heidegger along with the German translation of *The Human Condition*. But I was aware of the tenor of Heidegger's Marburg lecture courses attended by Arendt who was fascinated by them. The textual confrontation of the lecture courses predating *Being and Time* with *The Human Condition* was sufficient to convince me that her work would not have been possible without Heidegger's teaching. Heidegger's teaching was the necessary condition for her investigations. But in no way was it the sufficient condition, as Ms. Ettinger suggests, because as soon as one confronts what Arendt says on "world," "work," "speech," the "political," with what Heidegger says, one cannot fail to note that Arendt, far from being an intellectual epigone of Heidegger, at every point delivers a retort.

It is up to the reader to decide whether it can still make any sense to consider this retort—in which little by little the entire history of philosophy is implied as it was also, from another perspective, in Heidegger's thinking itinerary—under the simplistic psychologistic headings of the mechanisms of fascination and the blindness of infatuation.

I wish to thank Michael Gendre for his long-standing interest in my work and his care in translating it.

The Thracian Maid and
the Professional Thinker

INTRODUCTION

The History of an Irony

In *The Life of the Mind* Arendt evokes the "absolute seriousness" with which in *Theaetetus* Plato recounts the story of the young peasant woman from Thrace who burst out laughing when she saw Thales fall into a pit while observing the motions of celestial bodies: "In his eagerness to know about the heavens, he could not see what lay at his feet" (174a, ff.). And Plato adds: "Anyone who gives his life to philosophy is open to such mockery. . . . The whole rabble will join the peasant girl in laughing at him . . . [as] in his helplessness he looks like a fool" (*L.M.*, I: 82–83). Regarding the rigid demarcation between the speculative thinker and the average individual Arendt adds the following commentary: "Kant . . . seems to have been unique among the philosophers in being sovereign enough to join in the laughter of common man" (*ibid.*, 83). To the name of Kant she could also have added Aristotle's since he is the one who in *Nicomachean Ethics* alludes to the Thracian maid and, regarding Thales, notes that it is perfectly possible to be *sophos* without ever being *phronimos*. In any case, one may think that in Plato's dialogues there was more irony than Arendt seems to believe, and indeed more so than in texts by Heidegger. There is, however, a curious passage in *Die Frage nach dem Ding (What Is a Thing?)* in which Heidegger repeats the story of the maid from Thrace related in *Theaetetus* and adds the following commentary: "The question 'What Is a Thing?' must always be rated as one which causes housemaids to laugh. And genuine housemaids must have something to laugh about" (*What Is a Thing?*, trans. W. B. Barton and Vera Deutsch, New York: University Press of America, 1967, p. 3). By just saying this much in this commentary Heidegger seems merely to repeat the Platonic distinction between the thinker and ordinary persons and the condescension of the former for the latter. But he does not limit himself to this alone and adds:

Philosophy, then, is that thinking with which one can start nothing and about which housemaids necessarily laugh. Such a definition of philosophy is not a mere joke but is something to think over. We shall do well to remember occasionally that by our strolling we can fall into a well whereby we may not reach ground for quite some time. *(Ibid.)*

Such a commentary suggests that at the very least on certain occasions Heidegger was aware of the risks of professional thinking.

In any case, Arendt's irony for professional thinking was itself the result of a slow transformation of her intellectual relationship to Heidegger, a relationship whose first phase was characterized by an overwhelming fascination, soon thereafter to be followed by an extreme bitterness. I would like to attempt to show here that the eventual irony, which can be sensed in *The Life of the Mind*, has much to do with the combined interaction *[jeu]*—but also the overcoming—of both the initial fascination and the subsequent bitterness.

Let us consider the initial fascination. It began in Marburg in 1924. She was eighteen years old and he was thirty-five. He was in the midst of composing *Being and Time* and giving courses or seminars all connected to the elaboration of his fundamental ontology. She was no young peasant maid, but an educated young woman from the bourgeoisie, a brilliant student in philosophy. The account of their love affair is of no concern to me here. The reason of her fascination has something to do with the history of ideas, and Arendt herself mentions it in the text of homage she wrote for Heidegger on his eightieth birthday. She recalls in those pages, which allude to Heidegger as well as Plato, that at the beginning of the 1920s "the rumor of Heidegger's teaching reached those who knew more or less explicitly about the breakdown of tradition and the 'dark times' (Brecht) which had set in, who therefore held erudition in matters of philosophy to be idle play and who, therefore, were prepared to comply with the academic discipline only because they were concerned with the 'matter of thought' or, as Heidegger would say today, 'thinking's matter'" ("Heidegger at Eighty," in *Heidegger and Modern Philosophy*, ed. Michael Murray, New Haven: Yale University Press, 1978, p. 295). The rumor, she wrote, that attracted them to Freiburg-in-Breisgau and later Marburg, "had it that there was someone who was actually attaining 'the things' that Husserl had proclaimed, someone who knew that these things were not academic matters but the concerns of thinking men—concerns not just of yesterday and today, but from time immemorial—and who, precisely because he knew that the thread of the tradition was broken, was discovering the past anew" *(ibid.)*.

The very words by which Arendt describes Heidegger's teaching at Marburg were used again almost verbatim in her introduction to the Gifford Lectures she gave at the University of Aberdeen. When she used them again, it was no longer to describe Heidegger's teaching, but rather her own way of approaching the treasures of a legacy, which in the words of René Char "is preceded by no testament" (*L.M.*, 1: 12). This reiteration means that a common denominator exists between Arendt and Heidegger, consisting in the effort to discover the past anew simply because the thread of the tradition was broken. This reiteration further suggests that their approaches overlap, but this does not mean that they are similar. In order to understand their difference it is necessary to gain some clarity for the "things themselves" that fascinated Arendt in Heidegger's teaching in 1924–25. In fact, a certain light is already shed by the very sentences of the 1971 homage "Heidegger at Eighty" which immediately follow the ones I have just quoted.

The text of the homage in no way specifies what those problems were, but the very tone in which the mention is made suggests that they mattered as much to Arendt as they did to Heidegger. Let us try to determine what they were.

"The immediate and urgent importance" talked about by Arendt is all the more surprising since one does not find a trace—to say the least—of any reappropriation whatever of Plato in her own work, whereas by contrast there exist many manifest signs of such a reappropriation in Heidegger's first works. It so happens that the text of homage to Heidegger at eighty refers in fact to the memory Arendt had kept of a lecture course Heidegger had given during the 1924–25 winter semester with the title *Interpretation Platonischer Dialog (Sophistes)*. It is therefore appropriate to go back to this lecture course in the attempt to come to terms as much as possible with our surprise.

As it turns out, the lecture course on *The Sophist* pronounced by Heidegger three years before the publication of *Being and Time* is the document which articulates clearly for the first time the question on the meaning of Being into a problematic, one that Heidegger soon thereafter would term "fundamental ontology." This lecture course, of which Arendt was a fascinated listener, has been recently reconstituted and edited by Ingeborg Schüssler (*GA*, 19, 1992). Let me determine from the introductory pages of this lecture course the essential points allowing Heidegger's fundamental ontology to make a claim on certain basic concepts of Greek philosophy all the while integrating and reappropriating them in his own way. In this process, my only intention is to establish the way in which this lecture course could open up a whole set of problems that were, or became, "of immediate and urgent importance" for Arendt herself.

At the very beginning of the lecture course Heidegger's argument underscores that philosophy in its cardinal form, which is metaphysics, is not a doctrine, but rather a form of existence, and even the highest.

In *The Sophist*, he claims, "Plato considers human existence according to one of its extreme possibilities, namely philosophical existence" (12). He adds, however, that Plato does not clarify directly what makes philosophy an eminent form of existence; Plato proceeds only indirectly by raising objections against a mode of being which the philosopher must set aside, that of the sophist. The sophist never gets past *doxa*, which is a gaze narrowly focused on what comes to appearance and at the outset is manifest. To *doxa* Plato opposes *aletheia*, truth. The negative and privative structure of that word is significant; according to Heidegger it indicates that "the Greeks had understood the 'non-veiled character' of the world as having to be conquered: the world is not available at the outset; at the outset it is not uncovered. And what is uncovered in natural life is precisely that which was no sooner uncovered than covered up again—covered up again because of *doxa*. Moreover, opinions get hardened into propositions which are repeated in the absence of originary seeing." That is why, according to Heidegger, the work of the lives of Socrates, Plato and Aristotle was "a struggle against sophistry and rhetoric" (16). This struggle is the conquest of a mode of existence dedicated to the ultimate possibility of uncovering *(erschließen)*, namely the uncovering of Being itself.

At this point of his exposition Heidegger in order to elucidate this uncovering in terms of existence decides to draw upon an Aristotelian treatise which he claims is focused on a detailed description of the possible modes of uncovering characteristic of the human *Dasein*. He has in view *Nicomachean Ethics* which, from that point on, he holds to be the best introduction for the study of the struggle mounted by Plato against sophistry. "Truth is a character of beings inasmuch as they stand against us, but in its ownmost meaning *(eigentlichsten)* it is nonetheless a determination of being of *Dasein* itself. This is what emerges and is given expression to when Aristotle says *alētheuei hē psychē* (1139ab5). Inasmuch as *psychē* characterizes the ownmost being of man, being-in-truth is a determination of *Dasein*" (23). Because Aristotle carefully explores the various ways of being-in-truth accessible to man while giving the highest status to philosophical existence, i.e., to being devoted to *sophia* or to the "authentic understanding *(eigentliches Verstehen)*" (22) of the Being of beings, Heidegger holds *Nicomachean Ethics* as tantamount to an ontology of *Dasein*, whose study may clarify retrospectively the Platonic conquest of philosophic existence.

Let me recall briefly the essential points of the analysis made by Heidegger of what he holds to be the Aristotelian ontology of *Dasein*. Actually, those points sketch out the very structure of his analysis of the *Dasein*, i.e., of the first step of his fundamental ontology. By the same token, I would like to suggest that those essential points amounted for Arendt to decisive and urgent themes for her own interpretation of active life and the life of the mind.

What Heidegger perceives in Aristotle's descriptions of the possibilities of human uncovering is a hierarchy of two modes of being that correspond to two levels of comportment. On the inferior level there is a deliberative and active comportment and, on a superior level, there is a contemplative and theoretical comportment. Let us first consider the Heideggerian interpretation of the Aristotelian analysis of the deliberative comportment.

Deliberative comportment itself is divided in two types of activity that are not on the same level. They are the activity of fabrication called *poiēsis* and, on a higher level, the activity of action called *praxis*. To these two activities or to these two comportments correspond two forms of uncovering, or two ways of being-in-truth. The mode of uncovering corresponding to the comportment of fabrication or production is a know-how, or *technē*. In the activity dominated by the light of *technē*, the principle of the being that must be produced resides in the agent or the fabricating individual: it is the *eidos*, the type or the model of the work or product. But this *archē*, or principle, is in no way in the product, for the product does not emerge from within itself, is not brought spontaneously or naturally to the light of day. By contrast, the *telos*, end or goal, of both *technē* and *poiēsis* does reside in the product; it is the work itself in which the productive activity reaches its accomplishment, i.e., what Aristotle calls *energeia* or *entelecheia*. This *telos* is not in the producer because, once completed, the work becomes independent from the producer. Moreover, as soon as it is here, the product may become an instrument for various goals and it may be used to satisfy the needs of many individuals. In addition, it falls within an infinite circle of means and ends. Because of the lack of equilibrium between *archē* and *poiēsis*, the ontological dignity of the doublet *technē-poiēsis* is afflicted with a deficiency: the agent of the activity cannot in it be concerned with his or her ownmost mode of being (40–47).

It is easy to recognize in this reading of Aristotle the anticipation of the analysis of everydayness in *Being and Time*. And, indeed, the first thematic analyses of everydayness during the Marburg period—especially *The Prolegomena to the History of the Concept of Time*—teem with vocables such as *Werk* and *Herstellung*, which are overwhelmingly present in the interpretation of *technē* and *poiēsis* given in the 1924 lecture course.

Higher than the level at which *technē* and *poiēsis* reside is the level involving the doublet *phronēsis-praxis*. *Phronēsis* is a mode of uncovering or being-in-truth adjusted to action *(Handlung)*. Heidegger insists on the fact that *phronēsis* overcomes the ontological deficiency affecting *technē*. For the goal of *phronēsis* is nothing external to the agent, nothing which falls outside of him or her, nothing which may become indifferent to him or her: the end of *phronēsis* is not beside the agent, it is rather his or her being itself. The goal, says Heidegger, is "of the same ontological character as *phronēsis*." This goal is *eupraxia*, i.e., human *Dasein* itself taken in the how *(Wie)* of its acting. But this goal of acting is equally its principle: "In *phronēsis* the theme is the ownmost being of *Dasein* itself and in it are apprehended at the same time the principle and the end of deliberation." In other words "*praxis* is for *phronēsis* both *archē* and *telos*" (48–51).

The most striking feature of this reading—schematically presented here—is the way in which it channels what according to Aristotle pertains to the ethical realm and is connected with the plurality of human affairs into a debate strictly dealing with ontology. To this extent, it is not exaggerated to recognize in the Heideggerian analysis of *phronēsis* the anticipation of the maxim requiring that "*Dasein* exist for the sake of itself," in short the anticipation of the analysis of care and authentic existence in *Being and Time*. Two remarks are sufficient to suggest this anticipation. First, Heidegger insists on the fact that *phronēsis* is required because at the outset "*Dasein* hides itself from itself and forgets itself" (51–53). Second, the constellation of German words by which he highlights the structure of *phronēsis-praxis* is itself sufficient to suggest a parallelism with the future analysis of care and the specific sight adjusted to the ownmost mode of being of *Dasein*. These notions are *Durchsichtigkeit* (transparency), *Gewissen* (conscience), *Entschlossen-sein* (being-resolute) and *Augenblick* (moment of vision).

But the anticipatory character of this analysis is manifested with even greater clarity in the very question raised by Heidegger to lead to his inquiry into what in Aristotle beyond *phronēsis* and also *epistēmē* stands as the highest potentiality of uncovering. This eminent potentiality is *sophia*, i.e., according to Heidegger "the authentic understanding of Being." He begins by underscoring that *epistēmē* and *sophia*, which are forms of *theōria* or contemplation, are also forms of *praxis* or existence, aiming at conquering the unveiling of Being. He underscores, next, that for Aristotle *sophia* is higher in rank than *phronēsis* and that as *bios theōrētikos* it represents "the highest meaning of human existence for a Greek" (61). And it is at this juncture that his question is asked: Why is there room for *sophia*, which is deemed of higher rank than *phronēsis*, if this *phronēsis* is oriented toward *Dasein* itself? In other words, "Why isn't there in Aristotle an identification between *sophia* and *phronēsis*?" (136). Put differently still, in ontological terms, "what is the meaning of Being on the basis of which Aristotle grants to *sophia* a rank higher than to *phronēsis*?" (164).

The answer to this question, we can see fairly quickly, will have two stakes, Being and Time: Being, because for the Greeks *Dasein* is not the highest being there is on earth and thus the being of *Dasein* seems ontologically deficient; time, because for the Greeks the highest being is the one that is always and for ever, whereas human *Dasein* is mortal. Consequently, the Greeks believed that human *Dasein* reaches its highest possibility of being-in-truth not by turning toward *Dasein* itself but by "remaining as long as possible within the pure consideration and within the pure presence of what is eternal" (171). *Sophia* is the pure contemplation by means of which the Greek philosopher who experiences the *bios theōrētikos* is immortalized or reaches *eudaimonia*, a word which Heidegger translates without hesitation as "authenticity" (*Eigentlichkeit*) (see 172–79).

Thus, the meaning of Being in Aristotle is Time. It is with respect to time that he grants a higher dignity to *sophia*. But the time focused upon for understanding the meaning of Being is a specific time understood as the constant presence of the present. This poses for Heidegger the question of knowing why the present is being privileged in this fashion. "Why can't the past and the future claim such a right? Shouldn't Being be understood from temporality as a whole?"

This question, we can surmise, was a decisive one for fundamental ontology. Fundamental ontology would soon show that the very time in which past and future count as much as—and even more than—present is the finite temporality of a *Dasein*. It is this temporality which would become the new center of gravity of ontology and bring about a complete metamorphosis of the Aristotelian ontology of *Dasein* in the reappropriation sought and brought about by Heidegger. At the outcome of this metamorphosis-reappropriation, Heidegger is still in agreement with Aristotle and Plato in granting *bios theōrētikos* the status of the highest possibility for *Dasein*, i.e., authentic existence. But he parts entirely with Aristotle when he changes the orientation of *theōria*. Instead of considering the perpetual being of *physis*, *theōria* in Heidegger's fundamental ontology has eyes only for the being mortal of *Dasein*. As a result, instead of being separate from *phronēsis*, *sophia* in the Heideggerian sense intimately connects with it. More specifically, its essential task consists from now on in redoubling *phronēsis* inasmuch as the latter is understood in purely ontological terms as the pre-ontological discovery of *Dasein*'s being, a status which Heidegger attributes to the seeing inherent in resoluteness. In other words, the metamorphosis of the Aristotelian legacy is to consist in projecting *sophia* and *theōria* upon the axis of *phronēsis/praxis*. This very projection entails a deconstruction of the Greek privilege given to *ousia*, or to the presence of the present. The deconstruction aims at showing that it is by dint of a movement consisting in *Dasein*'s falling from its *praxis*, from the assumption of its ownmost potentiality for Being—i.e., by dint of a fallenness leading *Dasein* to granting superiority to the everyday comportment of *poiēsis* or production—that this *Dasein* is put on the way of focusing on *ousia*, on the *Vorhandenheit* or subsisting presence of the present instead of taking in view its own existence. In other words, the pollution of *sophia* by *poiēsis* and *technē* explains that the Greek ontologist grants more attention to the being of nature than to his own being. The reason is that Being in the sense of the subsisting presence of nature is that which the activity of production never ceases presupposing and taking for granted.

This brief sketch is sufficient to clarify the sense in which, for Heidegger, a methodical reading of Plato's *Sophist*—which celebrates *bios theōrētikos* in the light of *Nicomachean Ethics* interpreted as an ontology of *Dasein*—(indeed "opened up the way for a set of problems of immediate and urgent importance." For his reading reveals several of the essential problems of his own fundamental ontology. It is even the entire structure of his analysis of *Dasein*, namely the tension between on the one hand public and fallen everydayness and on the other one's ownmost possibility, that is being sketched out in this interpretation of the Aristotelian analysis of *poiēsis* and *praxis*.

Now all this actually renders all the more enigmatic Arendt's words in her text of homage. For never did she take a share in the task of a fundamental ontology. After she left Marburg to work on her doctoral thesis under the directorship of Jaspers in Heidelberg, she found her interest in the concept of love in Augustine and subsequently in the life of Rahel Varnhagen: these are texts without any trace of a concern for fundamental ontology. I do not mean that it is impossible to detect already in her doctoral thesis the first signs of an oblique debate with Heidegger: in a sense this debate is already announced in the resistance that Arendt feels toward the Augustinian theme of the nothingness of the world.[1] But the point is that already then as well as in her subsequent work no traces of a fundamental ontology are to be found. But then how could she seem to claim that Heidegger's course on *The Sophist* opened up the way for "a set of problems of immediate and urgent importance" for herself?

In order to elucidate this question, it is appropriate to consider briefly the extreme bitterness that followed upon her initial admiration, for I think it is because of this bitterness that the themes treated by Heidegger in the lecture course on *The Sophist* initiated the motion that gave rise in her to questions of "immediate and urgent importance."

Extreme bitterness about Heidegger is the foremost feature of the first philosophical article Arendt published in America immediately after the war. It came out in *The Partisan Review* (13: 34–56) under the title "What Is *Existenz*-philosophy?" Concerning Heidegger's fundamental ontology, the article is tantamount to a violent rejection of it in the name of Jaspers and his philosophy of communication. Arendt's bitterness was comprehensible. She could not ignore that it was in the language of fundamental ontology, which is the very one Heidegger was forging around 1924, that he defended the National Socialist revolution of 1933. She knew that the "Rectorial Address," after the 1924 lecture course, celebrated the *bios theōrētikos* of the Greeks and presented itself as a sort of remake of Plato's *Republic*. In light of these painful developments she might have recalled a surprisingly foreboding remark of 1924 on Plato's concept of the philosopher-king. Heidegger said: "Admitting that *phronēsis* is the most serious and decisive knowledge, then the science developing in the field of *phronēsis* would be the highest science. And inasmuch as man is a *zōon politikon*, inasmuch as his *Dasein* is with others, then authentic *sophia* would be political science. As a consequence, the philosopher might be the true politician" (135–36). Yet in her article of 1946 Arendt does not seem to consider the possibility of a link between Heidegger's political blindness and the peculiar style of his reappropriation of Plato and Aristotle affecting his fundamental ontology. In any case it is not this question that is at the center of the article. Its leading characteristic is rather the abrupt dismissal of any connection between Heidegger and herself. Self-centeredness, attraction for nothingness, irresponsibility, deceptive genius, despair, Romanticism—such are the terms she uses to dismiss fundamental ontology. In other words, limiting ourselves to this article, it seems almost impossible to understand why twenty-five years later she would claim that Heidegger's teaching at the time of the gestation of the fundamental ontology could have made her suddenly aware of "a set of problems of immediate and urgent importance." In any event, although Jaspers liked the article, we know from Elizabeth Young-Bruehl that Arendt always refused to include it in any of her collected articles.[2] But if we consider this small writing in hindsight and from the perspective of her subsequent work, we cannot fail to note in it the announcement, so to speak *a contrario*, not of a subsequent agreement but rather of a debate with Heidegger.

From this perspective let me recall a few significant points of the article.

Apparently in full agreement with Jaspers, she concluded her text in the following terms:

> Existenz itself is never essentially isolated; it exists only in communication and in the knowledge of the Existenz of others. One's fellow men are not (as in Heidegger) an element which, though structurally necessary, nevertheless distroys Existenz; but, on the contrary, Existenz can develop only in the togetherness of men in the common world. In the concept of communication there lies embedded, though not fully developed, a new concept of humanity as the condition for man's Existenz. In any case, men move together within this "surrounding" Being; and they hunt neither the phantom of the Self nor do they live in the arrogant illusion that they can be Being generally.[3]

These sentences—given in conclusion of a quick overview of the existential analytic, introduced under the title "The Self as All and Nothing: Heidegger" (46)—condense the import of Arendt's critique. In her view the Self in *Being and Time* is everything because it is within it that the answer to the question on the meaning of

Being is to be found: since its essence is to exist, the Self takes the place formerly occupied by God in traditional metaphysics and thus becomes "master of Being." But this Self is nothing because the authentic mode of being, which is the center of care for *Dasein* in its most intimate potentiality-for-Being, entails in the end the nothingness of all beings, of others as well as of itself: indeed, it is in the anticipation of its own death that *Dasein* becomes a *Selbst*. According to Arendt, the Heideggerian notion of resoluteness—"the arrogant passion to be a Self"—is therefore contradictory. Only a complete withdrawal from the world would allow it to succeed. But because this is impossible, the Self is condemned to a constant "fall" and its resolution is the admission of an insurmountable failure. This notion is not merely contradictory, it is also "really contrary to Man" (*ibid.*, 51).

> The most essential characteristic of this Self is its absolute egoism, its radical separation from all its fellows. The anticipation of death as existential was introduced to achieve this; for in death Man realizes the absolute *principium individuationis*. Death alone tears him from the context of his fellows, within which he becomes a public person and is hindered from being a Self. Death may indeed be the end of human reality; at the same time it is the guarantee that nothing matters but myself. With the experience of death as nothingness I have the chance of devoting myself exclusively to being a Self, and once and for all freeing myself from the surrounding world. (*Ibid.*, 50)

Reading this critique in light of her own subsequent work—especially *The Human Condition* and *The Life of the Mind*—it is not possible to avoid thinking that the bitterness of 1946 called for—beyond refusal and rejection—a future work of analysis, demonstration and justification. For it is one thing to deny that the anticipation of death is the unique principle of individuation; it is another to show that very different factors determine individuation. It is one thing to claim that the Heideggerian resoluteness is merely an arrogant and contradictory passion; it is another to demonstrate that the Self cannot be without public relationships. It is one thing to substitute the notion of a common world conceived as habitat for the Heideggerian concept of authentic world; it is another to determine how a human world is constituted as common habitat.

It is well known that as soon as Arendt attempted those demonstrations in *The Human Condition* she reappropriated in her own way the legacy of the Greek tradition. Regarding this point, many experts of political theory were surprised by the stress she was putting on Homer or Pericles and by her argument for *doxa,* or by her insistence on themes such as immortality and *eudaimonia.* All this is less surprising if one keeps in mind that, most of the time, these analyses are retorts to the reappropriation of the Greeks conducted by Heidegger at the time of the genesis of his fundamental ontology and already, more specifically, in the lecture course on *The Sophist.* When Heidegger considers the Greek world, it is with respect to one single criterion: the excellence of *bios theōrētikos* celebrated by Plato. In this fashion, he accepts as given and unquestionable the legitimacy of Plato's struggle against *doxa,* sophistry and rhetoric. He therefore lends no attention whatever to the previous criterion of excellence against which Plato stood opposed: that of *bios politikos.* Never therefore did Heidegger consider the possibility for *doxa,* the discourse of the sophists, and rhetoric, of being quite legitimate with respect to that previous criterion. No testimony to the excellence of that other *bios* is ever taken into consideration by him. There is no doubt in his mind—and he admits so much unambiguously at the beginning of *Being and Time*—that compared with Plato's *Parmenides* or Aristotle's *Metaphysics* all of Thucydides is superficial. This explains that when Heidegger is inspired by the Aristotelian analysis of *poiēsis* and *praxis,* he is led to inscribing the analyses within the strict framework of his ontology of *Dasein* and to subordinating them entirely to the superiority of *bios theōrētikos* conceived as understanding of Being. Because this *bios,* as philosophical and contemplative existence, is solitary and private, because it is deemed to be the highest form of action, all other activities, namely, the productions of works, public interaction, interlocution, are relegated within an anonymous sphere afflicted with fallenness. This Platonic bias in Heidegger is underscored by Arendt a few years after the violent 1946 article of *The Partisan Review* in a lecture on "The Concern with Politics in Recent European Philosophical Thought," in which she said:

> Thus we find the old hostility of the philosopher toward the *polis* in Heidegger's analyses of average everyday life in terms of *das Man* (the "they" or the rule of public opinion, as opposed to the "self") in which the public realm has the function of hiding reality and preventing even the appearance of truth." (*E.U.,* 433)

Arendt's analysis of active life in *The Human Condition* may be considered as the attempt to consider from a fresh perspective all the Platonic and Aristotelian themes reappropriated by Heidegger in the lecture course on *The Sophist* and subsequently in *Being and Time: doxa*, rhetoric, work, action, public and private, immortality, *eudaimonia*. This reexamination is carried out with respect to *bios politikos*. It is with respect to this non-Heideggerian criterion that Arendt was led to realize after the fact that the problems raised by Heidegger in the 1924–25 lecture course were in fact of "immediate and urgent importance" for her. To be sure, Heidegger's name is not even mentioned in the whole work; but the reason is merely that in it she does not address *bios theōrētikos* itself. The book as a whole however—in its structure as well as in its themes—may be viewed as a retort to Heidegger with respect to the previous type of excellence which *bios theōrētikos* aimed at supplanting. In any event, it is only by considering the matters from this perspective that I can understand why Arendt was so interested in having Heidegger read the German translation of *The Human Condition*. Heidegger did not like the book, perhaps because a former muse is rarely entitled to stand on the same footing as the one she inspired and perhaps because Heidegger never managed to confront directly the prejudices inherent in his fundamental ontology, in spite of many indirect retractations and his conceding—only once—that the publication of *Being and Time* had been a "disaster" *(Unheil)*.[4]

A few remarks on three themes of Arendt's book will suffice to highlight this feature of retort. They were already indicated in the very bitterness that marked her 1946 article. These themes are: the world, the principle of individuation, publicness.

Fundamental ontology establishes a clear cut distinction between what everydayness holds to be the world and the world in its ownmost, ontological sense. The world to which everyday comportment refers is the surrounding world, *Umwelt*, which presents itself as the functional context on the backdrop of which tools in general appear and the entities that are means for the sake of various ends. This environment is the intentional correlate of a concernful comportment, whose fundamental feature resides in the productive activity. The everyday world is pronounced inauthentic by Heidegger inasmuch as the production and preoccupation which animate it have eyes only for those beings whose mode of being is other than that of *Dasein*. By contrast, the world in the authentic sense is announced when the stability and the safety of the environment have been shaken and reduced to nothingness, as when tools break down or are revealed inadequate to the task at hand. Such a rupture foreshadows—but foreshadows only—the true experience of the world. Such an experience encounters nothingness face to face and is revealed in the fundamental mood of anxiety. By the agency of this mood what is being revealed is that the world in the ownmost sense is not at all a dwelling or a home that we inhabit in common, but rather strangeness, the absence of dwelling *(Unheim-lichkeit)* of the existing of *Dasein.* This world that is no longer a dwelling place is that for the sake of which *(Worumwillen)* a Self exists, outside of any relation with things and others and in a face to face with itself. What we recognize here is a very particular and highly metamorphosed reappropriation of an Aristotelian theme previously broached in the lecture course on *The Sophist,* namely the analysis of *praxis* as an activity that aims at *hou heneka,* at being for the sake of itself. But what is absolutely no longer Aristotelian in such a reappropriation is the fundamental solipsism entailed in the Heideggerian notion of *praxis* as being-in-the-world.

It is against this demarcation between a common or public world deemed inauthentic and an ownmost, solipsistic world that the descriptions of the world in *The Human Condition* are directed. Against any negative connotation of fallenness into the improper, the activity of production of works under description by Arendt is an activity that makes possible the duration of a properly human habitat—beyond the biological environment to which the activity of labor and the vital cycles that circumscribe labor are bound, inasmuch as labor and vital cycles leave nothing behind themselves. The activity of work or fabrication, starting with the fashioning of the most humble tools and ending in the production of useful artifacts beyond those consumer goods to which the labor activity is limited, is what gives "the world the stability and solidity without which it could not be relied upon to house the unstable and mortal creature that is man."[5]

In other words, whereas Heidegger attributes the persistence and stability of *Vorhandenheit* to nature, Arendt by contrast does not hesitate to consider insertion into nature as a renewed evanescence. Moreover, whereas Heidegger attributes to artifacts an intermediary status between natural persistence and the finite temporality of *Dasein,* Arendt's first step is to separate the artifact from nature and conceive nature as the cycle of being born and perishing—the artifact only being what endows the emerging human world with stability; likewise at the other pole, far from considering the time of the artifact as fallenness from the ownmost time of *Dasein,* she sees in the duration of the artifact the first condition of possibility for a properly human duration. This being said, a detailed analysis of the description Arendt makes of the activity of work would show that she accepts a great many aspects of the Aristotelian theory on *poiēsis*. Regarding this point, her debt to Heidegger's lecture course on *The Sophist* is beyond doubt, but there is no trace in her reappropriation of Aristotle of the movement leading Heidegger to emphasize the *Unheimlichkeit* of *Dasein*. There is a good reason for this. The life of a pariah to which Nazism condemned her for a number of years and her own trial of exile prevented her forever celebrating *Unheimlichkeit* in any fashion whatsoever.

And if the mentality of *homo faber* suffers in her eyes from a fundamental deficiency, the reason is not that it is linked as in Heidegger to a world that is a stable dwelling, but quite on the contrary that its fundamental utilitarianism leads to transform endlessly all ends into means for the sake of further ends, thus threatening the stability of every dwelling. Furthermore, if Arendt insists on the necessity of action as an activity of a rank higher than fabrication, it is not as in Heidegger in order to distance herself from the dwelling erected by *homo faber*, or for the sake of an ontological absence of dwelling. Instead, this higher rank points to the attempt of keeping dwelling safe, of maintaining a common and public world secure for the sake of *amor mundi*, which has no room in Heidegger's fundamental ontology.

What about the second theme, that of individuation? In fundamental ontology, individuation comes about by means of the face to face with nothingness, which means that every intercourse with things as well as every interaction with others must sink in order to allow *Dasein* to become individuated. More importantly, individuation is fundamentally hostile to communication and expression. At the outcome of his analysis of *Gewissen*, the internal forum and intimate knowing with the mission of calling every time each *Dasein* to assuming resolutely its own selfhood, Heidegger writes: "Dasein is *authentically itself* in the primordial individualization of the reticent resoluteness which exacts anxiety of itself" (*Being and Time*, 322; 369). In other words, to the celebrated question "Who is *Dasein*?" there can be an answer only in the ontological repudiation of every sharing of words and deeds. Such is the peak of the Heideggerian reappropriation of the Aristotelian teaching on the *hou heneka* of *praxis*.

The Arendtian concept of individuation is in many respects a reaction against such views. Indeed Arendt too poses the question "Who are you?" instead of the traditional question "What is the human being?" Moreover, in apparent agreement with Heidegger, she claims that individuation is not truly possible within the activity of production and that it requires action in order to come to light. Yet her notion of individuation contains no longer anything Heideggerian. Whereas Heidegger is focused on being-toward-the-end and on the anticipation of one's own death, which as a certain impossibility is the most individuated possibility, Arendt puts the burden of individuation on what she calls "natality," conceived not as the mere emergence of *zoē* but as a capacity to initiate something unforeseeable and exceptional. Whereas Heidegger divorces individuation from any interaction as a result of the anticipation of one's ownmost death, Arendt inserts it within human plurality. Where Heidegger separates authentic *praxis* from any communication and reserves its manifestation to the intimate and silent knowing of *Gewissen*, Arendt insists by contrast on the essential link between *praxis* and *lexis*.

> When I insert myself into the world, it is a world where others are already present. Action and speech are so closely related because the primordial and specifically human act must always also answer the question asked of every newcomer: "Who are you?" The manifestation of "who somebody is" is implicit in the fact that speechless action somehow does not exist or, if it exists, is irrelevant. (*L.W.A.*, 39–40)

It is hard to conceive of a clearer distancing from the analytic of *Dasein*. A final feature confirms this divergence. At the beginning of his introduction to his ontology of *Dasein*, Heidegger insists in full agreement with Plato's *Sophist* that the first philosophical step consists in "not *mython tina diegesthai*, in 'not telling a story'" (*S.Z.*, 6). On the contrary, in a gesture that reawakens Aristotle's *Poetics*, in opposition to both Plato and Heidegger, Arendt insists on the fact that "it is precisely in stories that the actual meaning of a human life finally reveals itself" (*L.W.A.*, 40–41). It is the narrative that reveals the individual "such as he is himself in the end" and grants him *post mortem* his *eudaimonia*. By contrast, after translating this word as *authenticity (Eigentlichkeit)*, Heidegger claims that the true meaning *(Bedeutung)* of human existence only reveals itself to the Self in the silence and solitude of an internal forum, in confronting one's mortality: *eudaimonia ante mortem*.

Not less patent is their disagreement concerning the public realm. Publicness in the Heideggerian sense is everydayness in which everyone is no one; it is the rule of the "they." Since everyday comportment is dominated by the activity of work, this is tantamount to saying that the public domain may be adequately understood in terms of fabrication. And when, by opposition to this comportment, Heidegger in the analytic of *Dasein* reappropriates in his own fashion the Aristotelian notion of *praxis* after metamorphosing it into authentic existence, it turns out that in his eyes this notion is entirely private and thus that a public *praxis* would be a contradiction in the terms.

Against this analysis, Arendt claims that the activity of *poiēsis* could never really be public because only the product is and may remain apparent, whereas *praxis* is essentially public because it is conditioned upon human plurality, upon the sharing of words and deeds in a common world of appearances. This reversal is the very fundament of her political thought.

It seems to me that, taken by themselves, the three previous points are retorts that sufficiently show that indeed for Arendt it became a matter of "immediate and urgent importance" to consider anew—from the point of view of *bios politikos*—the very themes of Heidegger's fundamental ontology and thus to surmount her bitterness. And if her reexamination was the target of many objections on the part of specialized scholars, historians and political scientists, it is because she was not aiming at some objective neutrality but rather at a hermeneutic reappropriation. In this measure only, as Heidegger had done previously, she came to make hers Nietzsche's recommendation in the second *Consideration Out-of-Season:* "It is only from the perspective of the highest force in the present. . . that we can discern what is worthy of being known and preserved, what is great in the past." But contrary to Heidegger, she assigned this highest force to one's active belonging in a common world of appearances.

What is the connection with the irony of the maid from Thrace in all of this? In fact the tonality of *The Human Condition*—when the time came for the task of identifying the various symptoms of blindness in the approach by various philosophers to active life—is not ironic yet. When she maintains that the status Plato grants to *bios theōrētikos*, and also Aristotle although less exclusively, induces a failure to acknowledge the specific articulations of active life and tends to subject action to the model of the fabricating activity, no irony looms in these views. In order for her to adopt an ironic attitude toward professional thinking, an extra step was necessary. Her irony emerged and gained substance when she realized that those who devote their lives entirely to *bios theōrētikos* not only fail to recognize the essential features of active life, but also wrap thought itself in various fallacies. I do not doubt that it is by comparing what she had retained of Heidegger's teaching at the time of the project of fundamental ontology with what he expressed in his post–World War texts that she came to realize this speciousness. I do not doubt also that the emergence of her irony toward the professional thinkers had something to do with a sort of self-critique. I mean to say that she came to realize along the way by reflecting upon *The Human Condition* that her 1958 book still remained influenced in spite of herself by the lecture course on *The Sophist*. Indeed, in spite of its implicit objections to Heidegger, in replies and retorts I highlighted, her book rests on the tacit presupposition that thought is ultimately contemplative, even though in the last page she wonders whether it is not perhaps an intense activity. Characterizing thought as contemplation: such is the central thesis of the 1924 thesis and of the entire project of fundamental ontology. At that time, Heidegger was saying repeatedly that thinking is a matter of knowing and that knowing is a matter of gaze. He claimed to agree with Plato on that point. Indeed fundamental ontology gravitates around the hierarchy of three forms of gaze, three levels of seeing. On the lowest level, there is according to Heidegger the intuitive grasp of what is at hand *(vorhanden)*. Once this intuition has been deconstructed, it turns out that the seeing that it contains is abstract and derived after a loss from a higher seeing, the one that illuminates productive and prospective circumspection, which Aristotle called *technē*. But this seeing also turns out to be derived and in a position of fallenness with respect to a still higher form of seeing, which is the moment of vision, or *Augenblick*, by means of which *Dasein* sees ontologically in full lucidity and transparency *(Durchsichtigkeit)* the finite totality of its potentiality-for-being. Fundamental ontology as a philosophical corpus claimed to limit itself to reflecting within the conceptual element of a theory on Being this eminent seeing, which sheds light pre-ontologically on existence itself. Of this pre-ontological seeing fundamental ontology claimed to be the anamnesis. As I have suggested above, the lecture course on *The Sophist*, which sheds light on the Platonic anamnesis by drawing upon *Nicomachean Ethics*, claims to show how this hierarchy of the levels of seeing rests upon a particular metamorphosis of the Aristotelian notions of *phronēsis* and *sophia*. Once metamorphosed, *phronēsis* is not longer what it was in Aristotle, the judgment on private and public matters; rather it becomes the silent seeing by an individual of his or her ownmost

potentiality-for-being. Consequently the new *phronēsis*, now become resoluteness, in addition to supposing a withdrawal from
human plurality and the common world of appearances in which
the mortals live, is deemed to be for each one the prelude to *sophia*,
conceived as understanding of Being. In 1924–25 Arendt had been
the fascinated witness of these metamorphoses. Her bitterness ex-
ploded when she came to realize that they had constituted the
backdrop for the arrival of Heidegger on the political scene in 1933.
Bearing witness to this bitterness, the 1946 article limited itself to
rejecting Heideggerian resoluteness as a contradiction and an impossible withdrawal from the world. Subsequently, *The Human
Condition*, which no longer bears any trace of this bitterness, takes
for granted also that the philosopher holds himself in a position of
withdrawal from the common world and that this withdrawal leads
to pure contemplation. Because of this feature, her book reiterates a
major theme of the 1924 lecture course, namely the thesis that in
the final analysis the accomplishment of *bios theōrētikos* is purely
contemplative and that thought consists in a sight by means of
which the mind *(nous)* extends beyond speech *(aneu logou)*. It is
after the fact only that irony appeared, when Arendt attempted to
question the very notion of "withdrawal" from the common world
of appearances, instead of abruptly rejecting this withdrawal or
defining it in terms of contemplation. This questioning was based
on the discovery that such a withdrawal is in fact essential to the
life of the mind and necessary in order to think, will, and judge.

Concerning thought, it would not be exaggerated to claim that
the analyses conducted by Arendt bear witness—at each step she
takes—to a renewed debate with Heidegger, but to a debate in
which her revived admiration is accompanied with irony. Her admiration was revived because, in her view, Heidegger was a living
testimony to what thinking is, the weaving of a Penelope, a task
with no end, an incessant *retractatio*, which burns today what
seemed to be valuable yesterday as stable product or work, an intense activity endlessly tracing new paths, which lead to still different ones, while these lead back to the first ones, in a labyrinth with
no way out. Her admiration can be explained also by the fact that
in her view Heidegger was not only one of the rare thinkers of the
West to have made his "residence" in the activity of thinking, but
also had been able to express the specific traits of this purely intransitive, "entirely non-contemplative" activity, an activity of
which one cannot say that it aims at knowledge, at a science where
it would find satisfaction, for it has no respite, never brings an

ultimate foundation to a seeing, edifies no doctrine or theory whatever. Her admiration, finally, was justified in that in the retrospective light of texts such as *What Is Called Thinking?*, *Zur Sache des Denkens*, *Gelassenheit*, she could make sense again of her initial fascination. It had not been owed to the talents of an architect of a new doctrine but to the fact that she had accompanied and shared an experience of thought, that is to say, as she herself wrote it in her text of homage for Heidegger at eighty, a "fresh rethinking of what was already thought" ("Heidegger at Eighty," *ibid.*, 298).

But her renewed admiration was doubled with irony. The very one who as early as the 1920s had devoted himself to the purely intransitive and non-contemplative activity of thinking was also the one who had proclaimed himself capable of an ultimate gaze. The very one who was in a constant dialogue with himself was also the one who claimed reaching a seeing *aneu logou*. The very one who claimed day after day to withdraw from the common world of appearances in order to think was also the one who suddenly claimed himself capable of giving advice to a tyrant. It was the same person in fact, who was involved in an endless questioning and also, all of a sudden, wanted to contribute a new solution of, and foundation for, human affairs.

The Life of the Mind should be read as an attempt to confront the irony of such contradictory developments.

I would like to conclude this introduction with a few remarks on her attempt. At the end of the first volume of that work Arendt wrote the following: "I have clearly joined the ranks of those who for some time now have been attempting to dismantle metaphysics, and philosophy with all its categories, as we have known them from the beginning in Greece until today" (*L.M.*, 1: 212). For those who read too fast this seems to say: "Ultimately I agree with Heidegger." But then why, at the beginning of the volume, did she underscore the loss of "the age-old distinction between the many and the 'professional thinkers' specializing in what was supposed to be the highest activity human being could attain to" (*ibid.*, 13)? Didn't Heidegger throughout his career repeatedly proclaim the privilege of that activity? Precisely, by contrast to Heidegger, the dismantling of metaphysics conducted by Arendt does not claim an exclusive privilege for thought. Her own experience of the horrible effects of totalitarianism taught her that dwelling was not in the thinking activity but in the common world of appearances shared in words and deeds by a plurality of human beings, a world that requires to be safeguarded as the public realm in which individuals express their judgment on human affairs. To be sure, she knew that, in order to protect this world, the thinking activity—an activity set in motion by *thaumazein* and whose questions in their quest for an ultimate are always without answers—is also necessary for it feeds both the capacity to judge, which is always inserted within a situation, and the movement of cognition, without ever being confused with them. But from the fact that "thinking" is necessary for the human condition, there does not result that the thinking activity should regulate the other activities—work-making, action, willing, and judgment. Consequently, instead of rekindling in a new fashion the ancient privilege of thought as in Heidegger post-*Kehre*, her own dismantling of metaphysics aimed at taking apart the fallacies brought in by this privileging. And concerning the thinking activity, the dismantling operated by Arendt consisted in locating thought with respect to a common world in which human beings interact, take initiatives on their own and express their judgments on specific events. In fact, the specious arguments she calls "metaphysical fallacies" all consist in hiding away the fact that the thinker belongs to the common world of appearances, even in hiding away the fact that the withdrawal necessary for the thinking activity cannot cut the link with appearances in spite of its intention to do so. The decisive point for Arendt—in *The Life of the Mind*—is that it is better to confront the existence of this link, as well as the tension that it entails between withdrawal and belonging, rather than covering it over. Such is the root of her deconstruction of metaphysical fallacies. The deconstruction aims at differentiating what the professional thinker tends to amalgamate.

Indeed, the irony of these "fallacies" emerges when the thinker —especially the professional thinker in whom *thaumazein,* upon which the thinking activity feeds, devours all other activities—returns to the common world of appearances where, in fact, we all have to act, will, and judge in the midst of our fellows in humanity. As a consequence of his total devotedness to the thinking activity, the professional thinker is inclined to claim the right of regulating all other activities and, therefore, to confuse or amalgamate thought and action, or thought and will, or thought and judgment. As I have attempted to suggest above, the lecture course on *The Sophist* was already exposed to such confusions and fallacies, for example when Heidegger amalgamated *sophia* and *phronēsis,* i.e., thinking and judging, but also when he attempted to understand the thinking activity in terms of willing, and vice versa. I cannot doubt that it is on the backdrop of recollecting those lectures that in her homage to Heidegger at eighty Arendt insists that the more intense the pathos of thinking is, the more risks of blindness the thinker runs when he exchanges his residence in the thinking activity for the common world of human affairs. In other words, there are great risks that for his passion for the rule of thought he will substitute the passion for tyranny seen in a similar rule in the common realm of appearances. One finds the first example of this substitution in Plato's *Republic*. We find it repeated in the 1934 "Rectorial Address." It is, Arendt says, a case in "déformation professionnelle" ("Heidegger at Eighty," *ibid.*, 303).

It was given to me to witness an instance of this kind of tyrannical bend. The event took place during Heidegger's last seminar, to which I had been invited, in 1973. Heidegger was speaking on the *Gestell* and its contrast with *Ereignis*. His meditation reached a great intensity; it evoked themes such as Technology, Dwelling, *Gelassenheit*. The five participants, all French speakers, were carried out by the "wind of thought." Heidegger was in a dialogue with himself, in front of us, his gaze reaching somewhere else. But all of a sudden, he came out of his retreat and was back among us. And this is what he said in a firm voice: "Tourism should be forbidden." On the spot, no one smiled. We were all under the spell of the intensity of his monologue. For myself, I was quite ready to admit that tourism is indeed one of the contemporary modes of the *Gestell*, conceived as the generalized enframing of beings and the picture-making of the world. But from there to conclude that it should be forbidden, there was a shift which seemed to me to betray a change of register and to precipitate meditating thought into some despotic decisionism. Back in my hotel and in the company of one of the participants, I could not prevent myself from waxing ironic: "Who is going to enforce this prohibition on tourism? How does it agree with *Gelassenheit*? Isn't this the proclamation of a strict and pure nationalism? Doesn't he realize that without any tourist infrastructure in the city of Freiburg we would never have able to attend his seminar?"

Subsequently re-reading Kant's *Project for Perpetual Peace*—an "ironic" text, as Arendt notes[6]—I could not prevent myself from favoring Kant, against Heidegger, for thinking that the right to visit foreign countries and to stay there temporarily belongs to every citizen of the world. Much later, upon reflection, this incident contributed to convince me of the appropriateness of the irony directed in *The Life of the Mind* at the professional thinkers.

NOTES

1. See Hannah Arendt, *Love and Saint Augustine,* ed. Joanna Vecchielli Scott and Judith Chelius Start, Chicago: The University of Chicago Press, 1996.
2. Elisabeth Young-Bruehl, *Hannah Arendt, For Love of the World,* New Haven: Yale University Press, 1982, p. 217.
3. *Partisan Review,* vol. 13, no. 1, pp. 55–56.
4. Correspondence Heidegger-Komerell, Paris: Minuit, p. 16.
5. See "Labor, Work, Action" in *Amor Mundi: Explorations in the Faith and Thought of Hannah Arendt,* ed. James W. Bernauer, Dordrecht: Nijhoff, 1987, hereafter *L.W.A.*
6. *Lectures on Kant's Political Philosophy,* ed. Ronald Biener, Chicago: Chicago University Press, p. 52.

ONE

The Phenomenologists of Action and Plurality

Could it be that phenomenology, although in many respects leading to a post-metaphysical way of thinking, often had the tendency of maintaining or favoring a very traditional approach to the phenomenon of action? In other words, could it be that the burden of the tradition weighed on the phenomenological gaze, thus preventing it from seeing what was to be seen, from being strictly focused on the *Sache selbst*, which in this case is the phenomenal articulations specific to action? I will first attempt to define the terms of this question in light of the teaching of Hannah Arendt, particularly in *The Human Condition* (hereafter *H.C.*).[1]

I

At the very foundation of the tradition of metaphysics, i.e., in Plato, we find the affirmation of a clear-cut distinction between two forms of life—active and contemplative. This distinction affirms a hierarchy between the first and the second: action, according to Plato, is inferior in kind to contemplation. Not only is action inferior to contemplation, but its specific dignity is spent entirely in the assistance it provides to contemplative ends. It is therefore nothing but a means toward contemplation. The one who devotes himself to contemplative life must maintain his body alive: he must therefore consume regularly a certain amount of goods, foods and beverages, which nature provides only after some corporeal pain has been taken in extracting them from it. He must also shelter his body and surround himself with a habitat propitious to the silent dialogue of the soul with itself. This presupposes the production and maintenance of a certain number of utensils and artifacts. He must finally preserve the tranquillity of contemplative life, which requires an atmosphere of civil peace secured only if the public interaction of humans is organized so that order dominates this life in common. As Arendt insisted a number of times, this characterization—one so to speak canonical of the representation of active life by philosophy—was set in place with respect to contemplation, i.e., the aiming of a pure noetic consideration of the immutable order of the *physis,* and thus was all the more prone to blurring the specific phenomenal articulations of active life as it now became conceivable to minimize the importance of active life in general and the activity of citizens in particular, which so far in the Greek world had incarnated excellence. It is striking to note that Plato, foremost among the founders of the metaphysical tradition, put a premium on *bios theōrētikos* and was also inclined to obliterate the distinction between the phenomenon of the activity of *poiēsis* and that of the activity of *praxis* and to interpret political activity in light of the activity of the artisan, or *technitēs,* who operates in conformity with a preconceived model and seeks to realize it by using adequate means. By the same token, Plato subordinated *praxis* to *poiēsis,* such a subordination being itself regulated by the primacy of contemplation because the artisan himself too is for a significant part of his activity a contemplative individual: antecedently, he takes into view a model, an archetype and an idea, and his gaze remains fixed upon it for as long as the process of shaping and finishing the product lasts.

In such conditions, in order to focus on and describe the phenomenal articulations of active life with respect to what they show from within themselves, Hannah Arendt was led to conduct both a deconstruction and a destruction of a great many structures carried on by the legacy of metaphysics since Plato. In the pursuit of this purely phenomenological task, she found an extremely important support in the pre-Platonic texts that bear testimony to the Greek way of assessing active life before the issue was to grant primacy to *bios theōrētikos*—for example Homer, Herodotus, Thucydides— but also in Aristotelian texts inasmuch as they reacted against the excesses and reductions which, in Plato, go hand in hand with the celebration of the excellence of *bios theōrētikos.* This textual support from the ancients did not, however, amount to exclusiveness in the phenomenological approach Arendt had chosen, for the passionate attention she paid to them was accompanied by a no less passionate vigilance in her questioning of our epoch. Because of these three features—deconstruction, memory, contemporary gaze —there can be no doubt in my eyes that her phenomenological approach is akin in its style to the one practiced during the Marburg period by Martin Heidegger. In its style, but not in its content, as I shall indicate later.

Let me recall the essential features of Arendt's teaching concerning the phenomenology of active life. Three basic statements on the human condition summarize it: "The human condition of labor is life itself"; "the human condition of work is worldliness" (*H.C.*, 7); "plurality is the condition of human action" (8). A distinction must be made at the very outset, according to Arendt, between the activities of labor and that of the production of works. Such a distinction is attested to in all Indo-European languages. In every one of them there is a verb (*ponein, laborare, travailler*, labor, *arbeiten*), which in its designation of the activity of labor connotes a painful bodily experience. The word, obviously, is in keeping with an activity connected with the biological processes of the body. It is this activity that Aristotle had in mind when he spoke of laborers who "minister with their bodies to the necessities of life" (Aristotle, *Poetics*, 1254b25). Life is tantamount to the realm of necessity because the reproduction of the species through the living individuals and their survival are subjected to the repetition of the same, to what Nietzsche, a philosopher of life, called "eternal return." As long as a singular living being stays alive, this condition entails a cycle whose phases keep repeating themselves: lack, pain taken in addressing it, satisfaction, new emergence of a lack. Being alive is—for each singular living being—being subjected to the law of this cycle, whose onrush gives rise to a whole process of incorporation, elimination, elaboration and destruction, in which the living being is so to speak not responsible for anything, and yet a process which is tantamount to the being alive of the individual. The cyclical character of life marks the labor activity that it conditions. It marks, namely, the painfulness associated with the body struggling against nature in its attempt to wrest from it those ephemeral products, which are no sooner produced than they must be consumed. Because it is nothing more than what Marx used to call "metabolism with nature," this activity of labor is bound to share the characteristics of the vital cycle in which it is inscribed: repetitiveness, multiplication, interdependence of the bodies, fundamental anonymity of the agent. With respect to life, the question "Who are you, you the struggling one?" (or "Who are you, you who find joy and comfort in the assured process of the vital cycle?") could not be asked because no irreplaceable singularity could emerge in a cyclical process regulated by the repetition of the same.

Contrasting with labor, which leaves behind no durable product inasmuch as the product of labor participates in the vital cycle, the activity consisting in producing a work produces, in the sense both of making and manifesting, a stable region of durable things beyond the circle of the eternal return of the same. Its products are not destined for consumption, for disappearance; they are meant to be used for a utilization that may wear them but will not destroy them at the outset. Whereas labor is inscribed within the cycle of nature, the activity of working interrupts, violates, subjugates or destroys natural processes. By wresting from nature those materials that enable it to fashion things that have no natural equivalent, this activity promotes an artificial environment that protects human beings from nature and ensures a durable dwelling between life and death, stabilizes their life, endows it with continuity and identity—features that could not emerge without the durability of artifacts. In other words, the activity of working starting with the incipient fabrication of the most modest tool erects a world that is irreducible to the natural environment of biological life. The activity of working is different from the laboring one not only because of the endurance of its product but also in its movement: the process of fabrication has a definite beginning and a determinable and foreseeable end. Its beginning is the plan established by the producer, its end is the conclusion of the realization of the product. The production itself is distinct from the product; the production is the means, the product is the end. In the laboring activity, by contrast, the body is both means and end: it consumes what it produces, it eats so as to be able to work, it works so as to be able to eat. Whereas the activity of labor is a cycle that dominates the laborer, the activity of working is a linear sequence of which the worker is master.

Yet, although indispensable for the erection of a properly human habitat beyond nature's devouring cycles, the activity of working—which was called *poiēsis* by the Greeks—is unable to take into view that which it constitutes, namely the world. This activity is indeed thoroughly determined by its reference to instrumentality. In it, it is the end that regulates the means, selects them, and rules over the entire process of fabrication. Yet no sooner is the end reached than it falls within a new sequence of means-and-ends and in its turn becomes a means for further ends. Henceforth, the stability instituted by the activity of working is being threatened by the utilitarian mentality of *homo faber*. No sooner is instrumentality generalized than it deprives everything of its intrinsic worthiness, destroys its permanent signification, and consequently erodes the objectivity and consistency of the habitat which the world is. As the mere condition for a world whose duration does not extend beyond the life span of mortals, *poiēsis* does not insure the safekeeping of the world. The anthropocentrism that animates it does not allow it to be cosmocentric. In order that the world be kept safe, another activity is required.

A world is the world, Arendt points out, only if it "transcends both the sheer functionalism of things produced for consumption and the sheer utility" (*H.C.*, 173). The two features which make this overcoming possible are *appearing* and the *human* dimension. The world is inasmuch as it appears. This appearing is publicly manifest: the world is perceptible, it can be seen by all, and all can talk about it. With respect to it, the old metaphysical distinction between being and appearing is not pertinent. Other distinctions are not more pertinent either, such as the distinctions between the one and the many or between identity and difference. Indeed, the identity of a world is inseparable from the plurality of perspectives that can be opened up on it. It disappears as soon as it is seen in a unique perspective. It is this differentiated identity that prevents all those who refer to the world from being confused with all other individuals. But the world also transcends the sum of the perspectives that are opened on it at a given time, for not only is it the in-between that both connects individuals together and presently differentiates the living ones from one another, but it is also what links them to those who inhabited it before and those who will inhabit it later. The world thus understood is strictly correlative to the human conditions of *plurality* and *natality*. Plurality is in no way identical with multiplicity. Every living species multiplies itself into a manifold of individual organisms of which each one is distinct from other organisms, but human beings alone have the ability to take upon themselves the naked fact of their distinction or alterity, they alone have the capacity not merely of being different, but of differentiating themselves. In other words, their birth inaugurates in them the power to express and render manifest not only what they are as representatives of a living species or the bearers of general capacities required for poietic activities, but also *who* they are in their exclusive, non-reproducible, singularity.

The only activity which corresponds fully to the world and to those two human conditions—plurality and natality—that are correlative to it is *action* properly speaking, or *praxis*, and not *poiēsis*. Action does not connect a living being to life, as labor does, it is not what relates general aptitudes to artifacts, as *poiēsis* does, it is what links an individual to other individuals all similar and all different, what causes the individual to appear with respect to other individuals who are no less conspicuous amidst appearances. Action, in this sense, is the life of someone, not as an ephemeral temporal flux amidst the cycles of nature, but as the irreversible sequence between life and death of singular events that can be told. It is about this life, *bios* and not *zoē*, that Aristotle used to say that "it is in a way a sort of *praxis*" (*Politics*, 1254–57). Because the manifestation of "who" someone is presupposes plurality, speech is essential to it. At the same time as plural, action is intrinsically interlocutory. That is why Aristotle used to connect closely *praxis* and *lexis*. Through *praxis* each individual actualizes in an open sequence of initiatives the fact that, from his or her birth onward, he or she has been a beginning. Through *lexis* this individual reveals who he or she is to others who address themselves to him or her. Because it emanates from a *quis* that can never be defined in general terms, action in this sense is never devoid of ambiguousness. Because action is interlocution and interaction and thus inscribes itself within a preexisting network of relations and speech acts *[paroles]*, every acting individual is a patient as much as an agent. Because the network is open, action is unforeseeable. Because the appearance of newcomers renews this network, the effects of action have no assignable limit. Intensely personal to him or her, someone's *bios* therefore remains both manifest and hidden to the individual. As the carrier of his or her history, the individual could not act as though he or she fabricated it as some finished product since this would negate plurality and every interlocution. All those features—unpredictableness, irreversibility, ambiguousness, illimitability—in addition to being distinguished clearly from the specific characteristics of *poiēsis* also denote the essential frailty of what the Greeks called human affairs, *ta anthrōpina pragmata*. The pre-metaphysical remedy they found against this frailty was the invention of the *polis*, conceived as a stable space for the sake of sharing and memorializing deeds and words publicly. In other words, political life under the specific Greek form of *isonomia* was instituted with respect to a common horizon of appearances, within which the being-together of *praxis* and *lexis* could be kept safe and flourish, within which this being-together could be the location for the emergence of *meaning* beyond the *necessities* of life and beyond *usefulness*.

This remedy did not overlook, but instead took into account the fragility of human affairs. But this same frailty is precisely what metaphysics at its inception was led to find intolerable. When he acknowledges the lack of clarity of human affairs, Plato deplores it and in *The Laws* says that mortals are as puppets manipulated by a hidden god who is the secret author of the show in which they are playing. This is tantamount to expressing the wish that a manifest author should replace the secret one and that the distinction between *poiēsis* and *praxis* be abolished. It is well known that Plato was inclined to think of the political remedy to the frailty of human affairs in terms of fabrication, the fabrication of a Republic in which everyone would fulfill his or her own specific function as it is the case in the workshop of the artisan.

II

In light of this short and schematic presentation of Arendt's teaching on the phenomenal articulations of active life, we may wonder whether the most noteworthy phenomenologists do not sanction their being passed over, as was the case in Plato.

Let me consider Husserl first. There is no doubt that unlike Plato in ancient thought or Descartes in modern thought, Husserl greatly contributed to rehabilitating the perceived and to giving right to its specific phenomenality. He showed that the carnal density *(Leibhaftigkeit)* of the perceived world is the strict correlate not only of my sense-related experiences, of my *Erlebnisse*, but also of the intersubjective communication by a plurality of perceiving subjects with respect to their experiences, and he insisted also on the unique contribution made by a legacy of artifacts for the constitution of a *Lebenswelt*. Thus Husserl seems to recognize—before Arendt—the specificity of what she calls "the common world" as an indispensable medium for *praxis*. In the Husserlian description of the perceived, the Platonic oppositions between the one and the many, identity and difference, no longer have currency. The unity of the perceived thing is not heterogeneous with respect to the diversity of its profiles *(Abschattungen)*, it is being attested through them. And the perceived is no solitary spectacle: "*Wir sehen, wir hören nicht bloß nebeneinander, sonder miteinander* (We see, we hear not merely individually, but with one another)" (*Manuscript, K* III, 1, III, 19–20). Yet this undeniable recognition of plurality from within the phenomenon of perception in no way leads Husserl to acknowledging an essential link between plurality and the phenomenon of action. There is no doubt, indeed, that his philosophical project was held together by the ambition to give life back to the age-old predominance of *bios theōrētikos*. The highest activity was, according to him, that of the philosopher devoting his attention to the problems of transcendental constitution, and pure *theōria* retained in his eyes a normative status with respect to action in general. It is not surprising, therefore, that when he considered problems such as the action of an individual, individual history, social interaction, politics and history, Husserl should tend to obliterate their link with plurality and, with respect to these themes, to reiterate the Platonic confusion between *poiēsis* and *praxis*. Indeed, when treating the interaction of humans, Husserl posits that in order to constitute a community, this interaction must rest not only on a baggage of commonly held cultural assets but also on a collective will, unified by a center, which is the collective equivalent of the Ego. In such an analysis, the correlate of what Husserl calls the common world or even the community world *(die gemeinschaftliche Welt)* is not a plurality but a "collective subject" in which, as he says, "the multiplicity in the process of communicating operates as a unique ego" *(G.G.,* II, 12–13). This phenomenology of interaction, therefore, tends to precipitate and condense plurality into a unique center, which of course is tantamount to destroying it. Following this tendency, Husserl sees the best example of community in the centralized state in the modern sense, i.e., endowed with a constitution, a government and an administration. The nation-state, he says, is a "unique will" that is "centralized in the fashion of an Ego, analogously to the individual Ego" *(ibid.,* 20). In this notion of community, the stress is not put on debating, on plural interlocution with one's peers, but on the execution of a centralized will, which means that functionaries are the true members of the political body and that interlocutory action gives way to unified executive management. In other words, the Husserlian concept of community is foremost poietic rather than practical. If one claims that *Gemeinschaft* reaches completion when those individuals that make it up act as if they were one single body, then the organization of work in the workshop is certainly a model of community. But the predominance of *poiēsis* over *praxis* is manifest also in the way in which Husserl treats history. Let it be sufficient for me to draw attention to a passage—very significant in my opinion—in a manuscript in which Husserl treats what he calls the "degrees *(Stufen)*" of historicity on the individual level:

> A vagabond who allows himself to drift aimlessly has his trials, his deeds and misdeeds. But he has no history, he is not a possible theme for a biography, if it is true that biography is to be a mode of history. There can be historicity in the proper sense only for a man who has foreordained the meaning of his life as one who has freely decided to

devote his life to a *Beruf* and prescribed thereby a rule and norm for all his future volitions and actions; by maintaining it throughout all vicissitudes, by remaining faithful to himself, he is conducting within the history of his mission a unified life full of meaning. (*K.*, III, 3)

The word *Beruf*, upon which the semantic weight of this text rests, is susceptible of two translations: it signifies either vocation and mission or profession. If one is tempted to translate it here as "vocation" or "mission," the reason is that one presupposes not without reason that what Husserl had in mind was the consecration of his own life to the philosophical activity. But if one posits that Husserl held his own vocation and mission as transcendental philosopher as normative for historicity in the proper sense or as an example of such a norm, then it is easy to object to Husserl that the history of his vocation, i.e., the incidents of his own research, can well indeed lend itself to a historical narrative, namely that of the evolution of Husserlian phenomenology, but can hardly, or can not at all, be a possible theme of biography. If a philosopher has fully devoted himself to the thinking activity, he withdraws from the common world, he seeks isolation from his fellow men, he ceases inscribing himself amidst the plural and interlocutory interaction that characterizes *praxis*. And to this extent, his biography, the narrative of his *bios* loses density, empties itself of events, and on the limit can be summarized in those few words in which in one of his lecture courses Heidegger presented Aristotle's biography: he was born, he worked, he died. If on the other hand it is admitted that by *Beruf* Husserl aimed not at his transcendental vocation but at a profession, there too it is easy to object to him that the professional activity as such—in particular if it is conceived on the model of management by a civil servant—is rarely a fascinating subject for biography. No more than the "civil servant of humankind" does the state civil servant have any history. My aim is not irony. At issue is only the question of knowing whether the very notion of historicity understood as a process ruled by the "foreordaining of the unified meaning of a life" accounts for the phenomenon of action understood as plural and interlocutory interaction. If it is true that the life of someone, the object of a biography, is a *praxis* intrinsically linked to the condition of plurality, not as multiplicity but as condition in which all are both similar to others and different from them—and if it is true that this life is intrinsically connected to the exchange of words *[paroles]*, i.e., to a linguistic relation, which is alive by pluralizing several foci of meaning and forbids concentrating them in a single one—then one may wonder whether the notion of a "foreordaining of unified meaning" does not (far from being called for by the phenomenon) forcibly remove the *bios* from shared words. Husserl proposes only this alternative: life may be either loitering, i.e., absolute drifting of meaning, or preordaining of an end, a rule, a norm, i.e., a unified meaning that no vicissitudes may impugn. If it is loitering, or in his words "allowing oneself to drift aimlessly," we may admit that this mode of life does not transcend mere *zoē*, that it consists in experiencing its thrust and impulses, and we can concede to Husserl that—since this life is not yet the life of someone and since no singular "who" could appear and stand in front of his or her peers—this situation would not provide any substance for a biography. Short of any plurality in the strict sense, such a mode of life would eschew historicity. But a mode of life integrally unified by the preordaining of a meaning would also eschew historicity and it would do so for the same reason: the absence of plurality. In addition, one knows that the most fascinating biographies are those of not vagabonds indeed, but adventurers. In actuality, the notion of a "preordaining of a unified meaning" originates not in the phenomenon of *praxis* but rather in that of *poiēsis*. In the domain of fabrication there must be a preordained design that will be maintained in spite of obstacles. In the case of *praxis*, by contrast, the fact that meaning would be given antecedently in a unified manner would be a threat for renewed plurality and the unending sharing of voices inherent in the phenomenon. This does not signify that this domain eschews any unification of meaning. The various modalities of promising and forgiving remedy its constitutive unpredictableness and irreversibility and by the same token establish a community of meaning which fluctuates and remains open. But respect of a norm is one thing, faithfulness to a promise another: the first is monadological, the second intrinsically referred to other human beings. And every one knows that the various modalities of *philia* between individuals owe their wealth of meaning not to a preconceived design remaining unchanged in spite of vicissitudes but to the fact that the relation is intrinsically open to the changes of those connected and that, consequently, *philia* contains an essential part of adventure.

In other words, *bios* as *praxis* does not owe its meaning to a preordained meaning that oversees everything and of which this life would be the implementation after selection of adequate means. Unlike *poiēsis*, the life of someone does not lend itself to this

clear-cut distinction of end and means. Because this life is intrinsically relational, it owes its meaning to the relations that constitute
it, to its way of taking them upon itself, favoring them, or moving
away from them.

Let us now turn to Heidegger.

I have already pointed out earlier that Arendt's analyses of *vita
activa* invited us to cast a critical, perhaps even suspicious eye on
Heidegger's fundamental ontology.

The Arendtian analysis leads to question the duality of, or the
alternation between, proper and improper, authentic and inauthentic, which regulates Heidegger's existential analytic. Indeed, the result from such an alternation is, first, that the "world" in what is
most properly existential about it *could no longer be a common
one* because it is being revealed only by the encounter with nothingness experienced through anxiety by a radically isolated existing
being. There results from this alternation, second, that the world
could in no way be a habitat since the being-in-the-world called
Dasein is in the end *unheimlich*, without a dwelling. There results
from that alternation, third, that there is no other individuation
than being-toward-death and, since one cannot discharge oneself of
one's death upon somebody else, it is not in facing another that the
individual declares who he or she is, but only in a face to face with
oneself in the solitude of one's conscience, in a fundamental absence of relations.

In short, if one reasons according to the distinctions set up by Arendt, one would be tempted to say that there is in *Being and Time*
an account of fabrication, but no account of action or *praxis*. There
is indeed an account of fabrication because all of everydayness,
from which *Dasein* must sever itself in order to exist in the proper
mode, is regulated by the concern for goals, results and products to
be obtained by means of the appropriate ready-to-hand entities. At
first sight, there is no account of *praxis* first because plurality, far
from being constitutive of individuation, is opposed to it and for
Heidegger is homogeneous with what he calls "they," i.e., a neu-
tralized and leveled-off way of Being, and second because generally
speaking "the sharing of deeds and words" is in keeping with everyday fallenness and is regulated by a fabricating or utilitarian mentality.

But we must go beyond this assessment.

In his letter preface to the book devoted by William J. Richardson
to his itinerary Heidegger claims that he rediscovered *alētheuein* in

the Greek sense by dint of a renewed study of the ninth book of Aristotle's *Metaphysics* and of the sixth book of *Nicomachean Ethics*, a study vitalized by Husserl's teaching. Now, if an important distinction is brought to light and underscored in these Aristotelian texts, it is—among others for I am not claiming it is the only one—the one between *poiēsis* and *praxis*, between fabrication and action. It is highly improbable that a reader as vigilant and penetrating as Heidegger could have vicariously confused what Aristotle distinguished. In any case, it is essential to consider more closely what might have attracted Heidegger's attention in these Aristotelian books.

If one scrutinizes these Aristotelian texts again while keeping the project of fundamental ontology in mind, one realizes that not only does Heidegger take this distinction—namely the dissociation between the activities of *poiēsis* and *praxis*—into account, but even that he turns it into the supporting structure of the first stage of his fundamental ontology, i.e., of the existential analytic. However, this Aristotelian distinction is now reappropriated by Heidegger within the ontological context that is specific to him, and no longer in an Aristotelian one, a change from which various consequences unfold: in particular, a true metamorphosis of the Aristotelian notion of *praxis* takes place, as well as an obliteration, or even a rejection pure and simple, of a certain number of features deemed essential to *praxis* by Aristotle, which are the very ones whose importance Arendt's book attempts to highlight.

This claim calls for an explanation.

Book vi of *Nicomachean Ethics*, to which Heidegger draws attention, treats those forms of excellence called "dianoetic," a term rendered by the various translators as "intellectual." These forms of excellence, or virtues, are classified by Aristotle into two groups, corresponding to the two aptitudes of the soul: the first one he calls "epistemic" or scientific, and the other "logistical" or deliberative. It is with the second aptitude, the deliberative one, that both *poiēsis* and *praxis* are in keeping. It is relevant, therefore, to investigate the differences noted by Aristotle between these two activities contained within the deliberative aptitude as well as the differences between two forms of epistemic excellence, all the while keeping fundamental ontology in mind.[2]

The activity of *poiēsis* in the Aristotelian sense is an action that only reaches its end—e.g., victory for the strategist, restored health in the patient for the physician, or a given work for the architect—if it rests on an aletheic, i.e., discovering disposition that is appropriate to it. This disposition is called *technē*, a word which may be translated as know-how. It is know-how that is the dianoetic form of excellence, or virtue, of fabrication. Whereas the absence of know-how amounts to a blind and ineffective groping, any know-how is itself an excellence inasmuch as it exerts a discovering function. The one endowed with this know-how deliberates successfully and therefore discovers correctly those means, materials, contraptions and measures that will guarantee the implementation of the product he or she intends to fashion or the manifestation of the effect he or she seeks.

The activity of *praxis* also is an activity that rests upon a discovering disposition that is appropriate to it. This disposition is not a know-how because, as opposed to *poiēsis* which reaches its completion or entelechy in the external production of things or effects, *praxis* does not reach an end outside the agent himself or herself. In other words, whereas *poiēsis* exteriorizes itself in things or effects, *praxis* is an activity that affects closely the way of being of the agents themselves, the very life of humans as individuals who may be capable of excelling in their ownmost individuality and of leading a beautiful and good life in front of others. The discovering disposition specific to *praxis* is called *phronēsis*, a word traditionally rendered either as prudence or practical wisdom. It deals with the clear-sightedness or discernment consisting before particular and changing circumstances in judging what is in keeping with the requirements of a beautiful and good life at a given moment in time. It is *phronēsis* that is the dianoetic virtue of *praxis*.

In *Nicomachean Ethics*—as well as in *Metaphysics*, ix, the other text claimed as paramount by Heidegger—Aristotle underscores the structural differences between the two kinds of activities, *poiēsis* and *praxis*. The difference becomes a striking one if we apply to these two forms of activities, which are movements and processes, the notions of *archē* and *telos*, that is, principle and goal. The principle of the activity of fabrication is in the maker: it is the blueprint that the producer has in mind, the model he or she aims at and seeks to implement. But the goal of this activity resides outside: it is the work or the effect coming as a result. By contrast, *praxis* contains within itself its principle and its goal. Its principle is the prior option in favor of acting well; its goal is the quality of the action itself. It is therefore an activity which in itself is its own end and is exerted for the sake of itself.

As a consequence, these activities can also be distinguished if they are considered with respect to the two notions of *dynamis* and *energeia*, that is, potentiality and effectiveness. In the case of fabrication as well as in the case of the production of effects, what is intended as an occurrence—e.g., the completion of a building—is something other than the building process, the *energeia* is in the thing built and, with respect to such a thing, the building activity is *dynamis* or potentiality. The completion of this activity, its entelechy, falls outside of it, in the product, which means that *dynamis* and *energeia* are external one to the other. But because *praxis* in no way contains its completion outside of itself, such externality does not apply to it. It is in the agent himself or herself that the *energeia* of *dynamis* resides, and *dynamis* is within *energeia*.

As a consequence, finally, these two activities differ with respect to time. Since fabrication finds its completion in a product that emanates from it, one cannot be at the same time the one in the process of building and the one having already built, or the one who is building a building and the one who has built it. By contrast, because *praxis* contains both *dynamis* and *energeia* in the agent himself or herself, he or she is at the same time the one who acts and who has already acted. And since his or her *praxis* is this person's specific way of living and responding to the changing and particular circumstances of the moment, since therefore his or her *praxis* is always cast anew and always to come, the discovering function adjusted to this *praxis*, i.e., *phronēsis*, is properly speaking clearsighted and sagacious only inasmuch as it takes stock in a past and remains directed toward a future. It requires a prior disposition in favor of acting well and the persisting pursuit, or *orexis*, of a life beautiful and good.

Aristotle says and repeats that it is *praxis* thus understood, and not at all *poiēsis*, which allows life to be properly human. Experiencing human existence consists not in producing but in acting. *Poiēsis* falls within the realm of things, *praxis* concerns human affairs; and the virtue of *poiēsis*, i.e., know-how, is inferior to the virtue animating *praxis*, i.e., is inferior to *phronēsis*. The reason for this ranking is the following: Not only does *poiēsis* have its product outside itself, but this product once realized becomes relative to other ends, toward which it becomes a means; it is instrumental for this or that other end, and for the benefit of this or that other individual. Thus, if human activity only consisted of fabrication, life would remain imprisoned within an infinite circle of means and ends, we would merely choose something for the sake of something else, and this endless process of usefulness would render every desire futile and vain, as Aristotle points out at the beginning of *Nicomachean Ethics*. This vanity does not affect *praxis*. *Pros ti*—which translates as the "for-this-or-that-end" to which *poiēsis* is bound and made subservient—is very different from *hou heneka* of *praxis*, the "for-the-sake-of-" directed at life, beautiful and good, and worthy of being sought for its own sake. *Poiēsis* is subservient, while *praxis* being oriented toward living-well is free because its desire is liberated from sheer necessities and usefulness and acting on this basis makes a singular existence worthy of being commemorated or commended as exemplary.

If one reads the previous Aristotelian analyses while keeping fundamental ontology in mind, it becomes clear very soon that after reappropriation by Heidegger they determine the famous opposition at the core of fundamental ontology between ownmost and improper, or between the authentic and inauthentic.

Heidegger's fundamental ontology—his first philosophical project—aims at finding within the entity that we are, i.e., within *Dasein*, the center of intelligibility for the meanings of Being; *Dasein* is the entity that understands what Being means, yet "proximally and for the most part" understands it in an improper mode. Understanding Being in an improper mode is for *Dasein* tantamount to understanding itself on the mode of Being of things endlessly offered to the various *everyday* modalities of use, fabrication, and production. By contrast, understanding Being in an authentic mode amounts for *Dasein* to understanding itself from its most singular potentiality-for-being. On close inspection, it appears that this contrast—with all the oppositions that specify it—resulted from the reappropriation Heidegger conducted of the Aristotelian distinction between *poiēsis* and *praxis*, that is to say, between on the one hand an active comportment, whose end is other than the comportment itself, and on the other hand an activity pursued for its own sake. The oppositions that specify this distinction are: on the one hand *Umwelt*, as public, everyday environment, and on the other hand *Welt*, which is proper to *Dasein*; on the one hand "they" and on the other hand Self; on the one hand concern and on the other care; on the one hand foreseeing and productive circumspection and on the other resoluteness; on the one hand *Wozu* and on the other *Worumwillen*.

If we maintain this perspective, immediately some light is shed upon Heidegger's belated acknowledgment of the role played by his study on Aristotle for his own discovery, beyond Husserl, of truth as uncovering, an uncovering inherent not in consciousness *(Be-*

wußtsein) but in existence or *Dasein*. Husserl had shown that truth does not have judgment as its single site or residence and that there are ante-predicative truths. He had shown also that truth—more deeply than is entailed in its definition as adequation of, or correspondence between, intellect and thing—consists in every mode of intentionality exhibiting *(aufweisen)* its specific correlate. If the Aristotle of *Nicomachean Ethics* appeared to Heidegger as more original than Husserl with respect to truth, the reason is that Aristotle conceives the capacity of exhibiting as specific not to consciousness but to comportment, more precisely, to the different ranks of comportment, especially those ranks occupied by *poiēsis* and *praxis*.

From this it is possible to recognize indications of a close parallelism between Heidegger and Aristotle.

When he treats *poiēsis*, Aristotle assigns a specific mode of uncovering, which is *technē* or know-how. In parallel, when he analyzes everyday comportment—the way in which we act "proximally and for the most part" as he says it in the technical language of *Being and Time*—Heidegger maintains that that comportment is ruled by the productive activity in the broad sense, in German *Herstellen*, a word which is the literal translation of *poiein*. Heidegger claims that this production ruling over everyday concern is animated by a specific gaze, *praktische Umsicht*, which is the circumspect sight on the surroundings and networks of means and ends looming inside it. It is obvious that an affinity obtains between this analysis and the Aristotelian analysis of *technē*.

When he treats *praxis*, Aristotle shows that it has no other end than itself. Likewise, when Heidegger treats the ownmost mode of being of *Dasein*, he underscores that it consists in being in the care of oneself: *Das Dasein existiert umwillen seiner*. Clear-sightedness adjusted to *praxis* is, according to Aristotle, *phronēsis*, of which I have pointed out that it consists at the moment of decision and given particular circumstances in causing the convergence between an antecedent option for acting-well and the always future pursuit of *eupraxia*. The transposition of this point can be noticed in Heidegger's celebrated analysis of the ownmost seeing of existence, namely resoluteness, or *Entschlossenheit*, which consists for a singular individual in taking upon itself what it already is and in anticipating in the instantaneous wink of the eye, or *Augenblick*, its ownmost potentiality-for-being, namely in assuming in its three ecstases its own finite temporality.

From this parallelism, which to be sure could be explored in greater detail, we can see that in Heidegger indeed there is, contrary to what it might have seemed at first, a taking into consideration of *praxis* and no confusion whatsoever between *praxis* and *poiēsis*.

A certain number of features of the Heideggerian reappropriation of Aristotle cannot, however, fail to surprise us. Indeed, in *Nicomachean Ethics* we would look unsuccessfully for themes equivalent to being-toward-death, anxiety in front of the nothing, existential solipsism, the absence of dwelling *(Unheimlichkeit)* and the non-relational character of authentic existence *(Unbezüglichkeit)*. Heidegger's insistence on such terms is tantamount to extracting *praxis*, metamorphosed into the finite existence of *Dasein*, from plurality and every form of manifestation in front of others. Whereas Aristotle essentially teaches that *praxis* is what individualizes someone in the midst of plurality, Heidegger teaches that *praxis* individualizes someone only in being face to face with oneself. This metamorphosis of the very notion of *praxis* entails—with respect to the Heideggerian analysis of *phronēsis*, now understood as resolute assumption of being-toward-death—the absence of a number of features essential in the Aristotelian *phronēsis*, especially features that concern plurality and political life in particular. For Aristotle is careful to underscore—by opposing Euripides—that one cannot be a *phronimos* individual endowed with *phronēsis* if one cares only for oneself. It is well know that Pericles appeared to him as a model of *phronimos* because of his sagacity and his sense of measure concerning the public matters of the City. Of this point there is no equivalent in *Being and Time* because ultimately resoluteness is radically private, opposed to anything public, and characteristic of a mode of being that relegates opinions into fallen everydayness, in contrast to Aristotle who says expressly that *phronēsis* is the *doxastikē aretē*, i.e., doxic excellence. Likewise, it is hard to see what in *Being and Time* the equivalents would be for the understanding of another human being, or *synesis*, and the indulgence for him or her, or *syngnōmē*, as these are two features which for Aristotle are in keeping with plurality and characterize *phronēsis*.

Concerning the question of what motivated the Heideggerian inflection of *praxis* toward a type of solipsism fundamentally foreign to the Aristotelian conceptions, there is ample reason to think that the answer must be sought in connection with Plato. Relation to death, the solitary dialogue of the soul with itself—these are Platonic themes before Heideggerian ones. They are introduced by Plato as well as Heidegger in order to promote the excellence of the particular way of life of the philosopher, *bios theōrētikos,* which is devoted entirely to the task of unveiling the Being of beings in their totality, a task which the tradition after Plato and Aristotle designated by the word "metaphysics."

I have indicated above that the Heideggerian reappropriation of the Aristotelian analyses of *poiēsis* and *praxis* is inscribed in the context of the project of fundamental ontology, i.e., that it is set in motion by the fundamental ontological question of knowing what the unique focus for the intelligibility of the various meanings of Being is. Since this question is not proximally one of *praxis,* but one of *theōria,* i.e., since it does not ask how to act but how to understand Being as such, we may wonder whether the ontological intent leads Heidegger to describe *praxis* phenomenologically as what it actually is or only inasmuch as it is susceptible of providing the grounding for the science of Being or metaphysics. And since this task mobilizes all the efforts of thought and imposes upon it the attempt of pursuing indefatigably a solitary dialogue with itself, one may wonder whether this mobilization does not lead to considering the activity of thinking Being as the only form of authentic action, the only authentic *praxis.* It is from the perspective opened up by this suspicion that we must seek to understand philosophically—not anecdotally—Heidegger's Nazi engagement. For it is beyond doubt that Heidegger's Nazi proclamations, first of all his "Rectorial Address," are expressed in the language of fundamental ontology. This "Address" is in profound continuity with the inaugural lecture of 1929, "What Is Metaphysics?" and in it Heidegger claims allegiance to one text, a text which is neither *Mein Kampf,* nor *Myth in the Twentieth Century,* or some writing by Abraham a Santa Clara, but rather Plato's *Republic,* i.e., a founding text for the entire tradition of metaphysics.

So far I have expressed myself as though only the distinction between *praxis* and *poiēsis,* drawn from *Nicomachean Ethics,* had inspired Heidegger. In actuality, the Heideggerian reappropriation, which includes a profound metamorphosis, did not bear exclusively on these two activities, both in keeping with what Aristotle calls the deliberative part of the soul; it bears also on what he calls *psychē epistēmonikē,* the epistemic part of the soul, on *theōria,* and this is also subjected to a profound metamorphosis. This combined reappropriation-metamorphosis is evidenced in an unpublished lecture course from Marburg on "The Fundamental Concepts of Greek Philosophy" (1926), which contains a general interpretation of Aristotle, as well as in the 1924 lecture course on *The Sophist,* which

Arendt attended, the first third of which is a general interpretation of *Nicomachean Ethics*. Let me evoke once again these lectures in the attempt to shed some brighter light on the Heideggerian concept of *praxis*.

According to the Heideggerian reading, all of Aristotle's philosophical inquiry is set in motion by one question, that of Being as the Being of beings, once it is conceived that Being is no being. When Aristotle treats physics, it is, Heidegger claims, so as to find a term of departure—the problem of motion—for his ontological problematic. When he treats life, it is to establish its ontology. When he treats *logos* and concept formation, he treats the modalities according to which Being is unveiled through speech and by means of which Being is understood. Finally, when Heidegger treats ethics, it is in the attempt to establish "an ontology of *Dasein*, that is, of human life."

This ontology, however, according to Heidegger suffers from two defects: equivocation and indetermination.

Aristotelian ontology suffers from equivocation because the question on Being as such tends to be confused with the question about beings, of which one among all beings is the most properly so; that is to say that ontology tends to be confused with theology, the science of the supreme being, which for Aristotle is the prime motionless mover of all the motions in *physis*.

Aristotelian ontology suffers from indetermination because, when Aristotle establishes that being in its Being can be said in manifold ways, he does not expressly pose the question about the meaning of Being.

The Heideggerian praise of Aristotle's speculative powers comes hand in hand, therefore, with the highlighting of two defects, which it is easy to see that his own project attempted to correct: it would lift the onto-theological equivocation and lift also the indetermination regarding the meaning of Being. Aristotle himself opens the way for the correction of the second defect. To be sure, Aristotle does not raise the question of what brings unity to the four manners in which Being is predicated (the categories, substance and accident, truth, potentiality and actuality), but he answers it implicitly with one single word, *ousia*. This word, according to Heidegger, means *Vorhandenheit des Vorhandenen* or *Anwesenheit der Gegenwart*, presence of the present. The meaning of Being is therefore for Aristotle the present, a mode of time. The lecture course on "The Fundamental Concepts of Greek Philosophy" concludes on the following notations:

Greek ontology is an ontology of the world in the sense of *physis*, Being is interpreted as presence and constancy *[Beständigkeit]*. Being is understood from the present, naively from the phenomenon of time, in which nevertheless present *[Gegenwart]* is only *one* mode. Question: "How come the present have this privilege?" Past and future do not have the same rights. Shouldn't Being be understood from the totality of temporality? (see p. 102 of the transcript made by Hermann Mörchen)

Lifting the indetermination on the meaning of Being is tantamount to understanding Being not merely in the light of the privileged present, but rather in the light of the totality of temporality, that is to say, a temporality in which future and past count as much as present. Such a temporality is no longer that of *physis*, but of *Dasein*; it is the finite temporality, upon which the ontology of *Dasein* carried out in *Being and Time* brings the focus and which it sees as the foundation of the being that we are.

I have mentioned previously that Heidegger also characterized *Nicomachean Ethics* as an ontology of *Dasein*. In order to confront successfully these two ontologies of *Dasein* and understand the metamorphoses brought to bear upon the Aristotelian ontology of *Dasein* by the Heideggerian one, we must take into consideration what Aristotle says not only of *poiēsis* and *praxis* but also of *theōria*. For it turns out that the Heideggerian project for lifting the onto-theological equivocation and the indetermination on the meaning of Being is articulated thanks to a metamorphosis of not merely the Aristotelian concepts of *poiēsis* and *praxis*, but also the Aristotelian concept of *theōria*. This is what is shown—inasmuch as the interpreter takes into consideration the totality of Heidegger's Marburg work—by Heidegger's reading of *Nicomachean Ethics*, for example in the introduction to the lecture course on *The Sophist* (*GA*, 19, Sec. 13–17).

Theōria in the Aristotelian sense contains two forms of excellence, i.e., two hierarchized epistemic virtues, *epistēmē* and *sophia*. In both cases *theōria* bears on what is immune to being born and perishing, i.e., immune to the finite time of mortals. In the case of *epistēmē*, the sight of *theōria* (the meaning of *theōrein* being "to watch") bears on immutable beings, e.g., mathematical entities. In the case of *sophia*, this sight bears on Being and the most elevated among beings, the immovable prime mover that stands as the principle of every motion in *physis*. The sight of this immutability by mortals amounts for Aristotle to the highest form of existence that they can reach, inasmuch as by means of this sight *praxis* overcomes itself, nears the eternal which is divine, and extracts itself—so long as *theōria* lasts—from the fragility that affects it when inserted in those shifting human affairs. In the case of human affairs, according to Aristotle, there is no corresponding *sophia*, because they do not permit us to grasp first principles and because only the always provisional measure of *phronēsis* or judgment is appropriate for them. These Aristotelian views bring out in Heidegger a double gesture, which is one of critical thematizing on the most apparent side and one of metamorphosed reappropriation on its most hidden one. When Heidegger treats these views in critical thematizing, he reproaches them with ignoring—as the result of privileging the eternal—what is originary in the finite time of *praxis,* which we should take to mean the mortal existence of human beings. The Heideggerian deconstruction views this privileging as owed to the fact that Greek *theōria* allegedly aligned itself on the concerns of everydayness at the very same time as claiming to have extracted itself from both *poiēsis* and *praxis;* and the concerns of everydayness are tantamount to the views of *technē,* which needs to count on the stable persistence, or *Vorhandenheit,* of *physis* in order to guide the handling of tools and the fabrication of artifacts, i.e., *poiēsis.* The Aristotelian prime mover is, therefore allegedly, nothing but a hypostasis of the *Vorhandenheit* of those beings offered to everyday concern. But this critical thematizing is accompanied by a transformed reappropriation. It is, I have argued the point earlier, by means of the Aristotelian confrontation between *poiēsis* and *technē* on the one hand and *praxis* and *phronēsis* on the other that fundamental ontology secures after a considerable metamorphosis its distinction between first an everyday inauthentic mode of being, which is animated by the circumspection of concern, and second an authentic mode of being which is animated by resoluteness in being a Self. It is also from Aristotle—and this is shown by the lecture courses I mentioned above—that Heidegger seeks inspiration when he says and repeats that the highest form of existence, or *praxis,* is *theōria,* conceived as the thought of Being. But he radically removes himself from Aristotle's views, or if one prefers he metamorphoses Aristotle *in toto,* when to this thought of Being he assigns the role not of being dissociated from *praxis* and *phronēsis,* but of compounding these very notions, which is to say, of compounding the finite movement of a mortal resolute existence in his effort to found it ontologically. To think Being, henceforth, means to think the finite time cf *praxis*. From which there results the fact that the thinker on Being is in the end the true judge on human affairs.

What does all this have to do with Heidegger's Nazi embroilment in 1933 and the following years?

In order to answer this question it is necessary to consider in succession what lays *upstream* of the Nazi engagement, in its *center*, and *downstream* of it.

What lays upstream of his engagement is fundamental ontology itself, roughly speaking *Being and Time* (1927). It seems to me absolutely unacceptable to argue, as Adorno does, that this text is already fundamentally Nazi and harbors all the seeds for the 1933 advocacy. The reason is that I search in vain for a political philosophy in *Being and Time*. By contrast, it is possible to find the conditions of possibility for blindness and deficiency in political matters, both in *Being and Time* and the contemporary lecture courses.

Let us first note that the very selection made by Heidegger of what is candidate for reappropriating in the Aristotelian doctrine of *praxis* and *phronēsis* seems to indicate a Platonic bias. Is it not surprising that neither opinion nor plurality belong to Heidegger's concept of *Entschlossenheit* after it is granted that this is what radicalizes the Aristotelian *phronēsis*? In its essence *Entschlossenheit* is linked with what Heidegger calls "existential solipsism" (*S.Z.*, 188): *doxa*, relationship to other human beings, and plural debate are excluded from it and relegated into the orbit of concern, i.e., the inauthentic comportment of *Dasein*. Consequently, the very distinction between inauthentic and authentic seems to coincide with the distinction between public and private. We are justified to suspect here the echo of the Platonic disdain for human affairs. Doesn't this disdain emerge as early as *Being and Time*'s introduction when Heidegger opposes the "unprecedented character of [the] formulation" (*ibid.*, 39, 63) of Plato's *Parmenides* and Aristotle's *Metaphysics* to the platitude of the narratives owed to Thucydides, who remains nonetheless a remarkable witness of the City of Pericles? And indeed the very way in which Heidegger describes everydayness as subjected to the weight of the productive mentality and the equivocations of *doxa* is in full agreement with the Platonic description and depreciation of human affairs, which were made to justify *bios theōrētikos*, the solitary activity of the soul in dialogue with itself, as the highest activity. The insistence on the supremacy of the "they" in the public character of everydayness echoes the disdain evidently felt by Plato for *hoi polloi* in his *Republic*. And the very reappropriation of the notion of *doxa* for characterizing in-authentic understanding and speech which allegedly rule over everydayness is certainly more indebted to Plato's critique of *doxa* than to Aristotle's justification of it in connection with *phronēsis*. In fundamental ontology, there is no place for what Aristotle called "right opinion." But there are many echoes, on the contrary, of the Platonic dichotomy between *sophia* and sophistry, or between science and rhetoric.

This Platonic bias, upon which Hannah Arendt insisted, deserves more attention than it usually gets and raises the question of whether the Heideggerian reappropriation is a radicalizing of the teaching by Aristotle or a combination of radicalizing and obliterating. I choose the second possibility. Indeed, Aristotle was in agreement with Plato in thinking that *bios theōrētikos* is the highest form of *praxis*. But it is hardly doubtful that at the same time he rejected the Platonic ambition to subject the entire realm of *praxis* to the rule of *bios theōrētikos*. His *Nicomachean Ethics* is a case in point of this disagreement with Plato. After indicating at the beginning of that work that his inquiry is "in a way the study of politics," Aristotle underscores—to the contrary of Plato—that his own treatment of political science will be adjusted to the subject entailing "much difference of opinion and uncertainty," a subject matter which for this reason cannot be subjected to the same certainty and exactness as "may be expected in other parts of philosophy." Consequently, he writes, "it is the mark of an educated mind to expect that amount of exactness in each kind which the nature of the particular subject admits. It is equally unreasonable to accept merely probable conclusions from a mathematician and to demand strict demonstration from an orator" (1094b). The mentality presiding over Pericles' City resonates in these words. Difference of opinion and uncertainty are inherent in *praxis*, the issue being how to give right to them instead of dismissing them. The political philosopher in the Aristotelian sense is no rhetorician; but unlike what is the case in Plato's work he is certainly closer to the public orator than the mathematician or the metaphysician. The reason of this proximity is in keeping with the sense Aristotle had of the essential link between *praxis* and plurality. By dint of plurality—the *plēthos* that Aristotle opposes in his *Politics* to the monist and unanimous views cherished by Plato—*praxis*, in the Aristotelian understanding of the term, is essentially fraught with ambiguousness and henceforth cannot be the basis for, and the subject matter of, a science devoid of ambiguities. But isn't this essential link between *praxis* and plurality and the ambiguousness inherent in it precisely what the attempt to edify fundamental ontology on the basis of *praxis*—conceived as the free transcendence of *Dasein* understanding Being inasmuch as it exists resolutely for the sake of itself—obliterates? In fundamental ontology the concept of transcendence is totally dominated by the resistance of the ownmost against the improper or, in Platonic terms, of the One against the Many. That is why this concept prevents inscribing *praxis* within a common domain for the sharing of deeds and words, as the Greek city and in its wake Aristotle conceived it.

The deliberate orientation of the Heideggerian reappropriation of *praxis* to the exclusively solitary understanding of Being bears therefore witness to the rejection of Aristotle's resistance to Plato. In fundamental ontology everything happens as though *bios theōrētikos* had devoured, and now ruled over, *praxis* totally. Everything happens as though this *bios,* essentially solitary, were the only authentic form of individuation. In the 1928 lecture course on Leibniz, Heidegger writes: "Philosophy is the central and total concretization of the metaphysical essence of existence" (*Metaphysische Anfangsgründe der Logik in Ausgang von Leibniz*, 202; *The Metaphysical Foundations of Logic*, sec. 10, appendix, 158). Or in the lecture course on *The Sophist*: "It is in *theōrein* conceived as the inquiry on Being as such that man conquers the highest proximity possible to the highest mode of being accessible to him. This mode of being, Aristotle not only taught it, but experienced it; *philosophy in those days had no need to get closer to life*." In other words, living truly is to philosophize. So much for what lays *upstream*. Now what lays in the *center*?

The famous "Rectorial Address" on "The Self-Affirmation of the German University" may be viewed as the confirmation of this Platonic bias. Its theme is the normative position of metaphysics as the queen of all sciences: the framework of the "Address" when dealing with human affairs is borrowed from Plato's *Republic,* which proposed to eliminate the sufferings and the many cases of ambiguousness and tension inherent in the democratic city and its *praxis* and thus proposed to transform the city into a sort of vast workshop in which everyone would be assigned one defined task within a well-defined organ of the political body. This is echoed in the Heideggerian image of a corporatist State in which each of the corporate bodies, or *Stände,* fulfills a determined service: (1) the service of labor, (2) the service of defense, which are both topped by (3) the service of knowledge. And concerning the

Greeks, in response to the question of what *theōria* was for them, Heidegger wrote:

> It is said that *theōria* is the pure consideration which remains linked to the thing solely in its fullness and requirements. It is by appealing to the Greeks that this contemplative comportment is deemed to happen for its own sake. But this appeal is erroneous. For on the one hand "theory" does not occur for its own sake but as the passion to remain close to beings and under their constraint. And on the other hand the Greeks fought precisely in order to understand and accomplish this contemplative questioning as a very high way, even as the supreme modality of *energeia,* of the "being-at-work" of man. Their intention was not to equate *praxis* to theory, but on the contrary to understand theory itself as the highest setting-into-work of the true *praxis.* For the Greeks, science was not a "cultural asset" but the medium that determines in the most intimate fashion the whole Dasein of a people and of the State.

There is no need for a special exegesis to detect in this text the repetition and the further underscoring of what we have noted so far. By being applied to a whole people *(Volk)* organized in a State, the concept of *Dasein* does not lose the features it had in *Being and Time.* These features are conserved: the *Dasein* of a people-State is a *praxis* and its highest actualization is the articulated understanding of beings as such, that is to say, the science of the Being of beings; these features are now further accentuated because applying the concept of *Dasein* to a people-State is tantamount to intensifying the monadic features I have highlighted earlier; it is tantamount, in other words, to turning the State and its Commander into the sole, true Individual in the wake of dismissing the citizens individually. Positing that the people-State is a *Dasein* is equivalent to negating the plurality and the sharing of deeds and words and, consequently, to substituting the unanimous passion for the Being of beings for the plural debate on what appears to various individuals *(dokei moi).* The Platonism of these lines is obvious and in strict continuity with the disdain affected in *Being and Time* for Thucydides. Everything happens as though Heidegger, who claims allegiance to the Greeks throughout the "Address," never takes into consideration the fact that the Platonic science of Being instead of accompanying the blossoming of the City of Pericles emerged rather in connection with its decadence. He wants to believe that the Greeks invented the *polis* for speculative reasons. He does not seem to suspect that the Greeks of the City at the time of its splendor considered *nomos*, i.e., the legal forms of the debate in connection with the pluralism of their *doxa*, and not at all the science held by some sages and experts, as the true pivot of their being-together. As Hegel who in the preface to his *Philosophy of Right* interprets the Greek City in light of Plato's *Republic*, Heidegger unquestionably holds that the Platonic image of the *Politeia* exactly reflects the essence of the *polis*. Everything happens therefore as though, when hearing the word *Kampf*, so terribly overloaded in Hitler's Germany, Heidegger translated immediately as "*gigantomachia peri tēs ousias*" of which Plato speaks in his *Sophist*. There is no doubt indeed that the "Rectorial Address" is in close agreement with the Platonic concept of the philosopher-king. And there is no doubt in addition that the Heideggerian conception of "theory . . . as the highest setting into work of the true *praxis*" is very far from the pluralistic spirit of the Greek city which animated—in opposition to Plato—the Aristotelian concept of *praxis*.

There remains what lays *downstream* of Heidegger's political commitment, i.e., after 1934, as it is in June of that year that Heidegger resigns the Rectorship. Those readers of Heidegger who were attentive to the explanation he gave after the war of his embroilment with the regime might have expected to find in the following lecture-courses the expression of his disillusionment and the recognition of his errancy. More specifically, they could have expected to find in these lecture-courses the first traces of the famous "turning" which shifted the project of fundamental ontology—the science of the meanings of Being—toward the more thinking thought on the historical withdrawal of Being in the age of technology and nihilism. They could have hoped, therefore, to see the first traces of a surmounting of metaphysics, heeding Hölderlin, the poet of finitude and of the Sacred, and opposing Nietzsche, the philosopher of the will to power. But things were far from being this simple.

If one looks at the first lecture course on Hölderlin (1934–35), the lecture course *An Introduction to Metaphysics* (1935) and the documents now available concerning the genesis of the famous essay "The Origin of the Work of Art," one realizes that the project of completion of metaphysics continues to inspire such texts and even that Heidegger is more metaphysician than ever. These texts are therefore aligned with fundamental ontology.

This project is totalizing: what it attempts to do is to extract from *beings in their totality*—this syntagm being a refrain in the texts of 1934 and 1936—the secret of their Being. This project is voluntarist: thinking, questioning on Being, is tantamount to *wanting to know* and Prometheus is viewed as the first philosopher. The only difference is that the location of this will—a fundamentally historical one—is no longer the resolute existing of a singular *Dasein* for the sake of itself as in *Being and Time;* the location is now the unique *Dasein* of a unique people, the German people. *Being and Time* taught, in short, that the singular *Dasein* is a metaphysical being. The writings of 1934–36 teach that the German people is the metaphysical people and since metaphysics is of Greek origin, the project inhabiting the German people must lay claim to the two German thinkers who took their inspiration in Greece, i.e., Hegel and Nietzsche. The writings of Heidegger at that time celebrate the "greatness of German Idealism" and they view Hegel's *Principles of the Philosophy of Right* as the relay of Plato's *Republic.* As for Nietzsche, it must be noted that he is the only philosopher quoted without any reservations in *Being and Time,* where his second *Consideration Out-of-Season* is brought to task for developing the notion of historicity; the first lecture course on Hölderlin is replete with Nietzschean terminology: the "superfluous," "power," "overpower," "will," "overwill," "creation," the "Overman." At the same time as it claims a legacy from Hegel and Nietzsche, this first reading of Hölderlin broadens to an entire people the terminology of being-for-death characteristic of fundamental ontology.

The reason why I evoke this lecture course in the context of an exposition on the Heideggerian thinking on action is that it contains a serious amendment to theses held in *Being and Time.* This serious amendment concerns *poiēsis* and therefore *technē,* which is its uncovering or aletheic function. Let us recall that, according to *Being and Time* and the connected lecture courses, both *poiēsis,* i.e., the concern relative to means and ends, and the *technē* animating it, i.e., productive circumspection, are relegated entirely to inauthentic everydayness. Everydayness is in a position of fallenness with respect to what *Dasein* is in the ownmost. What we witness in the first lecture course on Hölderlin—and this is maintained in *An Introduction to Metaphysics* as well as in the first draft of the essay on "The Origin of the Work of Art"—is the emergence above this fallen *poiēsis* of everydayness of a non-fallen *poiēsis* with three modalities: the setting-into-work of the thinker, the setting-into-work of the poet and—alas!—the setting-into-work of the State Founder. Such men raise setting-into-work to the level of creation, for ownmost in the authentic time of a people is the fact that only a few individuals, the *creators*, can measure up to it. The thinker, in his work which is a mixture of *theōria* and *poiēsis* since he not only thinks but also writes texts, calls his people to confront their historical being in the midst of beings in their totality. The poet, by dint of his work and Singing, calls his people to welcome the gods. As for the State Founder—which of course means the Führer—the opposition maintained by Heidegger between an everyday fallen *poiēsis* and an authentic and creative one is enough to clear him without any hesitation of any wrongdoing and to dismiss as part and parcel of fallen everydayness and talk of the "they" such mundane realities as: racism, *Volkstum*, culture and science for the people, the slogan *Blut und Boden*, mass organization, and normalization of which Heidegger, however, is afraid that it might soon make the activity of thinking impossible.

Of course, all of the voluntarist and totalizing *pathos* relative to the destiny of the metaphysical people will later on be left out of the Heideggerian thinking on the withdrawal of Being in the age of technology and nihilism. But it is not at all certain that the speculative and Platonic bias that I evoked earlier—with the concomitant blindness to human affairs, their plurality, their ambiguousness—also disappeared. Ten years after the "Rectorial Address" in the 1942–43 seminar on *Parmenides* in which Heidegger makes numerous references to Plato's *Republic* we find the following definition of the Greek city:

> What is the *polis*? The word itself leads us to the answer, inasmuch as we know how to reach an essential view of the Greek experience of Being and truth—an essential view that illuminates everything. *Polis* is *polos*, the pivot, the location around which in its specific manner everything gravitates, which to the Greeks appears [as emerging] from within beings. As this location the pivot allows the appearance of beings in their Being according to the totality of its involvement . . . Between *polis* and Being an originary relation reigns. (*GA*, 54: 132–33)

These lines appear to me to be in strict continuity with the "Rectorial Address" with respect to the concept of City. By turning it into the location for the uncovering of beings in their totality and of their Being, they say in short that the essence and foundation of the public domain are of speculative order. They suggest, consequently, that those individuals devoting their lives to thinking the Being of beings are the best qualified to rule human affairs, or at least to be the advisors of the Prince. These lines are aligned with the views of

Plato in the *Republic* and they are not without betraying some Hegelian resurgences. It seems to me extremely significant in this regard that shortly thereafter and in the same seminar Heidegger should have added the following: "The Germans would not be the people *[Volk]* of thinkers if their thinkers had not thought likewise. Hegel says in the introduction to the first edition of his 1812 *Logic* that 'an educated people without a metaphysics is like a richly decorated temple without holy of holies'" (*GA*, 54: 148). We find in the same seminar a passage that is just as telling on *phronēsis*. Plato says somewhere in the *Republic:* "Those that are not saved by *phronēsis* drink beyond any measure" (621a7, ff.). Heidegger comments: "*Phronēsis* is the penetration of that sight which has a view of what is authentically visible and uncovered. The seeing alluded to here is the seeing of the essential sight, i.e., philosophy. *Phronēsis* means philosophy, and the word says: to have an eye for the essential" (*ibid.*, 178). Although those lines may interpret correctly the Platonic concept of *phronēsis*, we can suspect them of saying something far and away from the Aristotelian understanding of the same word. We can suspect by the same token Heidegger's agreement with the Hegelian concept of "educated people" to put him far and away from the Aristotelian notion of "education" with respect to human affairs *(vide supra)*.

It is not certain that this Platonic bias did ever disappear from Heidegger's views. Let us limit ourselves to recalling the beginning of *The Letter on Humanism*, which is the first text published by Heidegger after the war and in which he now declines any pretension to complete metaphysics as the science of Being:

> We are still far from pondering the essence of action decisively enough. We view action only as causing an effect. The actuality of the effect is valued according to its utility. But the essence of action is accomplishment. To accomplish means to unfold something into the fullness of its essence, to lead it forth into this fullness—*producere*. Therefore only what already is can really be accomplished. But what "is" above all is Being. Thinking accomplishes the relation of Being to the essence of man. (*B.W.*, 193)

Here too we witness the reappearance of the Platonic bias: the accomplishment of action is nothing but thinking. Heidegger was to reiterate the point in his lecture on "The Turning": "Thinking is acting in what is ownmost" (*The Question Concerning Technology and Other Essays*, trans. William Lovitt, New York: Harper Torchbooks, 1977, 40, mod.). Indeed this new thinking no longer aims at the Science of Being, it is no longer metaphysical; but is it not a sign of Platonism to consider action—"engagement" is the term used by Beaufret—without granting the least attention to insertion within human plurality as connoted in the word and to orient immediately the written response toward a modality of *bios theōrētikos*? Even if this modality is careful not to confuse thinking on Being and knowledge about Being, which was a confusion made in fundamental ontology, even if it takes care to dissociate thinking from willing and especially from willing to know, it could not be said that Heidegger takes care to dissociate the thinking on Being from a judgment relative to human affairs. What was at issue for the *praxis* of the Greeks of the isonomic city was the aiming at an excellence strictly conditioned by the free manifestation of individuals, by their sharing through deeds and words of a common world whose identity cannot be separated from the plurality of the perspectives taken on it. It is this plural and ambiguous manifestation that Aristotle aimed to preserve against Plato when in his *Nicomachean Ethics* he stood opposed to the complete absorption of *phronēsis* by *sophia*. *Phronēsis*, as Aristotle conceived it, was in essence the aptitude granted to everybody, and not merely to the professionals of thinking, of having a judgment in political as well as private matters. But if the only manifestation to which *praxis* is attuned is the unveiling of Being— which happens essentially when it is confused with the thinking activity—then, whatever the ambiguousness of this unveiling, it relegates the eventful course of human affairs into margins of irrelevance. The plural and ambiguous manifestation of these affairs does not deserve in Heidegger's view more attention than in Plato's: with respect to the history of Being, the turns of human affairs are equivalent to a foam, which hides the essential, or that with which only the rare few—thinkers and poets—are entrusted.

This questioning could be continued with an examination of French phenomenology. A few words will suffice concerning Sartre.

Indeed Sartre—no more than Merleau-Ponty—lent any attention to the Greek world. There is therefore no reason to expect from him any explicit repetition of the Greek philosophical approach to active life. But philosophers cannot escape the tradition because they decided to ignore it.

I shall limit myself to introduce what I have in mind by means of a short quotation: "Truth is one, error is manifold. It is no coincidence if the [political] right professes pluralism."[3] These words are not by Sartre, but by Simone de Beauvoir. The sentence means that the public realm in which the *praxis* of human beings unfolds must be approached according to a clear-cut distinction between truth and error, the one and the many. This is the type of approach dictated by Plato. The sentence quoted is tantamount to denying that plurality is essential to human affairs, to negating that their light results from the expression of this plurality. It is equivalent to opposing plural *doxai* to a unique *epistēmē* and, consequently, to conferring upon those that are devoted to the latter the right of bringing their solution to human affairs. To be sure, in the Sartrian phenomenology of action, the theoretician's domain is no longer the heavens of Ideas, it is existence itself, the existence of each individual in its original movement. In *Being and Nothingness* this movement is described as a conscious project endowed with internal unity and transparency, to which others constantly pose a threat. It may be a relevant question to ask whether in its very principle that description does not consist in subordinating *praxis*, as relational insertion in the midst of plurality, to the ideal of mastery of a *technitēs* absorbed in the activity of fabrication. In *The Critique of Dialectical Reason* the theme is no longer the movement of consciousness in its opposition to the objectifications with which others threaten it but the relation between the *praxeis* of individuals. An existential repetition of Marx is enacted by Sartre who in agreement with his forerunner considers the *praxis* of an individual not in terms of interaction but in terms of a transformation of nature by the means of tools. In its essence such a transformation supposedly constitutes and shapes the individual at the same time as it elaborates nature. The description of *praxis* understood in this fashion maintains the fundamental features of consciousness described in *Being and Nothingness:* unifying project, transparency, understanding of the situation and goal. Individual *praxis* is therefore in *The Critique of Dialectical Reason* what in the previous *Being and Nothingness* was described as the movement of the "for itself" understood in terms of *poiēsis.* Yet it does not seem any more that the relation between individuals is still to be viewed as essentially fraught with conflicts. Conflict has become contingent and surmountable: it depends on the contingent fact of the scarcity of economic resources, which generates and perpetuates inhuman conditions. The overcoming of scarcity and the advent of abundance will be sufficient to bring about properly human relationships between individuals—relationships which would consist in reciprocity between the *praxeis* as each one recognizes the other.

In light of the phenomenological distinctions I was recalling earlier in the wake of Arendt, the blindness of this description is almost transparent. Everything happens as though unbeknownst to him Sartre repeated the ancient metaphysical ignorance of the phenomenal articulations of active life. To be sure, what is totally non-Greek in his analyses—non-Greek both from the point of view of the men of the *polis* and from the theoretical perspective of the philosopher—i.e., what is typically modern is the idea that the total unbridling of laboring activity and the production of abundance in consumer goods would lead to a properly human interaction. On the other hand, what Sartre calls "individual *praxis*" corresponds strictly to the specific features of what the Greeks called "*poiēsis.*" Understanding "individual" *praxis* as *poiēsis* means that once the fetters of scarcity have been removed we are the author of our life, we make it, we are the author of our history to the same extant that the maker is the lucid master of the work. This predominance of the model of *poiēsis*, an activity in which we saw plurality is not essential, affects and determines the Sartrean concept of recognition. Sartre writes:

> Each individual *praxis*, in its practical structure and for the sake of the completion of its project, *recognizes* the *praxis* of others, . . . it sees the duality of activities as inessential and the unity of *praxes* as such as what is essential. (Jean-Paul Sartre, *The Critique of Dialectical Reason*, trans. Alan Sheridan-Smith, New York: New Left Books, Verso, 1991, p. 131)

These words explicitly praise fusion and explicitly deny plurality. The sentence means that human affairs and their history would be fully endowed with meaning if they were not an adventure experienced by humans in their interaction but a fabrication process carried out by a single one.

NOTES

1. A first version of this text appeared in *Archivio di Filosophia*, 1986, 1–3, pp. 741–57.
2. See my *Heidegger and the Project of Fundamental Ontology*, trans. Michael Gendre, Albany: State University of New York Press, 1991, chap. 3.
3. "La pensée de droite aujourd'hui" (Rightist Thinking Today), in *Les Temps Modernes*, 1955, p. 1539.

TWO

Speculative Individuation
and the Life of Somebody

A ll of *Being and Time* gravitates around the question on the
meaning of Being rebounding on the following question,
"Who is *Dasein?*"

The analysis of active life, which in *The Human Condition* culminates in that of action, gravitates around the question, "Who are
we" (*H.C.*, chap. 1, sec. 1, p. 11).

Arendt's question may be viewed as a reply and retort to the Heideggerian question. Let me therefore attempt to confront the way
in which each one of these questions is articulated.

THE "WHO" IN HEIDEGGER

Let us begin by asking what the ins and outs of the Heideggerian
question, "Who is *Dasein?*" are. This question aims at the *Selbst,*
the self in the sense of *ipse* and not at all of *idem.* It seems to me
that in order to question successfully the ins and outs of this question, we cannot spare ourselves the trouble of inquiring into the
traces of a Husserlian legacy in Heidegger's text with respect to this
theme. To be sure, it is hard to see at first glimpse how the *ipse* of
Dasein, or its ownmost response to the question "Who?," might attest to whatever kinship with the Husserlian *Bewußtsein.* It is
however this "at first glimpse" that I would like to dispel. With respect to my topic, it so happens that it was Heidegger's own words
in his last seminar—the Zähringhen seminar—that prompted me
for the first time to begin this attempt. To the question asked by
Jean Beaufret of whether the *Seinsfrage* could claim a Husserlian
legacy, Heidegger's response in his last seminar was that, indeed,
the Husserlian doctrine on categorial intuition, such as it had been
exposed by Husserl in the *Logical Investigations,* had provided him
with the ground for the problematic of *Being and Time.* Discreetly
though this recognition was made, it nevertheless immediately

alerted me to the connection and finally left me with the conviction that a certain Husserlian legacy ruled the problematic of fundamental ontology in its center. This center also concerns the question of the *Selbst*. It is that conviction that I should like to justify in
this chapter.

I have just recalled that in Heidegger's own admission it was the
intuitionist theme of Husserl's *Logical Investigations* that allowed
him to articulate the *Seinsfrage* into a problematic. It is around the
motif of intuitionism that my analysis[1] is going to gravitate.

In *Being and Time* Heidegger does not shy away from expressing
a number of reservations with respect to Husserlian descriptions.
But upon closer inspection of the book it turns out that when he
refers his reader without critical commentary to Husserl's writings—which Heidegger does discretely in footnotes at the bottom
of pages—the texts that he sanctions with approval are precisely
ones that insist on privileging intuition. It is the case with the first,
fourth and sixth *Logical Investigations*. It will be useful at this
point of my presentation to reintroduce the teaching of the first
Logical Investigation, more specifically its beginning, the very text
that was questioned masterfully by Jacques Derrida in *Speech and
Phenomena*.[2] Heidegger himself alluded to the Husserlian teaching
and declares himself in agreement with it in the 1927 lecture
course (the year of the publication of *Being and Time*) on *The Basic
Problems of Phenomenology*.[3] We can read the following:

> Only in recent times has this problem of the sign been pursued in an
> actual investigation. In the first of his *Logical Investigations*, *"Aus-
> druck und Bedeutung"* (Expression and Meaning), Husserl gives the
> essential determinations concerning sign *[Zeichen]*, mark or symp-
> tom *[Anzeichen]*, and designation *[Bezeichnung]*—taking all of them
> together in distinction from *Bedeuten*. (*G.P.*, 263; *B.P.*, 185)

To agree with Husserl on this distinction and to consider it essential is tantamount to delineating a clear demarcation between the
order of *Bedeutung* (meaning) on the one hand and the order of the
symbolic, the first one being immediately amenable to an adequate
seeing and the second not being amenable to it because it is intrinsically affected with inescapable mediateness. What in Husserl justifies this distinction is the phenomenological privilege of *Bedeutung*
and the brushing aside of the symbolic realm. For *Bedeutung* in the
Husserlian sense is properly a phenomenon only inasmuch as it is
an ideality amenable to exhibiting itself with complete obviousness

and presence to a signifying intention which is fully present to itself and finds total fulfillment in ideality. It is by contrast this possibility of certainty that is lacking in the order of indication in general since its characteristic is simple motivation defined as follows:

> [Here] certain objects or states of affair the existence of which someone has a current knowledge indicate to him the existence of certain other objects or states of affair in the sense that the conviction about the being of the ones is lived by him as a motivation (and as such a non-obvious motivation) for the conviction on the presumption of the others. (*Logical Investigations*, sec. 2)

The order of indication is a domain in which absence intrinsically affects presence, in which what is being given is not a full phenomenon but the mere *announcement* of what is never given. This domain is what must be set aside in order to gain access to the phenomenon properly speaking.

Method is what circumscribes the first point of my inquiry: Husserl's phenomenological approach is held in place at the outset by a clear-cut demarcation between the intuitive register and a merely symbolic one. My first question is to know whether this demarcation can be found in the Heideggerian concept of method practiced in *Being and Time* in order to reach the *Selbst*, in the sense of *ipse*, of *Dasein*.

This concept is defined provisionally in a few famous pages of the introduction of the work (sec. 7). In those pages Heidegger elucidates the two stems of the word "phenomenology," i.e., phenomenon and *logos*. Concerning the first stem, he maintains that the expression "phenomenon" means "that which is apparent within itself" *(das sich-an-ihm-selbst-zeigende)*, the manifest *(das Offenbare)*. From this phenomenon in the original and positive sense appearance or semblance *(Schein)* derives as a privative modification. To say that semblance is a privative modification of the phenomenon in the original sense amounts to saying that in its very derivation semblance remains founded upon that which it modifies. For semblance is "what shows itself within itself as that which *it is not*." "Now it is only inasmuch as something claims according to its meaning to show itself, that is, to be a phenomenon, that it can show itself *as* something that it *is not*." Semblance is said of the phenomenon merely claimed for, yet precisely a phenomenon upon which a claim is made.

Now, Heidegger insists, there is reason to oppose to both the phenomenon in the original and positive sense and its negative modification, i.e., semblance, something that is different from both. This something is *Erscheinung*. This term—in the way Heidegger understands it—is closely akin to the Husserlian term of *Anzeigen*, index, as it appears in the first *Logical Investigation*. In the extension of the Heideggerian notion of *Erscheinung* are included "all indications *[Indikationen]*, *Darstellungen*, symptoms and symbols." Husserl evokes also the stigmata, flags, distinctive marks, traces, mnemonic signs, designations, etc. but he says that "those distinctions and other ones that are analogous do not suppress the essential unity with respect to the concept of index" (sec. 2), whose function is to indicate and establish a non-obvious *(uneinsichtig)* relationship between a given indicator and a something indicated that is not given. In full agreement with Husserl's description Heidegger defines *Erscheinungen* in the following fashion: they are "events that show themselves and in the showing-forth 'indicate' *[indizieren]* something that does not show itself." Or elsewhere: "*Erscheinung*, as the *Erscheinung* 'of something' does not precisely mean showing itself but the being announced of something which does not show itself by means of something which shows itself" (*S.Z.*, 29). It is not unjustified to decipher in this Heideggerian description of *Erscheinung* something like a mere terminological transcription of the Husserlian description of *Anzeige*. When Husserl speaks of *Anzeichen*, Heidegger speaks of *Erscheinung;* when Husserl speaks of *Anzeige*, Heidegger—little inclined though he is to use vocables of Latin origin—speaks of *Indikation* or of *indizieren;* when Husserl uses the word *kundgeben*, Heidegger uses *melden*, but these vocables are interchangeable, and the same thing is at issue on one side and the other.

Consequently, in the same fashion as Husserlian phenomenology was at the outset held in place by a clear-cut demarcation between an intuitive register and a symbolic one, likewise the phenomenon in the sense of Heideggerian phenomenology is defined as "what shows itself within itself" and is at the outset delineated from the register of mediateness and the symbolic in general. On this topic, the 1925 lecture course on *The History of the Concept of Time*,[4] which in many respects can be considered as the first version of *Being and Time*, contained the following:

The characteristic feature of the referential function in appearance, in appearing, is the function of *indicating, of the indication or announce-*

ment of something. Indicating something by means of something other, however, means precisely not to show it in itself but to represent it indirectly, mediately, symbolically. (*P.G.Z.*, 112; *H.C.T.*, 82)

The order of the phenomenon, although doomed to, and threatened by, its privative modification, i.e., semblance, is clearly demarcated from the order of the symbolic.

It turns out that the same demarcation is repeated when Heidegger elucidates the second stem of the word "phenomenology": the Greek word *logos*, which he usually translates by *Rede*, discourse. Regarding this theme, it is enlightening to consider as part of the same position its treatment in *Being and Time* and the 1925 lecture course, which is more explicit. It is in keeping with every discourse, Heidegger claims, to reveal, make manifest *(offenbar machen)* and to show *(zeigen)* that which it is in the process of treating. But amidst the discursive function in general, it is appropriate to distinguish carefully two modalities of showing forth. On this point, Heidegger claims allegiance to Aristotle, who establishes in *De Interpretatione* that every *logos* is semantic but not apophantic. The fact that every *logos* is semantic means, in the Heideggerian commentary, that every *logos* shows something understandable. The fact that a part only of *logos* is apophantic means that what it shows consists in "allowing something to be seen within itself and from—*apo*—itself," thus offering it to a gaze, to a *theōrein*. There is thus a clear distinction between a merely semantic discourse and one properly apophantic. Only apophantic discourse, Heidegger insists in *Being and Time* (32–33), has "the function . . . of letting something be seen by pointing it out" *(im Sinne des aufweisenden Sehenlassens)* (33). It seems to me remarkable that the verb *aufweisen* is precisely used in Husserl's first *Logical Investigation*, where it characterizes the fulfillment of the inherent aiming of the act of *Bedeutung* by putting in view that at which it aims—by contrast to the mere *hinweisen* (to refer), which is the function of the index and symbolic in general. One can recognize the echo of this opposition in the Heideggerian opposition between apophantic and semantic *logos*.

It is only inasmuch as *logos* is apophantic, i.e., only inasmuch as it allows one to see, that it can be true, i.e., unveil that about which it speaks. In the same fashion as the phenomenon (in the original and positive sense of what shows itself from within itself) is being threatened with its privative modification, i.e., semblance (that which shows what it is not within itself), likewise the unveiling showing of apophantic *logos* is threatened with the privative modification of falseness under the guise of a belying veiling, which consists in placing something in front of the thing that is talked about and in passing the thing for what it is not.

By contrast, merely semantic discourse is neither true nor false in the sense of being unveiling or veiling. As being part of the extension of this type of discourse Heidegger mentions exclamation, request, wish, prayer. I would be tempted to add, given the strict isomorphism between this elucidation of *logos* and *phenomenon*, that the highlighting of merely these forms of semantic discourse refers exactly to the symbolic part of discourse, the one in which what is shown refers to something that cannot be made visible. In any case, Heidegger's clarifications with respect to both terms display a clear-cut demarcation between an intuitive register that is open to the phenomenon understood as "what shows itself from within itself" and a symbolic register in which such a manifestation does not obtain.

Concerning *logos*, the primacy of the intuitive register turns out to be all the more strong since Heidegger insists on the fact that even apophantic *logos* is not the first site of truth, in the sense of unveiling. The first sight is *aneu logou*, without speech. It is, for example, *aisthesis*, which cannot fail to intend the sensible data that are relevant to it: colors for sight, sounds for hearing. Yet, "pure *noein* . . . the perception of the simplest determinate ways of Being which entities as such may possess . . . is what is 'true' in the purest and most primordial sense" (*S.Z.*, 33). With respect to this noetic vision, *logos*, even apophantic *logos*, stands in second position.

Regarding this secondary position of apophantic *logos* with respect to noetic vision, it happens again that Heidegger is indebted to Husserl. He himself recognizes it discretely when he points out in a note of *Being and Time* that pages 255 ff. of *Ideen I* radicalize the problematic of the first *Logical Investigation*. What is at issue in those pages? Husserl begins by inviting his readers to reflect on the experience of reading, to pay attention to the understanding of what may be called the "thought content" of reading, and to consider "what, in the understanding of what is read, gains the status of an effectively originary actualization with respect to what may be called the thought infrastructure of expressions" (255). It is this actualization that is dealt with in section 124 of *Ideen I*, whose title is "The Noetic-Noematic Layer of *Logos*. Signifying and Signification *[Bedeuten und Bedeutung]*." The thought infrastructure of expressions according to that section lies in expressing acts, i.e., according to Husserl in the layer of specifically logical acts. The specifically logical layer of an expressing act consists in the act of signifying, *Bedeuten*. This act is intentional and has therefore a noetic-noematic structure. But its intentionality is merely that of a medium "whose specific characteristic is by essence to reflect, so to speak, every other intentionality" (257). In other words, "the layer of expression—in this resides its originality—is not productive, except that it is it precisely that which confers expression to all other intentionalities" (258). To express is merely to explicate by means of *Bedeutungen* "pre-expressive" or even "non-expressive" intentionalities, which are themselves endowed with a specific productivity. Thus, perception as an intentional act is referred noematically to a "pure intended as such" which is of a perceptual nature, of which it is the first, pure and simple apprehension *(die erste, schlichte Erfassung)*. When we state "this is white," this expressing as an act effective by means of significations is merely a second layer that replicates and reflects accurately—in its noetic-noematic structure—the very noetic-noematic structure of the first, pure and simple apprehension. This perceptive apprehension is the intentional substratum upon which the expression rests. Such a substratum is amenable to "a gaze of the 'I' *[Ichblick]* formed of a unique ray which is directed upon it and gets hold of the considered noematic object in one undivided grasp" (255).

It matters little that in his analysis of *logos* Heidegger claims to be inspired by Aristotle rather than Husserl: it does not seem doubtful to me that he is reading the former in light of the latter.

From this double elucidation, it appears that the very notion of phenomenology does nothing more than gather together the intimate relationship between what is thought under the word "*phenomenon*" and what is thought under the word "*logos*." Phenomenology therefore means "showing-forth from itself what shows itself, such as it shows itself from within itself." This is what expresses, according to Heidegger, the maxim "*Zu den Sachen selbst.*" It could not be better suggested that the Self has to be approached not at all by means of the symbolic, but rather of the intuitive.

The second phase of my inquiry is to determine how this methodological demarcation—one originally Husserlian—between the intuitive and the symbolic regulates the analysis of the modes of Being of *Dasein*, that is to say, the existential analytic conceived as ontology of *Dasein*. One of the first versions of this ontology is provided to us by the 1925 lecture course on *The History of the*

Concept of Time quoted earlier. This version begins with Heidegger recalling the three Husserlian discoveries to which he claims to be indebted in his inquiry. It seems to me significant that the intuitionist motif plays a determining role in Heidegger's assessment of the import of each discovery.

The first discovery is intentionality. Heidegger insists that it is a structure that concerns "the very being of comporting" and in it designates a "directing-itself-toward" (*P.G.Z.*, 40; *H.C.T.*, 31) Yet, there is "a traditional tendency not to question that of which it is presumably the structure, and what this sense of structure itself means" (*ibid.*, 63; 47). That is why it is essential, Heidegger says, to resist this tendency and to adopt as "a methodological rule for the initial apprehension of intentionality . . . not to be concerned with the interpretation but only to keep strictly to that which shows itself, regardless of how meager it may be" (*ibid.*). He continues:

> Only in this way will it be possible to see, in intentionality itself and through it directly into the heart of the matter, that of which it is the structure and how it is that structure. Intentionality is not an ultimate explanation of the psychic but an initial approach toward overcoming the uncritical application of traditionally defined realities such as the psychic, consciousness, continuity of lived experience, reason. But if such a task is implicit in this basic concept of phenomenology, then "intentionality" is the very last word to be used as a phenomenological slogan. *(Ibid.)*

There is no doubt that the entities in question—consciousness, continuity of lived experience, etc.—are part and parcel of the terminology of Husserl, who is thus under attack. Yet he is coming under attack only for not measuring up to the rule of intuitive vigilance he had himself imposed; it is in the name of this vigilance, which in the end presides over reduction, that Heidegger will direct the "phenomenological gaze," but no more toward the transcendental life of consciousness and the noetic-noematic correlations inherent in intentionality and rather toward the openness of *Dasein* to beings and to itself as well as toward the understanding of Being inherent in this openness, in short toward transcendence.

The second Husserlian discovery praised by Heidegger is that of categorial intuition. The clarification of this discovery offers the opportunity of "following intentionality in its concretion" *(ibid.)*. It is therefore a discovery—intuitive in nature, as the term indicates— playing a privileged role in the seeing of that of which intentionality is the structure, i.e., in the seeing of the intentional entity. The point is thus to see transcendence as the understanding of the Being of beings by the human entity.

At the outset, Heidegger stresses the ontological importance of this intuitive discovery. It is "the demonstration, first, that there is a direct *[ein schlichtes Einfassung]* apprehension of the *categorial*, such constituents in entities which in traditional fashion are designated as *categories* and were seen in quite crude form quite early" (*ibid.*, 64; 48 mod.), which alludes to Plato and Aristotle. More importantly, we find Being among the categorial intuitions dealt with in the *Logical Investigations*. Being—inasmuch as it is in *surplus* with respect to the "real" properties of given states of affair or inasmuch as it is a non-real predicate according to the Kantian formulation quoted by Husserl—is amenable to an intuition: such is the Husserlian discovery, which according to Heidegger's belated recognition provided him with the ground for his existential analytic. It taught him that understanding Being inasmuch as it is different from understanding beings is a matter of *seeing*. Inasmuch as this understanding is not an intentionality among others but is primordial and constitutive in the deepest of the being that we are, it taught him to *see* that the concretion of intentionality consists in the movement which exceeds beings toward Being, i.e., in transcendence. In this connection it seems to me significant that in one of the densest presentations of what he means by transcendence, Heidegger should say that *Dasein* is in itself *überschüssig*, excessive. *Überschüß*, surplus, is the term used in the *Logical Investigations* to qualify the status of categorial intuition with respect to sensitive intuition (*GA*, 26: 248). It is not less significant that this presentation took place in the lecture course on *The Metaphysical Foundations of Logic*.[5]

The third discovery evoked by Heidegger is that of the *a priori*. Here too Husserl is being praised for attempting to give the discovery a universal ontological import in spite of certain limitations, since the Husserlian *a priori* is immune to the traditional division between a subjective and an objective sphere. Husserl granted that the *a priori* is "in itself demonstrable" in a "simple apprehension" and "originary intuition" (*P.G.Z.*, 102; *H.C.T.*, 74–75) and thus he can be credited for providing with a "preparation for the specification of the structure of the apriori as a feature of the being of entities" (*ibid.*, 103; 75).

Since the remarks by Heidegger on this third discovery underscore at the outset that the clarification of the meaning of *a priori* presupposes the understanding of time, as the terms *prius* and *proteron* already suggest, it is perhaps not exaggerated to recognize in this the admission that he himself felt indebted to Husserl when it came to making temporality the principle of transcendence as understanding of Being. It seems to me significant in this connection that the lecture course on *The Metaphysical Foundations of Logic* should praise Husserl for having "seen for the first time with the aid of the intentional structure . . . the phenomena" of expectancy, retention and making-present. Although this praise comes hand in hand with reservations because Husserl remained prisoner to a problematic of consciousness, it also contains the following admission: "What Husserl still calls *Zeitbewußtsein,* i.e., time-consciousness, is precisely time, itself, in the primordial sense" *(im ursprünglichen Sinne)* (*M.A.L.,* 264; *M.F.L.,* 204, mod.).

In any case, it is indeed an intuitionist motif that is put forward by Heidegger in these three Husserlian discoveries, which he sets out to ontologize.

This ontologizing presupposes an analysis of *Dasein*, the entity for which, in its own being, Being is an issue. It is therefore appropriate to ask whether and how the privilege of the intuitionist motif regulates the analytic of *Dasein* and concerns *Dasein* within itself, in its Self.

The analytic of *Dasein* is held in place by a distinction of principle between the way in which *Dasein* in the everyday comports itself "proximally and for the most part" and the way in which it is in the ownmost and authentically. Now this distinction between (1) a *Dasein* mindful of tasks and the means or instruments serviceable to their implementation and with the tendency to allow *Vorhandenheit,* the mode of Being of things, to reflect upon its own condition and (2) its seeing of the mode of being that is its ownmost, authentic existence, this distinction seems upon closer inspection to correspond strictly to the distinction between the symbolic in general and *Bedeutung,* which was posited at the outset by Husserl in the *Logical Investigations* and was held as essential by Heidegger. More precisely, given the ontologizing I just evoked, this distinction undergoes simultaneously a reappropriation and a metamorphosis. One could even say that it is because the tension between ownmost and inauthentic regulates ontologically the comportment of *Dasein* that in his detailed description of everydayness Heidegger can analyze the order of the symbolic, which in the *Logical Investigations* Husserl limited himself to characterizing briefly so as to demarcate immediately the sphere of the pure logical. I argued that it was in the wake of Husserl that Heidegger enforces a demarcation between (1) the phenomenon in the phenomenological sense of what shows itself from within itself, and in addition semblance, the privative modification of the phenomenon and (2) the mediate level of the symbolic in general. Now, if it turned out that a phenomenon for the most part is not itself or does not manifest itself from within itself precisely because it is embroiled in the mediate order of the symbolic in general, it goes without saying that this notional and formal demarcation should be nuanced. We cannot merely oppose: on the one hand the phenomenon and its privative modification, i.e., semblance, and on the other the mediate character of signs. We should rather say that semblance is the privative modification of the phenomenon in the ownmost sense inasmuch as it is embroiled within the mediating order of signs. Now such is indeed the everyday status of *Dasein*, the being which the ontologizing of the Husserlian discoveries had made essential to analyze. In its everydayness *Dasein* falls into the realm of semblance with respect to its ownmost phenomenality inasmuch as it is concerned with signs. In this fashion we can explain that in 1927 the lecture course on *The Basic Problems of Phenomenology* could characterize section 17 of *Being and Time*, which consists in a thematic broaching on sign in general, as both a "complement" to Husserl and a radicalizing of his teaching thanks to an "orientation toward principles" (*G.P.*, 263; *B.P.*, 185), an expression that we must take to mean orientation toward ontology. It is this ontological orientation that allows Heidegger to take up as a theme signs and references, which were no sooner focused upon by Husserl than reduced. But this thematic treatment, as we shall see, is in no way a rehabilitation of the symbolic: it aims rather at justifying ontologically this reduction which, in the Husserl of the *Logical Investigations*, opened up the field of *Bedeutung* beyond every symbolism.

Let us recall broadly this thematic treatment and reduction. As I indicated previously, the thematic treatment takes place in section 17 of *Being and Time*. That paragraph, which should not be dissociated from the adjacent ones, is entitled "Reference and Signs" *(Verweisung und Zeichen)*. It argues that, far from being a thing over here *(vorhanden)* that would stand in a showing-forth relation to another *vorhanden* thing, the sign appears as such only with respect to *Dasein*'s everyday comportment, i.e., in its concernful minding of the production and manipulation of tools in the midst of the *Umwelt*. It results from this that the sign is merely a particular instance of the ready-to-hand, or a *zuhanden* entity, and that the reference it publicizes rests upon a more radical referring, that of "usefulness-for," which is the ontological trait of anything *zuhanden* in general with respect to the *Dasein* that is connected with it in the register of concernful minding. Inasmuch as this *Um zu* founds the sign ontologically, it is not itself a sign. By dint of this ontological foundation what the sign shows at the outset or *a priori* is not the relation of this given thing to that non-given other thing but rather that "wherein one lives, where one's concern dwells, what sort of involvement [or *Bewandtnis*, as the relation that allows *Dasein* to be near this with the help of that] is linked with the concern" (*S.Z.*, sec. 17, 80; 111). But since each given functional involvement is cut out from within the totality of functional involvements, it is this totality—in which each everyday *Dasein* is inscribed—that the sign indicates *a priori*. Such is, schematically reconstructed, the general thematic treatment of the symbolic in *Being and Time*. It is obvious that no privilege is granted the symbolic when one realizes that it is not sufficient unto itself but is a stepping stone before the ontological equivalent of a reduction, or suspension, of the symbolic. For following this thematic treatment, section 18 stipulates that the totality of functional involvement *(Bewandtnisganzheit)*

> itself goes back to a "towards which" *[Um zu]* in which there is no further involvement . . . [and] is not an entity with the kind of being that belongs to what is ready-to-hand within a world; it is rather an entity whose being is defined as Being-in-the-world and to whose state of being worldhood itself belongs. This primary "towards-which" . . . is a "for-the-sake-of-which." But the "for-the-sake-of" always pertains to the being of *Dasein*, for which in its being, that very being is essentially an *issue*. (*S.Z.*, 84; 116–17)

This change, or turn, of *Um zu* into *Worumwillen* is what precipitates the thematic treatment of the symbolic into the reduction of it. For if the symbolic is everywhere present in what pertains to *Um zu*, it has no room in what pertains to *Worumwillen*. The relationship of *Dasein* to its being and the "for-the-sake-of" that characterizes it have no need for symbols, signs, indexes, etc. The distinction between *Um zu* and *Worumwillen* is in fact tantamount to establishing a delineation between the order of the symbolic and the intuitive, non-symbolic order of pure vision.

Against my presentation it will perhaps be objected that the characterization of *Dasein* by means of a fundamentally hermeneutic mode of being renders this delineation problematic. Doesn't the very choice of the word "hermeneutic" reveal that attention is brought to the symbolic and the interpretation of signs? On closer analysis, however, it turns out that the symbolic is essential merely at the first level of the famous hermeneutic circle, the circle of interpretive understanding.

This first level is that of concern, which is in relation with an everyday environment already familiar and receives the light of a specific seeing, that of foreseeing circumspection. Generally speaking, this concern is permeated with the interpretive understanding in the sense that *Dasein* at the outset grasps those beings with which it deals "as" being such and such instrument. At the outset, therefore, *Dasein* interprets those beings by projecting its own being upon within-the-world possibilities while resting on the previously secured basis of its familiarity with the environment. Thus its own environment appears to it as endowed with meaning or significance *(Bedeutsamkeit)* or pregnant with signs. And since every sign is connected to others on the backdrop of a region of functional involvements—which, beyond its proximity to other regions, is cut out from a totality of involvement *(Bewandtnisganzheit)* functioning as a horizon—concern is inscribed within an endless circuit of interpretations. At this level, we could say that the field of the symbolic is inexhaustible.

Matters are different on the second level of the hermeneutic circle. This level is no longer that of concern but care. In care *Dasein* does not project its being on within-the-world possibilities but upon the ownmost possibility of its own end. On this level, instead of being absorbed in an indefinite circle of references, *Dasein* takes its own Self into view and refers to its own mortality as its ownmost can-be. It is on this level that Heidegger's reappropriation of the Husserlian *Bedeutung*, dissociated from the symbolic in general, is conducted for the sake of ontology. After reappropriation the *Bedeutung* is no longer a logical ideality but consists rather in *Dasein*'s "giving itself of an originary understanding of its being and its can-be with regard to its Being-in-the-world" (*S.Z.*, 87, mod.); in other words, in making clear to itself that it exists for the sake of itself. Now this *Bedeutung* as self-referential in no way belongs to the symbolic order; indeed, it belongs to the intuitive inasmuch as, similar to the Husserlian *Bedeutung*, it is amenable to a seeing. Heidegger writes:

> In its projective character, understanding goes to make up existentially what we call Dasein's "sight" [*Sicht*], . . . sight which is di-

rected upon Being as such, for the sake of which *[umwillen dessen]* Dasein is each time as it is. The sight which is related to primarily and on the whole to existence we call *"transparency" [Durchsichtigkeit]*. (*S.Z.*, 146)

Here the symbolic has no validity, no more than either the overlapping of the visible and the invisible or the indefinite movement of interpretation; what has validity, instead, is the total transparency which *Dasein* reaches when, in the midst of anxiety, it gets the instantaneous and resolute sight of its ownmost possibility.

In this ontology of *Dasein* the thematic treatment of the symbolic is therefore accompanied by its reduction. With respect to the primordial *Durchsichtigkeit* symbolism as a whole is far from being privileged and is rather in a position of fallenness. Indeed, according to the Heideggerian analytic, it is inevitable that when everyday concern takes the signs found in its environment seriously—and this takes place by dint of the *a priori* of the *"um zu"* structure—it should be forgotten that this very structure has a deeper ontological foundation, which is the reference of *Dasein* to its ownmost can-be. To take signs seriously is forgetting what is fundamental.

At this juncture it could be objected against me that my analyses are limited to too narrow a conception of the symbolic and that they tend to equate the universe of symbols with the system of signs, with which everyday concern is confronted in the technical tasks that involve it. Symbols are also the elements of great myths, which humankind keeps in memory: It may be objected against me that it would be surprising if Heidegger reduced those symbols to a variety of the ready-to-hand in general.

In order to answer those objections let me open a parenthesis on myth. It so happens that the theme of myth is not absent from *Being and Time* and that shortly after the publication of that treatise and in the wake of its conceptual apparatus Heidegger wrote a rather detailed presentation of the second volume of Ernst Cassirer's *Philosophy of the Symbolic Forms*, which is devoted to *Mythic Thought*. Although these texts are not—relatively speaking—very dense, they are nonetheless sufficiently precise to allow us to determine what status Heidegger gives to mythical symbols.

It is precisely at the end of section 17 on "Reference and Signs" that *Being and Time* treats myth at greater length. What does Heidegger say? On the basis of the analysis I recalled earlier Heidegger begins by granting that it could be tempting to consider "the abundant use of 'signs' in primitive Dasein, as [well as] in fetishism and magic" (S.Z., 81) as the illustration of the "remarkable role which they play in everyday concern when it comes to our understanding of the world" (ibid.). But he rejects this temptation: "But on closer inspection it becomes plain that to interpret fetishism and magic by taking our clue from the idea of sign in general, is not enough to enable us to grasp the kind of 'being-ready-to-hand' [Zuhandensein] which belongs to entities encountered in the primitive world" (ibid., 82). In other words, on the assumption that the primitive world relates to the realm zuhanden, it does not, strictly speaking, relate to signs. Indeed, "for primitive man, the sign coincides with what it indicates" (ibid., mod.), for him the sign itself always "is the indicated" (ibid.). This remarkable coinciding shows that in the primitive world "the sign has not yet become free from that of which it is a sign" (ibid.) and that therefore "what is zuhanden within the world does not have the kind of being that belongs to equipment" (ibid.).

The primitive world is therefore affected with the index of "not yet." In it "signs" are not signs yet, "tools" are not yet tools, perhaps even the "zuhanden" is not yet zuhanden, if it is true that Zuhandenheit, equipmentality and serviceability are almost indissociable. To characterize this world by means of the index of a "not yet" is quite obviously tantamount to postulating that the myths of the primitive world and its symbols may not appeal to the philosopher, much less provide him with food for thought. More deeply, to apply to this world the index of "not yet" is tantamount to having decided at the outset that the so-called primitive Dasein would be considered only with respect to a teleology of Dasein's Eigentlichkeit, of its ownmost proper being, in short to a teleology of the understanding of Being, whose key the philosopher is deemed in possession. This is indeed how Heidegger himself defines his method at the end of section 17 of Being and Time:

> If an understanding of Being is constitutive for primitive Dasein and for the primitive world in general, then it is all the more urgent to work out the "formal" idea of worldhood—or at least the idea of a phenomenon modifiable in such a way that all ontological assertions to the effect that in a given phenomenal context something is not yet such-and-such or no longer such-and-such, may acquire a positive phenomenal meaning in terms of what it is not. (S.Z., 82)

It could not be said more clearly that the ultimate methodological criterion is the phenomenological seeing enjoyed by the philosopher. This seeing is what functions as *telos*. It is this seeing alone that allows Heidegger to decree that in the case of mythical symbols the only "positive meaning" is properly speaking *not yet* of the order of *Zuhandenheit*, as treated in the analysis of everydayness in the analytic of *Dasein*.

But it may be objected that Heidegger nonetheless grants an understanding of Being to primitive *Dasein*. What about this understanding? It is thematized not in *Being and Time* but in the review of Cassirer's book. This thematic treatment confirms the teleological presupposition I just evoked. In order to answer the question of what sort of understanding of Being determines mythical existence, Heidegger insists that "we must presuppose a prior elaboration of the ontological constitution of existence in general. If this constitution resides in 'care' understood ontologically [and here Heidegger refers the reader to *Being and Time*], it is being-thrown *[Geworfenheit]* that reveals itself as primordial determination of mythical existence" (*Deutsche Literaturzeitung*, Heft, 1928, 21: column 1009). To be thrown in is to be delivered over to that in which one is thrown and exposed to its overpower. Because the primordial determination of primitive existence lies in *Geworfenheit*, thrownness, this existence is "thus referred to overpower, . . . is annexed by it and cannot be therefore experienced in any other way than as belonging and being closely akin to this very reality. Consequently, in *Geworfenheit*, every being unveiled in one way or another will have the existential character of overwhelming power *(mana)*" (*ibid.*, columns 1009–10). From the priority in it of *Geworfenheit* there results that mythical existence is harassed *(umgetrieben)* by the beings to which it is delivered over, possessed by *mana* represented itself as a being, such that the "ontic representations of *mana* are not absolutely false" (*ibid.*, 1010).

Schematic though it is, this presentation of the understanding of Being inherent in mythical existence reveals nonetheless its teleological presupposition. Everything happens in this picture as though the understanding of Being—precisely because it is regulated solely by thrownness, *Geworfenheit*, in the absence of the project, which is its counterpart in authentic existence—was doomed to fail to recognize the ontic-ontological difference, to flatten Being to the level of beings and to interpret it in terms of the latter. Consequently it is as though in myths and symbols existence could only command a diminished understanding of Being, which turns out to be nothing more than a truncated and blind "modification" of the authentic understanding of Being. Indeed, this modification as such presupposes that mythical *Dasein* "has already understood itself" (*S.Z.*, 313), that it already understands the distinction between existence and *Realität*, yet understands it without understanding it since this *Dasein* interprets existence in terms of reality.

There is therefore here a reduction of the symbolic. Everything happens as though fundamental ontology prevented itself from discovering in the symbols any type of inspiration for its specific task.

One may still object to me that, in light of the texts I have just considered, reduction merely concerns the symbols and myths of the so-called primitive *Dasein* and that I have not demonstrated that the same reduction affects those myths which Greek and Roman antiquity has bequeathed to the Western world. But it does not seem to me that this objection stands the test of a confrontation with the texts. It so happens, in fact, that *Being and Time* contains an allusion—to my knowledge the only one—to ancient mythology. This allusion evokes the fable of Caius Julius Hyginus, of which Heidegger quotes and analyzes *cura* in section 42 and of which he recalls that Goethe, who held it from Herder, had been inspired by it in the second part of his *Faust*. But this very allusion is to me indicative of the reduction I was talking about. First, the allusion to ancient myth is made by means of a fable, i.e., a literary document that tends to make myth into a mere allegory, the imaginative rendition of a philosophical meaning which may be apprehended beyond the external image. Second, the quoted fable was written in Rome during Augustus's century, that is to say, in an epoch and place no longer dominated by myths but by late philosophical currents such as Stoicism, which reduced myths to mere allegories. Finally, everything happens as though Heidegger further underscored these reductionistic tendencies by granting no other meaning to the mythological and symbolic elements of the fable than that which brings light on his own analytic of *Dasein*. Thus, when the fable recounts that in the end it was Saturn who arbitraged the feud between *Cura* (care), *Tellus* (earth) and Jupiter with respect to what name should be given to the human being fashioned by *Cura*, Heidegger immediately translates: "In care this entity has the 'source' of its being" and "the decision as to wherein the 'primordial' being of this creature is to be seen, is left to Saturn, 'Time'" (*S.Z.*, 198).

The symbol here is not the trace of a lost treasure or of an enigma which it might be appropriate to become aware of. It gives nothing unusual as food for thought to fundamental ontology. At

the most it can illustrate, while confirming it, that which fundamental ontology claims to be capable of seeing on its own.

Let me close this parenthesis. It confirms the extent to which
the Husserlian distinction between symbolic and intuitive was indeed held as essential by Heidegger with respect to his own project.
For this distinction governs the existential analytic and the polarity
instituted between improper and ownmost.

At this point it still can be objected to me that my considerations
are limited to a formal analogy inasmuch as the question "Who is
Dasein?" does not have any equivalent, even distant, in the Husserlian problematic. The objection calls for me to question—in the
third part of my presentation—whether there still is a trace of some
Husserlian legacy in the Heideggerian determination of the *Selbst*,
the *ipse* of *Dasein*. It invites me, in other words and more specifically, to wonder whether the movement ontologizing intentionality,
categorial intuition, and the *a priori*—a movement conducted toward transcendence—still betrays a kinship with that movement
which in Husserl leads to the constitutive transcendental ego. What
do the transcendental ego and the Self of *Dasein* have in common?

It is well known that in Husserl access to the original region of
transcendental experience is managed by successive *epochai:* there
is first the *epochē* or suspension of the empirical inscription amidst
the totality of occurrences making up the "natural world" so as to
discover the immanent pure psychic domain; then there is the suspension of the pure psychic in order to gain access to transcendental consciousness. Yet, Husserl insists that "phenomenological psy-
chology and transcendental philosophy are allied with one another
in a particular and inseparable manner in virtue of the alliance of
difference and identity between the psychological ego (i.e., the
human, worldly ego in the spatial-temporal world) and the transcendental ego" (*Krisis*, 205). It must be said simultaneously that
the transcendental ego is and is not the transcendental ego. Husserl
characterizes this strange alliance of identity and difference as parallelism. This parallelism is nothing like a doubling because the
transcendental ego remains what it is—in spite of the destruction
of the world, i.e., the totality of the spatial-temporal occurrences
making up nature—and because it is a monad without body, even
without soul, yet is the constituting element of body, soul, other individuals and the world, not in their existence but in their phenomenality. The transcendental problematic of constitution is the result of successive stages of neutralizing and purifying with respect

to anything contained in the initial experience of the natural and human "I," of which, however, the transcendental ego is the ultimate condition of possibility.

One might believe that in searching for an answer to the question "Who is *Dasein*?" Heidegger would be worlds apart from the monadological purifying, which may be held as one of the last avatars of the philosophies of the *cogito*. Not only is Heidegger's question no longer Husserlian, but unlike the Husserlian *cogito* at the outset *Dasein* is characterized by Being-in-the-world. Hence the temptation to think that it is fully incarnated, that it dwells near things and that its Selfhood is indissociable from an intercourse with others. Nonetheless, a monadological purifying is what takes place in the unfolding of the analytic of *Dasein*.

The series of Husserlian reductions is ultimately an affair between me and myself, and it is a matter of seeing. The Heideggerian approach to the core of the Self is nothing else. It is the same *Dasein*, each time mine, that alternatively is absorbed in the realm of everyday concerns and is related to its ownmost can-be. So much so that Heidegger can both say that (1) everyday *Dasein* is a modification of authentic *Dasein* and (2) authentic *Dasein* is a modification of everyday *Dasein*. The everyday *Dasein* is my Self in a position of fallenness with respect to my Selfhood. The authentic *Dasein* is my *Selbst* severing itself from everything that links it to such a fallenness. Regarding the psycho-transcendental parallelism and Husserl's struggle against transcendental psychologism, Jacques Derrida observes that this is "a difference that distinguishes nothing in actuality, that separates no beings"[6] and yet "one which, without altering anything, changes all the signs." *(ibid.)*. Soon thereafter he adds: "Transcendental consciousness is nothing more and nothing other than psychological consciousness. Transcendental psychologism misunderstands that if the world needs a *supplement of soul*, the soul, which is in the world, needs this supplementary nothingness, which is the transcendental and without which no world would become visible."[7]

It goes without saying that this "nothing" is not named by Husserl: nothingness is not among his themes. But it behooves Heidegger to name this "supplementary nothingness" and make it a central theme in line with the very ontologizing of the Husserlian discoveries, particularly of the categorial intuition of Being. This discovery teaches that Being is not a real predicate and is therefore *nothing being*, yet manifests itself to a seeing in its very difference. If the understanding of Being is the issue of phenomenology, then *epochē* must by the same token take on the feature of reduction to the nothing. And if the understanding of the ontic-ontological difference concerns every *Dasein* in its very mineness even in what it is "proximally and for the most part"—in the same fashion as the Husserlian transcendental ego is what the empirical ego presupposes—then it becomes necessary to show that this ontological reduction to the nothing, as metamorphosed *epochē,* must be attested to ontically and pre-ontologically at different levels and depths. This task is accomplished by the successive analyses: of the everyday experience of the dysfunctional character of tools, of anxiety, of the relation to one's own death, of the *Gewissen* (conscience). Those analyses are well known, and I shall not consider them anew. I note, however, that, each time, the description is accompanied by urging caution against confusing ontic and ontological, *existentiell* and existential, i.e., against a confusion linked in its form with what Husserl used to denounce as "transcendental psychologism." I note in addition that at every step the issue is for a *Dasein* which each time is mine to promote a suspension and to experience a seeing. This is what the analysis of *Gewissen* puts perfectly in evidence.

I have argued that ontologizing the Husserlian logical discoveries and the subsequent privileging of the intuition of Being resulted in the notion of an originary *Bedeuten* of *Bedeutung,* which consisted for *Dasein* in the self-givenness of the understanding of its being and its can-be; this self-given understanding is no longer mediated by signs but culminates in an intuitive clarification, the sight of *Durchsichtigkeit* (transparency). This is what is attested to ontically—and pre-ontologically—in the *Dasein* which each time is mine by the phenomenon of *Gewissen* (conscience).

The term *Gewissen* should not be translated as "moral conscience" because the Heideggerian analysis of the phenomenon referred to by the name expressly excludes any moral connotation and attributes the ontological origin of the notions of good and evil, and more generally of value, to *Vorhandenheit,* the mode of being of those entities that, precisely, are not of the same type as *Dasein.* Since in the Heideggerian appraisal the prefix *Ge-* connotes a gathering, collecting, and centering, I would see no objection in translating it as "internal forum." But since in *Gewissen* there is also *-wissen,* namely knowing, I prefer translating it as "internal knowing" or "intimate knowing."

This intimate knowing is presented by Heidegger as the existential attestation of "an authentic potentiality-for-being-Self" *(Selbstseinkönnen).* In assessing the characteristics of this intimate knowing connected with *Selbst*, it is no exaggeration to say that Heidegger subjects it to a monadological purifying, which happens by welding together in the register of intuition alone—after excluding all signs and therefore in the wake of Husserl—*phenomenon* and *logos*.

There is a monadological purifying because in every feature of this intimate knowing *Dasein* is in a circle with itself. The characteristic features are the *existentialia* themselves, here detached from any referent other than the potentiality for being a self. Here the only state-of-mind called forth is fundamental anxiety inasmuch as it reveals the nakedness of facticity, bare *[pure]* strangeness and the "uncanniness which is basically determinative for individualized *[vereinzelt]* Being-in-the-world" (*S.Z.*, 276). Here, the understanding involved has nothing to do with interpretation: it is gathered in the resolute insight of the moment of vision *(Augenblick)* concerning one's ownmost can-be. Here, finally, discourse *(Rede)*, or *logos*, is purified of any communication whatsoever, of any expression, even of any monologue, so as to be collected in the silent hearing of a call with no other referent, no other caller, no other aim than the *Selbst*, inasmuch as it is still in debt *(schuldig)* of its ownmost can-be.

There is an ultimate welding of *phenomenon* and *logos* because what this calling brings to a hearing, i.e., the Nothing, mere *Nichtigkeit*, is also what is given to a sight.

Heidegger insists that this intimate knowing moves within its own circle. He says that hearing the call of *Gewissen* means nothing except willing-to-have-intimate-knowing *(Gewissen-haben-wollen)*.

I find the confirmation of the fact that this monadological purifying is indebted to Husserlian monadology—no matter the extent of its metamorphosis—in two hints. I have argued that the Heideggerian project of fundamental ontology is held in place by an ontologizing of logic. This ontologizing is acknowledged by Heidegger in the very first lines of the supporting text by which he presented his application for professorship in Marburg and Göttingen: this text sketches out an interpretation of Aristotle in light of what Heidegger then called a "hermeneutic of facticity."[8] It is still to this ontologizing of logic that he alluded at the beginning of the Freiburg years in the lecture course on *The Metaphysical Foundations of Logic*. This lecture course, which claims to be phenomenological, contains two parts, one historical and the other thematic.

The first hint in keeping with my argument is to be found in the historical part of the course. It consists essentially in a debate with monadology. The fact that the monadology at stake is Leibniz's or

Husserl's is no objection: Heidegger was fond of allowing texts to overlap. I gave an example of this practice in the analysis of the notions of *phenomenon* and *logos:* this analysis takes place in the language of Aristotle but strictly overlaps a specific Husserlian teaching.

The second hint is to be found in the thematic part of the lecture course. It consists in a metaphysics of the principle of reason, which announces *Vom Wesen des Grundes* and brings a number of clarifications on *Selbst.* After recalling that his question was the fundamental question of metaphysics "What does 'Being' mean?" which alone governed the analytic of *Being and Time,* Heidegger states several leading principles of the analytic.

First and foremost, the notion of *Dasein* is neutral, of a neutrality which is one of essence, prior to any factual concretization in an ontic individuality, prior to any embodiment and consequently prior to belonging to one sex. This neutrality goes hand in hand with innermost *(innerlichst)* isolation. Heidegger grants an originary and transcendental status to this isolated neutrality. It is the ultimate condition of possibility: in it alone the transcendental origin must be sought beyond the splintering *(Zersplitterung)* in a body and sexual division *(Zerspaltung).* More deeply than this bodily splintering and sexual division, which are ontic, there is an ontological and transcendental dispersion *(Zerstreuung)* at the core of the neutrality and metaphysical isolation of *Dasein.* This transcendental dispersion, which goes hand in hand with an equally transcendental *Mitsein,* is founded upon *Geworfenheit.* Finally, it turns out that the world to which this neutral and isolated *Dasein* refers is nothingness: "*Die Welt: ein Nichts, kein Seiendes—und doch etwas; nicht Seiendes—aber Sein*" (The world: a nothing, no being—and yet something; nothing of beings, but Being) (*M.A.L.,* 252; *M.F.L.,* 195). In this hyper-transcendental characterization of *Dasein* we may suspect an echo as well as a profound ontological transformation of the Husserlian reduction considered in its monadological core, which is the pivot for the problematic of embodiment and intersubjectivity. This suspicion is confirmed when we learn that it is this *Dasein,* which is transcendentally neutral and isolated as well as dispersed, that properly speaking is a *Selbst.* It is of it that it can be said "*Dasein* exists for the sake of itself." In a gesture whose style is also Husserlian in inspiration Heidegger insists that this proposition is not the expression of a *Weltanschauung* but concerns an ontological and metaphysical *egoity,* identical with ipseity itself, or *Selbstheit* (see *M.F.L.,* sec. 10 and 11). The suspicion is reinforced when we think that the transcendental problematic called "fundamental ontology" constitutes the "internal and hidden life of the fundamental movement of Western philosophy," a status that until *Krisis* Husserl never ceased granting to pure phenomenology. It is further increased when we learn that this transcendental problematic, a radical one, is also universal in the sense that it leads meta-ontologically to a thematic treatment of beings in their totality. Didn't Husserl conceive of pure phenomenology as the science of the foundation of all sciences and the regions to which they refer?

One final point. The paradox of the search for an answer to the question "Who?" is that after demarcating itself at the outset and in the wake of Husserl from the symbolic in general—and after deliberately taking upon itself Plato's dismissal of *diagesis* and his view that an end should be brought to plots, or *mythoi*—the answer has in the end hardly anything to do with the avatars of someone's life in the midst of plurality and the connected interlocution. The *ipse* which it treats in the wake of the successive reductions is ultimately an *idem*.

Heidegger takes great care to specify that *Dasein*, intrinsically isolated and transcendentally dispersed inasmuch as it is thrown in its existence, is free and that its freedom also is transcendental and metaphysical. He adds that the conquest of this neutrality and metaphysical isolation is itself possible only because of a free projection, which resides only in its being enacted. As such this projection emerges from the existential involvement *(Einsatz)* of a projecting *Dasein* and this involvement is termed "extreme" because it consists in this *Dasein* projecting "the constructive articulation *(Konstruktion)* of one of the most extreme possibilities of authentic and total can-be" (sec. 10), a construction that is identical with philosophic existence.

> The more radical [the philosopher's] existentiell involvement, the more concrete the ontological-metaphysical project. But the more concrete this interpretation of Dasein is, the easier it becomes to misunderstand it in principle by taking the existentiell involvement for what is essential and for the single most important thing, whereas this involvement itself becomes manifest only in the project, with all its indifference to the particularity of the person *[im seiner jeweiligen personalen Belanglosigkeit]*. (M.A.L., 177; M.F.L., 140)

This is tantamount to saying that ultimately—and this is the paradox at which I am aiming—the true authentic response to the question of "Who?" is given by the philosophical act, or in other words that individuation is nothing but speculative.

We should be careful not to claim that, on the issue of the "Who?" at least, Heidegger is not indebted to a Husserlian legacy: in fact the lines I just quoted may be read as designating the vanishing point—in the pictorial sense—of Heidegger's reappropriation of the Husserlian struggle against transcendental psychologism. In the margins of his copy of *Being and Time* Husserl jotted down a considerable number of remarks, which in general accuse Heidegger of anthropologism. In one of them he charges: "Against all that I opposed the natural apprehension of the world in natural worldly life to the philosophical, transcendental apprehension, transcendental understanding—i.e., to a life which is not naturally given to the naive valuing of the world, which does not consist in holding oneself as man in naive valuation, but is the very Idea of philosophical life determined by philosophy" (p. 16, ll. 38–41). Notwithstanding Husserl's objection I have suggested that it is, indeed, an opposition of this very type that regulates the Heideggerian notion of *Selbst* albeit after some considerable metamorphosing. In the process, I did nothing more than take literally this well-known footnote of *Being and Time:*

> If the following investigation has taken any steps forward in disclosing the "things themselves," the author must first of all thank E. Husserl, who, by providing his own incisive personal guidance and by freely turning over his unpublished investigations, familiarized the author with the most diverse areas of phenomenological research. (*S.Z.*, 38; *B.T.*, 489)

We may now view these lines as more than sheer politeness. Inversely, we may assess that something other than blindness dominates Husserl's following remark, penciled in his copy of the book:

> All of this is the translation and transposition of my thinking. Where I say *"Bewußtsein,"* Heidegger says *"Dasein,"* **etc.** (bold characters added)

All that my commentary has purported to do was to investigate, and substantiate, Husserl's **"etc."**

THE QUESTION "WHO?" IN ARENDT

"The human condition of labor is life itself." "The human condition of work is worldliness." "Plurality is the condition of human action" (*H.C.*, 8). Such are the basic statements of Hannah Arendt's master work, *The Human Condition.* By the word "condition" we must understand here what links, locates, and exerts a power of conditioning that is never a power of absolute determination. In other words, "condition" is not an essential component of the human being and Arendt insists at the outset that she finds the notion of a "human nature" worthy of suspicion: not only would our access to such a concept require that we leap above our own shadow, but more importantly this concept—assuming it is secured and presumably enables us to answer the question "What are we?"—could only do so in the wake of ignoring another question, which alone is crucial to her eyes, "Who are we?"

In what sense does life—since this is my theme—exert a power of conditioning? Inasmuch as this question does not aim at ascertaining a single essential component of being human, it can set us only on the path of an intrinsically historical inquiry. It is tantamount to asking how up to this day life has conditioned human beings? "Up to this day" for Arendt means Western history throughout its specific phases—the Greek City, the Roman Republic, the Christian Middle Ages, the birth and development of the modern Nation-States, the various revolutions (the American, the French, the Russian), finally the advent of the totalitarian regimes, which put their seal upon the twentieth century. In each case memory and reflection require that we determine how the "condition" that life is functions with respect to the other two—plurality and worldliness—and how in each case these conditions demarcate themselves or not from each other, i.e., how they form a hierarchy, or interfere with one another, or end up fusing. But this memorialized reflection here evoked with respect to life obviously requires that the status of "condition" attributed to life be clarified. Now such a clarification, even though it is governed by the question "Who are we?," cannot avoid the question "What are we?" Indeed life, as the basic condition for human existence, rightfully responds to the old metaphysical question of essence. In the same text where she underscores that "condition" is not an essential feature of human nature (or human essence), Arendt notes that the "modes of human cognition" applicable to those things endowed with "natural" qualities may also be applied to us "to the limited extent that we are specimens of the most highly developed species of organic life" (*H.C.*, 11). In other words, although human existence, which is basically conditioned by life, does not have an essence, this basic condition called "life" has an essence. But Arendt warns that it is only "to a limited extent" that human existence falls within the field of the question of essence. What does this mean? Does this limit only concern the inclusion of human life within biological life? Not at all. It concerns instead what in human existence prevents human beings from revealing "who" they are and what tends to reduce them to the specimens, or instances of a kind, of a species, hence to absorb them in the anonymity of an essence. For life in the organic sense offers the paradigm of such a reduction.

Arendt writes: "A philosophy of life that does not arrive, as did Nietzsche, at the affirmation of the 'eternal recurrence' *(ewige Wiederkehr)* as the highest principle of all beings, simply does not know what it is talking about" (*H.C.*, 97). Concerning life, indeed, the question "Who?" may never arise because irreplaceable singularity cannot emerge in a cyclical process regulated by the repetition of the same. Concerning life, the birth of a living being is neither an advent nor an event because in no way does the new living being open up a new unique path, an irreplaceable sequence of adventures and unforeseeable events; rather, the living being merely reproduces or repeats the species. Similarly, the death of a living being does not come to seal a singular destiny; it too is something repeatable in the perpetual cycle. "Everything goes under the earth and comes back into the play."[9] And this repetition of the same, affecting the beginning and end of each living being, affects also the moments of the life allotted to it. So long as the individual stays alive, this very maintaining is itself a cycle, a repetition of alternating phases—a coming and going of needs, of efforts made to produce what satisfies them in consumption, of pleasure and rest, and of the reappearance of needs. In this process every individual being experiences in itself through the onrush of its bodily functions a work of incorporation, expulsion and destruction wherein this individual counts for nothing, a work that, however, is the individual.

Because reproduction and individual survival are subjected to the repetition of the same, life is the realm of *necessity*. For the same reason, life prevents any differentiating that goes beyond the exercise of a vital or generative function. Inasmuch as it governs what it dispenses, life can be the source of a profuse *multiplicity* but could not tolerate that individuals emanating from it express their singularity, be destined to exhibit their uniqueness and make it recognized by others. In other words life multiplies itself, but in no way does it favor what Arendt calls plurality, i.e., the condition consisting for each individual in being both similar to others and different from them and unique. The groupings that life brings out have as their goal not the manifestation of singularity but life itself, for whose support the group members are in a relation of *mutual dependency*. In such groupings there is intrinsic monotony and conformism, which in the end are rooted in the unity of the concerned species.

All these features of life as eternal return of the same are also those of the human activity which life conditions, namely labor—they are the features of the effort of the body struggling against nature in order to wrest from her its own subsistence, i.e., the essentially ephemeral products that are no sooner brought into the world than consumed. Because this activity is both body-dependent and body-directed and because in the words of Marx it is "a metabolism with nature," it is bound to share the characteristics of the vital cycle in which it is inscribed: necessity, repetitiveness, multiplication, interdependency of the bodies, fundamental anonymity of the agent.

This picture may seem unduly negative but Arendt underscores that at the same time as the periodicity of the vital cycle—and consequently of the labor inscribed within that cycle—generates monotony, it is also a factor of equilibrium or security and confidence. In the very periodicity of a cycle there is a renewed adjustment and compensation between opposed phases, which allows Arendt to speak of an "economy of nature." And because nature is inscribed in this self-sustaining cycle, the cycle shares in its security and in the very joy of living.

> The "blessing or the joy" of labor is the human way to experience the sheer bliss of being alive which we share with all living creatures, and it is the only way men, too, can remain and swing contentedly in nature's prescribed cycle, toiling and resting, laboring and consuming, with the same and purposeless regularity with which day and night and life and death follow each other. The reward of this toil and trouble lies in nature's fertility, in the quiet evidence that he who has "toil and trouble" has done his part, remains a part of nature in the future of his children and his children's children . . . The blessing of labor is that effort and gratification follow each other as closely as producing and consuming the means of subsistence, so that happiness is a concomitant of the process itself, just as pleasure is the concomitant of the functioning of a healthy body. (*H.C.*, 106–8)

And because labor is so closely connected with the vital cycle and the tranquil evidence within which it moves, the joy it owes to its participation in the felicity of life is the only durable one.

There is no lasting happiness outside the prescribed cycle of painful exhaustion and pleasurable regeneration, and whatever throws this cycle out of balance—poverty and misery where exhaustion is followed by wretchedness instead of regeneration, or great riches and an entirely effortless life where boredom takes the place of exhaustion and where the mills of necessity, of consumption and digestion, grind an impotent human body mercilessly and barrenly to death—ruins the elemental happiness that comes from being alive. (*Ibid.*, 108)

This summary recall is sufficient to delineate the essential features of the Arendtian concept of life. We must hold these features in view if we want to avoid any misunderstanding concerning the expression *animal laborans*. In addition to not being associated with any kind of disdain, this expression does not refer to a special segment of the population. Every human being is an *animal laborans* as long as he or she lives, because the metabolism that allows a body to function is a labor and, quite obviously, survival depends upon the daily performance of a certain number of repetitive tasks. Yet, if his or her existence were merely limited to the life cycle, this individual would never be able to answer the question "Who are you?" and never could the phenomenon of "who he or she is" be seen, appear, and be recognized. The vital cycle within which labor participates would, no doubt, confer an essence upon the *animal laborans*, an essence which by definition would be generic and anonymous, it would be a "what," or *quid*, never a "someone," or *quis*. In order for life to be the life of somebody, it is necessary that another condition should superpose over the vital cycle of nature, or basic condition, while this new condition rests upon but also resists the previous one. This other condition is worldliness or the belonging to a world. The world is not at all nature, conceived as living environment or, even less, universe. The world is held in place by a whole set of artifacts conquered over nature but resisting the flux of its cycles. It is at this juncture that the disagreement between Arendt and Marx is the most marked. Although Marx superbly delineated the features of labor, he remained totally blind to the distinction between nature and world. In agreement with Marx Arendt maintains that human beings become human by inventing artifacts. In disagreement with him she views this invention as entirely separate from the goal of helping in the life cycle. This invention rather is motivated by the goal of resisting this life cycle in order to superimpose on the eternal return the consistency, the stability and the permanence of a dwelling upon which the "who" might appear.

Because the condition of the production of artifacts is the world, work cannot be confused with labor. The product of working is not destined to be consumed as that of laboring, it is destined to last; and because the institution of things that last is the end of the working activity, this activity is linear whereas labor is cyclical. Whatever the disparities between these two activities, the important thing for us is to note that there must be a world before the life of someone may appear. Arendt writes:

> The birth and death of human beings are not simple natural occurrences, but are related to a world into which single individuals, unique, unexchangeable, and unrepeatable entities, appear and from which they depart. Birth and death presuppose a world which is not in constant movement, but whose durability and relative permanence makes appearance and disappearance possible, which existed before any one individual appeared into it and will survive its eventual departure. (*Ibid.*, 97)

With respect to the world, life and death lose their status as phases in a repetitive and anonymous cycle. Now the word "life" no longer designates the eternal return of the same:

> [It] has an altogether different meaning if it is related to the world and meant to designate the time interval between life and death. Limited by a beginning and an end, that is, by the two supreme events of appearance and disappearance within the world, it follows a strictly linear movement whose very motion nevertheless is driven by the motor of biological life which man shares with other living things and which forever retains the cyclical movement of nature. The chief characteristic of this specifically human life, whose appearance and disappearance constitute worldly events, is that it is itself always full of events which ultimately can be told as a story, establish a biography; it is of this life, *bios* as distinguished from mere *zoē*, that Aristotle said that it "somehow is a kind of *praxis*." (*Ibid.*)

We encounter therefore the life of someone only inasmuch as the stability of the world allows the interval between life and death to be extracted from the vitalistic repetition of the same. But we just saw that this interval—conceived as a linear sequence encompassing singular, irreversible events—is what Aristotle calls "a kind of *praxis*." Now, in Aristotelian terminology, *praxis* designates neither labor nor the production of artifacts *(poiēsis)* but the third mode of activity, which Arendt calls "action." Not only does the life of someone presuppose a world which *poiēsis* works to erect, but since it is *praxis* it presupposes also its correlative condition, plurality. I pointed out earlier that *praxis* is the very condition that consists for each individual in being both similar to and different from others and thus unique. In what sense is action intrinsically conditioned by plurality, and what does action amount to if it is thus determined? Unlike on the one hand labor, of which we saw that by virtue of its inscription within the eternal return of the same it is an activity where the "who" could not appear, and unlike on the other hand the activity of production of artifacts, which as such is never anything else than the setting-to-work of general or generic aptitudes likely to be found identical among a certain number of individuals thereby revealing not "who" but "what" he or she is, action in the strict sense is that by which a singular individual exhibits who he or she is. And this individual can make appear who he or she is only in facing others who accept this appearing and themselves too show who they are. For such a showing forth, which is intrinsically interpersonal and connects one to one's peers, speech is indispensable. Speech permits each one to say who he or she is. Exception made for the singing of refrains, which facilitates individual or group efforts, labor is silent; likewise, with the exception of commands, which allot tasks or provide explanations, the process of the production of artifacts is silent too. At any rate, it is not indispensable that the agent declare who he or she is. By contrast, action in the strict sense is both intrinsically plural and interlocutory. Hence, Aristotle's close association between *praxis* and *lexis* (speech). As a result of this close association the world reveals itself as much more than the sum of durable artifacts. It becomes a common habitat that keeps in itself the traces and monuments of those who preceded us, a habitat perceived in common and whose consistency is owed to the diversity of perspectives that relate to it as well as to the diversity of the speech acts expressing the diversity of perspectives.

It is sometimes reproached to Arendt that she reserves the activity of action proper to a small group of elect ones and that she came to conceive it after the feats of heroes in the *Odyssey*. This reproach is hasty and groundless. Action for Arendt is in no way the privilege of a few, widely known, public figures, of individuals called "men of action." It consists in the very life of each individual, in his or her *bios*, inasmuch as in virtue of the stability of the world which is conquered over the devouring cycle of nature—i.e., conquered beyond the vital cycle to whose thrust each individual is subjected—this life inscribes itself within a network of interpersonal relations inherited from our predecessors and renewed with the incessant arrival of newcomers; this network is as much inherited as renewed when speech is exchanged. Although each human being has to a degree the status of *animal laborans*—an ascription dictated by organic life—and although some have the status of *homo faber*—an ascription that comes as the result of certain aptitudes—all of them have at their birth been endowed with action not as a result of the generic fact of procreation but merely because all emerge in a common world and have the capacity to initiate an absolutely unique sequence of events. It is sometimes asked: But what does this action do? Silly question this is. For the question suggests that "living" as applicable to the unique existence of someone mortal is tantamount to "making something" or that *poiēsis* and *praxis* are identical. *Poiēsis* aims at a product that is external to it, in which it reaches its term, and shares its reproducibility with those general aptitudes required to produce it. *Praxis* has no external product that may be generalized. What action introduces into the world is the *uniqueness* of someone: not the initiative he or she has of making something, but the initiative open to the individual for being somebody. Arendt liked to quote Dante who wrote: "For in every action what is primarily intended by the doer . . . is the disclosure of his own image . . . Thus, nothing acts unless [by acting] it makes patent its latent self" (*De Monarchia*, 1: 13; quoted in *H.C.*, 175).

But the uniqueness of this self has nothing monistic about it. Far from requiring the withdrawal within a egocentric sphere, it only reveals itself in a network of relationships and speech acts; and since its being is tantamount to appearing to others, the uniqueness of the "who" always remains hidden to the one acting. Intensely personal and yet non-revealed to the agent, action is first and foremost the very existence of someone in the unforeseeable and irreversible sequence of events that happen to him or her within this network of relationships and words. It is because action is inscribed within this network that it always produces stories. It is for that reason too that although someone is indeed the sole bearer of his or her own history and the one innovating in it, the same person is not its author or its producer: he or she does not make his or her own history. This very plurality brings out another radical divergence between *poiēsis* and *praxis*: the outcome of production is determinate and entails a "finish"; nothing of the sort happens in the case of action, since its inscription in a plural network makes it unlimited as a result of the unforeseeable character of the reactions it brings about. This means that recounting the past is a task always to take anew in light of the distant effects which the present seems to reveal. There is, therefore, a sort of fundamental frailty of *praxis*, and the life of someone would run the risk of loosing its identity and the claim implicit in this person's uniqueness if the irreversibility of every deed and every word were not compensated for by forgiveness and if their unpredictability were not corrected by promising and giving one's word.

We can measure now the distance separating the two answers given to the question "Who?"

The first answer commits the asking to an inventory of *existentialia* and to the progressive purifying, with respect to the public world of appearances, the sharing of words and deeds, the expounding of narratives, and more generally any symbolizing. This movement leads to the radical isolation of being *Selbst*, whose activity—prior to its dispersion in a body and a *Mitsein*—is strictly limited to the solitary and silent seeing of *Dasein*'s ownmost can-be.

The second answer commits other persons for its coming to pass and, to this extent, consists in each person replying to others and in identifying himself as the agent of his deeds by announcing to others "what he is doing, what he did, and what he intends to do" in the midst of a plurality that precedes and will succeed that person, so that this individuation in words and acts gives full right to narratives and opens the door, so to speak, to unlimited symbolizing.

NOTES

1. See "'Voix' et 'phénomème' dans l'ontologie fondamentale de Heidegger," in *Revue philosophique*, 2: 1990, pp. 395–408. A first version of the current essay was published in *La Phénoménologie aux confins*, Mauvezin: TER, 1992.
2. Jacques Derrida, *La voix et le phénomène*, Paris: P.U.F., 1967; see *Speech and Phenomena*, trans. David B. Allison, Evanston: Northwestern University Press, 1973.
3. *Die Grundprobleme der Phänomenologie*, Vittorio Klostermann, 1975, hereafter *G.P.*; see *The Basic Problems of Phenomenology*, trans. Albert Hofstadter, Bloomington: Indiana University Press, 1988, hereafter *B.P.*
4. *Prolegomena zur Geschichte des Zeitbegriffs*, Vittorio Klostermann, 1979, hereafter *P.G.Z.*; see *The History of the Concept of Time*, trans. Theodore Kisiel, Bloomington: Indiana University Press, 1985, hereafter *H.C.T.*

5. *Metaphysische Anfangsgründe der Logik im Ausgang von Leibniz*, Vittorio Klostermann, 1978, hereafter *M.A.L.*; *The Metaphysical Foundations of Logic*, trans. Michael Heim, Bloomington: Indiana University Press, 1984, hereafter *M.F.L.*

6. Jacques Derrida, *La voix et le phénomène*, Paris: P.U.F., 1967, p. 10. See *Speech and Phenomena*, trans. David B. Allison, Evanston: Northwestern University Press, 1973, p. 11, mod.

7. *Ibid.*, French text, pp. 12–13; English text, p. 13, mod.

8. The text appeared in *Dilthey Jahrbuch*, 6, 1988.

9. See Paul Valéry's poem "Le cimetière marin" ("Sea Cemetery").

THREE

From Aristotle to *Bios Theōrētikos*
and Tragic *Theōria*

Heidegger, I have argued, put *Nicomachean Ethics* to the task of establishing the existential foundations of *bios theō-rētikos* conceived as aletheic *praxis* aiming at the seeing of Being, inasmuch as it is no being. Along the way we have detected some of the biases of that reappropriation: it presupposes that there is no discontinuity whatsoever between Plato and Aristotle: *Nico-machean Ethics* would supposedly limit itself to clarifying the on-tology of *Dasein* already implicit in the Platonic struggle against those everyday modes of veiling such as the *doxa*, the persuasive discourse of the rhetorician and the mythical discourses that relate plots. Since the *bios theōrētikos* which solicits this struggle entails the existential choice of the thinker devoting himself to the soli-tary seeing of Being, this reappropriation is part of the elaboration of a purified monadology which strikes with fallenness the entire public sphere of plural interaction and interlocution. According to the terms of this monadology, *phenomenon* in the purest sense is the only singular can-be of finite *Dasein* and *logos* in the purest sense is the silent voice by which *Dasein* signifies to itself its own-most can-be.

It can be said that contrasting with this speculative reappropria-tion of Aristotle *The Human Condition* introduces an entirely praxeological reappropriation.

With the exception of Marx, who will not concern us here, the two authors most often quoted in the book are Plato and Aristotle. But a close examination of the treatment Arendt gives of both would show that she underscores in Plato what is unfaithful to *praxis*, whereas she highlights in Aristotle what has remained faithful to it. It is the insistence on that faithfulness that I would like to bring to clarity by means of an examination of some central notions of her analysis of action: speech, the doublet *idion* (private)

-*koinon* (public), appearance, the opposition immortality-eternity, *dynamis*. In the interpretation she gives of those notions Arendt claims to be indebted to Aristotle. But in each case what she detects in Aristotle with whom she is in agreement is not at all a privileging of *bios theōrētikos*, but rather the echo of *bios politikos*. We may therefore view Arendt's position with respect to these notions as so many retorts and replies to Heidegger.

The topic of speech is treated by Heidegger in the lecture course on *The Sophist:* at the outset he connects with truth conceived as unveiling:

> *Alētheia* reveals a specific ontological character of a being, inasmuch as it holds itself in relation to seeing. Seeing is itself a mode of being of the entity that we call human Dasein: openness *[Erschließung]*. This openness of the world itself, inasmuch as it is, is characterized as *alētheuein*, uncovering which consists in wresting the being from its closedness and covering-over. It is a mode of being of *Dasein*. It shows itself first in *legein*. In speech human Dasein expresses itself, and in such a way that it talks about something, about the world. To express oneself in such a way was for the Greeks, who used to speak liberally and a lot, something so pressing and ordinary that it is from this phenomenon that they conquered the definition of man: a living being endowed with speech . . . Aristotle defined *logos* in its fundamental function as *apophansis* or else as *dēloun*. (17–18)

This definition of the Aristotelian *logos* is a strictly theoretical and ontological one. Speech unveils inasmuch as it is tightly bound to a seeing *(theōria)* of beings themselves. But, what is thus unveiled, Heidegger insists, is threatened with being "immediately covered over by opinion. Opinions crystallize in propositions that are repeated in such a way that what had been seen originarily is veiled anew, covered over" (16). Hence the necessity of fighting against *doxa*.

Against this stance Arendt's reading of the Aristotelian definition of man as *zōon logon echōn* can be opposed term for term. This definition, she claims, is strictly indissociable from the other Aristotelian definition of man, *zōon politikon*. She stresses that by characterizing humans as living beings endowed with speech Aristotle was neither aiming at a definition of man in general nor pointing at his highest potentiality, which for him was not *logos*, but *nous*, "the capacity of contemplation, whose chief characteristic is that its content cannot be rendered in speech" (*ibid.*, 27). She adds:

In his two most famous definitions, Aristotle only formulated the current opinion of the *polis* about man and the political way of life, and according to this opinion, everybody outside the *polis*—slaves and barbarians—was *aneu logou,* deprived, of course, not of the faculty of speech, but of a way of life in which speech and only speech made sense and where the central concern of all citizens was to talk with each other. *(Ibid.)*

One could not say better that the Aristotelian formula *zōon logon echōn* has nothing to do with the *bios theōrētikos,* toward which Heidegger nonetheless immediately directs it, and that far from containing the traces of an opposition to the realm of opinion, this expression aims at giving right to it, and that the "speech" it evokes is not first and foremost veritist, but rather interlocutory, active sharing of a *lexis.* Precisely because this speech is exchanged, it is inconceivable without repetitions of what others have said and its aim could not conceivably be to coincide only with those perspectives that are the individual's own, since this restriction would be tantamount to abolishing the plurality of interlocutors for the benefit of a unique spectator of the true.

There is more. Precisely because Heidegger channels the Aristotelian formula exclusively toward *bios theōrētikos,* he reactivates a gesture that we find first in Plato, second in the views of Aristotle concerning the speculative (as Arendt also points out, and we saw it), and closer to us in Husserl's *Logical Investigations.* This gesture subordinates *logos* to a seeing that is reserved for the *nous.* Conversely, because at the outset Arendt connects *logos* to *bios politikos* and even, further upstream chronologically, to the prepolitical experience of action recounted in the Homeric legends— legends which inspired the playwrights of the tragic theater—she underscores the secondariness of thought with respect to speech. She writes:

The stature of the Homeric Achilles can be understood only if one sees him as the "doer of great deeds and the speaker of great words." In distinction from modern understanding, such words were not considered to be great because they expressed great thoughts; on the contrary, as we know from the last lines of *Antigone,* it may be the capacity for great words *(megaloi logoi),* with which [we fence] striking blows, that will eventually teach thought in old age. Thought was secondary to speech, but speech and action were considered to be coeval and coequal, of the same rank and of the same kind; and this originally meant that most political action, in so far as it remains outside the sphere of violence, is indeed transacted in words, but more fundamentally that finding the right words at the right moment, quite apart from the information or communication they may convey, is action. (*Ibid.*, 24–25)

We can notice an analogous reply and retort to Heidegger in Arendt's notion of appearance. Appearing is phenomenon. For Arendt as well as for the Heidegger of fundamental ontology Being is Appearing. But it is one thing to say, as Heidegger did then, that the being of *Dasein* can appear to it inasmuch as it transcends every being, it is another thing to say, as Arendt does, that to be truly human is to appear. In the first case what is at issue is the ownmost can-be of *Dasein* appearing to it exclusively, inasmuch as relinquishing all intercourse with beings it transcends itself toward Being. In the second case, what is at issue is a form of publicly manifested excellence, which presupposes liberation from everything strictly private. The same formula "Being is Appearing" lends therefore itself to two antithetical readings. The formula designates, for Heidegger, the wresting of *idion* (private) from *koinon* (public); for Arendt, that of *koinon* from *idion*. And it is the same Greek texts, primarily *Nicomachean Ethics*, that inspire these two readings, of which the first is focused on *bios theōrētikos* and superbly overlooks that which in Aristotle's words makes it a treatise of political philosophy, while the second points out all that may be objected against this neglect.

When in *Nicomachean Ethics*, book 10, Aristotle writes "*ha gar pasi dokei taut' einai phamen*" (for what appears to all, this we call Being, 1176b36 ff.), Arendt does not fail to detect in these words the expression of the public space of appearance in which action is inscribed in the sense of linguistic and plural interaction:

> To be deprived of this space means to be deprived of reality, which, humanly and politically speaking, is the same as appearance. To men the reality of the world is guaranteed by the presence of others, by its appearing to all; "for what appears to all, this we call Being," and whatever lacks this appearance comes and passes away like a dream, intimately and exclusively our own but without reality. (*Ibid.*, 199)

By contrast during the time when he sought his inspiration in *Nicomachean Ethics*, particularly book 6, in order to elaborate his fundamental ontology, Heidegger would indeed say—this was recorded by Gadamer, who was one of his assiduous listeners—that ultimately Aristotelian *phronēsis* was tantamount to *Gewissen*.[1] This admission is a pregnant one if it is true that, on the one hand, *phronēsis* is in *Nicomachean Ethics* the excellence of practical wisdom of which Aristotle finds a model in the public shining forth of a Pericles and if it is true, on the other hand, that *Gewissen* in the Heideggerian sense is the intimate knowing by means of which *Dasein* in the throws of anxiety is extracted from the common space and relates exclusively to what is strictly its own. It is for this intimate knowing that it turns out that *"Dasein* exists for the sake of itself."* This key formula of fundamental ontology results, as we saw, from the reappropriation by Heidegger of the Aristotelian doctrine on *praxis*.

In this reappropriation appearance, i.e., phenomenon in the Heideggerian sense, is at issue. Since another reading of the same doctrine is at the basis of Arendt's notion of appearance, confronting these two interpretations of appearance will put us on the way to realizing what in Arendt is tantamount to a reply and retort to Heidegger.

I have already argued that the structural support of the existential analytic, i.e., the distinction between ownmost and improper, authentic and everyday, care and concern is inspired—before a process of ontologizing—by the distinction established by *Nicomachean Ethics* between the comportment of action, or *praxis*, and the comportment of fabrication, or *poiēsis*. In this distinction appearing is at stake. Indeed, following Aristotle, *praxis* is really what it is only inasmuch as it is given over to its own manifestation, to its own shining forth, inasmuch as it aims at its own excellence, i.e., as it is *hou heneka* (for the sake of itself). As a result, one could say that it is fundamentally apophantic, which by contrast *poiēsis* is not because, so long as it exists as an activity, it is solely the product of its work that needs to appear: the productive activity is merely its means, no sooner effective than erased; in addition, once a work exists, its very manifestation is subjected to a sort of loss in an indefinite cycle of means and ends, of references *pros ti* or *pros tinos*. But from Aristotle's praxeological proposition *"praxis* is *hou heneka"* to Heidegger's ontological proposition *"Dasein* exists for the sake of itself" the inference is one of total metamorphosis, inasmuch as it transposes what for Aristotle is public, or *koinon*, into what is private, or *idion*. It is against this transposition that Arendt's analysis of action is directed. Her analysis is indeed also inspired by the Aristotelian concept of *praxis* as when she writes of action that "this specifically human achievement lies altogether outside the category of means and ends; the 'work of man' [ergon tou anthrōpou] is no end because the means to achieve it—the virtues, or aretai—are not qualities that may or may not be actualized, but are themselves actualities" (ibid., 207). But this Aristotelian idea that action has no other meaning than its own completion resonates for her with a double echo. The first echo is that of pre-philosophical, even pre-political experience of action and speech as "pure actuality," an essentially frail experience of the fact that someone may appear as the one "who" he is only by speaking and acting in the midst of a plurality of equals. The second echo is that of the experience of the polis, which, she argues, was founded as a remedy against this fragility and has a double function. Thanks to the sharing of words and deeds, the polis may both "multiply the chances for everybody to distinguish himself, to show in deed and word who he was in his unique distinctness" (ibid., 197) and "establish . . . everlasting remembrance" (ibid.) of these words and deeds. In other words, the Aristotelian concept of praxis subscribed to by Arendt echoes first the Funeral Speech that Thucydides attributes to Pericles and second, even further upstream chronologically, the Homeric epos. As connected with the space of public appearance of "who" each one is, this concept is indissociable from that of mythos (plot) as well as from that of bios politikos.

Heidegger too thinks that praxis is the appearing of each one in his ownmost individuality, his own way of excelling. Yet, because excellence in his eyes resides in bios theōrētikos given over to the solitary contemplation of Being, he merely retains from the Aristotelian praxis what puts him on the way to speculative excellence. Recently a lost Heideggerian text of 1922 reemerged: it was a research project on Aristotle by which Heidegger supported his candidacy to a teaching position at the University of Marburg. Gadamer once had a copy of it and always claimed that this text had been decisive for his own work of hermeneutics inasmuch as in it Heidegger developed the idea that in phronēsis interpretation is always in situation or "applied" to a situation. When he reread this text several decades later, Gadamer told his surprise to observe in hindsight that "in Heidegger's manuscript phronēsis is not quite so prominent as theoretical life, or sophia."[2] He adds that "this means that what preoccupied then the young Heidegger more than the relevance of practical philosophy was its meaning for the Aristotelian ontology, Metaphysics" (ibid.). It is exactly this deliberate orientation and privileging of theoretical life and ontology that rules over the Heideggerian analysis of *praxis* in the lecture course on *The Sophist* and it is against this bias that Arendt reacts in *The Human Condition*. This state of affairs appears unmistakably when one confronts on the one hand the treatment she conducts of the themes of immortality and eternity and on the other the one owed to Heidegger.

Commenting on the famous pages of book 10 of *Nicomachean Ethics* (1177a, ff.) on *energeia theōrētikē*, the setting into act of contemplation, Heidegger notes that in Aristotle's eyes there is preeminence of the theoretical excellence, in which *sophia* consists, over the practical excellence of *phronēsis*. Whereas *phronēsis* relates to something other than itself, namely action, *sophia* consists in the human being standing in pure *theōria* and is the only mode of being "that could be sought for its own sake *[um ihrer selbst willen]*." He comments that this standing is pure only if

> as authentic comportment, it maintains itself and reaches in fact over the totality of human existence. In this resides the specific tendency to measure human Dasein, with respect to its temporal being, against the being-always of the world (in the sense of the heavens and *physis*). This *theōrein* must not be sustained on demand from time to time but in uninterrupted fashion throughout life. It is in this that resides for man a certain possibility of *athanazein* (1177b33), of not dying, therefore of the mode of being of man in which he has the highest possibility: of not going toward the end. This is the most extreme position to which human Dasein might be conducted in the Greek interpretation. (177–78)

To be sure we find in *The Human Condition* no sign opposing the pertinence of this analysis of *bios theōrētikos* in the sense given by Aristotle and, before him, Plato. We can find however many an implicit objection against the reduction entailed by the analysis. To reduce the Greek pursuit of *athanazein*, of immortalizing, to *bios theōrētikos* amounts to hiding the fact that, before the Platonic invention of this *bios*, such a pursuit was conducted solely in the realm of *praxis*, that is to say, of linguistic and plural interactions and that it corresponded—as I am going to show it—to another *theōria* than that of the philosophers absorbed in the contemplation of *physis*.

In addition it amounts to hiding that the inventors of this new *bios* were aware of the fact that they were breaking with quite a different pursuit of immortality and that, in the attempt to have theirs accepted, they had to justify it with respect to the still dominating criteria of practical immortalizing. On the contemplative pursuit of immortality we may think with Heidegger that it turns us away from the condition of being mortals and gets us as close as possible to what in nature is being always, and for ever, and to that extent is divine. But unlike the pursuit of contemplative immortalizing, practical immortalizing, whose signs Arendt detects in Homer, in the life of the City, and also in Aristotle does not turn us away at all from the affairs of the mortals: it consists rather in bringing glory upon their very fragility. Is it not significant that one of the most noteworthy expressions of this glory *(doxa)* should be found in a Funeral Speech? And if it is true that *Nicomachean Ethics* is in Aristotle's view a treaty on political philosophy and not on first philosophy, is it arbitrary to think with Arendt that the very passages in which Heidegger himself detects the Greek privileging of *bios theōrētikos*—which conquers immortalizing by turning away from human affairs in order to contemplate the eternal in nature— still contain a tribute to the *bios politikos*? Concerning *Nicomachean Ethics* she writes:

> The famous passage in Aristotle, "[Regarding] human affairs, one must not . . . consider man as he is and not consider what is mortal in mortal things, but think about them [only] to the extent that they have the possibility of immortalizing," occurs very properly in his political writings. For the *polis* was for the Greeks, as the *res publica* was for the Romans, first of all their guarantee against the futility of individual life, the space protected against this futility and reserved for the relative permanence, if not immortality, of **mortals**. (*Ibid.*, 56, bold characters added)

Interpreting *Nicomachean Ethics* for the sake of his fundamental ontology, Heidegger, in summary, argues that Aristotle is right to claim that the *praxis* of a mortal is for his or her own sake, right also to claim that *theōria* is also, or even more so, for its own sake, but is wrong dissociating *theōria* from *praxis*, because this is tantamount to turning away from being-toward-death, which is constitutive of *Dasein* in the ownmost. Arendt, in summary, objects— without aiming the objection explicitly—that the condition of mortals does not reach authenticity in the seeing of one's own mortality but in the manifestation in deeds and words of an individual distinguishing himself or herself "with a recognizable life-story from birth to death" (*ibid.*, 19).

Finally, we are now able to confront two approaches to *dynamis*. Ontological manifestation or *phenomenon* in the Heideggerian sense is the appearing of the ownmost can-be. The theme of potentiality thus forms the loom of the existential analytic. Its conceptual articulation owes much to the Aristotelian analysis of the intimate relationship linking *dynamis* and *energeia* in the case of *praxis*. Aristotle shows that in the activity of *poiēsis dynamis* is external with respect to *energeia* because no sooner is the work, or *ergon*, produced than it falls outside this activity, which is as a potentiality, or *dynamis*, external to the end and effacing itself in front of the actuality of the product. By contrast, Aristotle teaches that in the activity of *praxis*, *dynamis* is internal in *energeia*, it is not abolished in its enactment, which must always be taken up again and therefore ever remains potential. Metamorphosing *praxis* into *Dasein*'s existence for the sake of oneself, Heidegger underscores that this existing is entirely potential: it is the resolute confrontation of one's ownmost can-be. But at the outcome of this metamorphosing, one may easily see that potentiality has become strictly monadological.

By contrast, those pages devoted by Arendt to "power" are tantamount to a reply or retort, although one not explicitly aimed. Because the condition of *praxis* is plurality, she insists that there is no power, or potentiality, except in being-together which shall not be understood as unanimous community, as this would amount to a large monad. She insists on

> this peculiarity of the public realm, which, because it ultimately resides on action and speech, never altogether loses its potential character. What first undermines and then kills political communities is loss of power and final impotence; and power cannot be stored up and kept in reserve for emergencies, like the instruments of violence, but *exists only in its actualization.* . . . Power is what keeps the public realm, the potential space of appearance between acting and speaking men, in existence. The word itself, its Greek equivalent *dynamis* . . . indicates its "potential" character. Power is always, as we would say, a power potential and not an unchangeable, measurable, and reliable entity like force or strength. (*Ibid.*, 200)

In addition, strength is individual and powerless against power, whereas force—indispensable though it is to the activity of *poiēsis* and the violence with which this activity wrests artifacts from nature—could only, if applied to human affairs, be destructive of their plurality, although it is ultimately powerless in front of the manifestations of this plurality. More importantly, it is inasmuch as it corresponds to plurality that "power can be divided without decreasing it, and the interplay of powers with their checks and balances is even liable to create more power, so long, at least, as the interplay is alive and has not resulted in a stalemate" (ibid., 201). By contrast, she insists that "whoever, for whatever reasons, isolates himself and does not partake in such being together, forfeits power and become impotent" (ibid.). For what is, we may ask, the solitary confronting of one's ownmost death if not the admission of a fundamental impotence in facing it?

This brings us to our last theme, that of the theōria prior to the invention of bios theōrētikos, namely the tragic theōria echoed by Aristotle in his Poetics. It is striking to note that Heidegger's lecture courses devoted to Aristotle at the time of the genesis of his fundamental ontology all neglect his Poetics.

It is not less striking to note, by contrast, that in her analyses of action Arendt devotes to it a long page, which deserves to be quoted in full:

> The specific content as well as the general meaning of action and speech may take various forms of reification in art works which glorify a deed or an accomplishment and, by transformation and condensation, show some extraordinary event in its full significance. However, the specific revelatory quality of action and speech, the implicit manifestation of the agent and speaker, is so indissolubly tied to the living flux of acting and speaking that it can be represented and "reified" only through a kind of repetition, the imitation or mimēsis, which according to Aristotle prevails in all arts but is actually appropriate only to the drama, whose very name (from the Greek verb dran, "to act") indicates that play-acting actually is an imitation of acting. But the imitative element lies not in the art of the actor, but as Aristotle rightly claims, in the making or writing of the play, at least to the extent that the drama comes fully to life only when it is enacted in the theater. Only the actors and speakers who re-enact the story's plot can convey the full meaning, not so much of the story itself, but of the "heroes" who reveal themselves in it. In terms of Greek tragedy, this would mean that the story's direct as well as its universal meaning is revealed by the chorus, which does not imitate and whose comments are pure poetry, whereas the intelligible identities of the agents in the story, since they escape all generalization and therefore all reification, can be conveyed only through an imitation

of their acting. This is also why the theater is the political art par excellence; only there is the political sphere of human life transported into art. By the same token, it is the only art whose sole subject is man in his relationship to others. (*Ibid.,* 187–88)

In a footnote Arendt underscores that:

the decisive point is that tragedy does not deal with the qualities of men, their *poiotēs,* but with whatever happened with respect to them, with their actions and life and good or ill fortune (1450a15–18). The content of tragedy is not what we would call character but action or the plot. (*Ibid.,* 187)

This analysis is short. Arendt used to write quickly, which often owed her the accusation of being a mere journalist. But in its very conciseness this analysis of Aristotle's *Poetics* seems to me flawless in its perspicacity. Let me then try—using it as well as some notations scattered in her text or notes and with the assistance of works of others that seem to me to agree with hers—to determine at my own risk the links that connected tragic spectacles with *bios politikos* and to delineate the nature of the gaze, or *theōria,* that corresponded to this spectacle before the invention of *bios theōrētikos.* This will present us with the opportunity of questioning a peculiar propensity of gazing toward the speculative, which philosophers from Plato to Heidegger—Aristotle being set aside—have had when considering tragedy.

It is originally in Plato's *Republic* and subsequently in Aristotle's *Poetics* that the first philosophical approaches to tragedy are articulated. In both cases the notion of *mimēsis* plays a capital role. Yet Plato and Aristotle draw upon it from very different perspectives. The angle that determines Plato's considerations is a function of the quasi-exclusive privilege he grants to the *bios theōrētikos,* to the philosopher's speculative mode of life. By contrast, the Aristotelian perspective is entirely praxeological. In this respect Arendt notes that, in light of the *Poetics,* "it is obvious that Aristotle's model for 'imitation' in art is taken from drama" (*H.C.,* 187). In addition, it is striking to observe that the *Poetics* contains no allusion to any theme of first philosophy.

Before questioning this contrast and in order to do so fruitfully, I have to point out that in the days when Plato first and then Aristotle—to a large extent against him—attempted to subject tragedy to a philosophical examination, the heyday of the tragic masterpieces and playwrights from Aeschylus to Sophocles belonged to the past. Two facts are worthy of attention concerning this age of Aeschylus and Sophocles.

First, it seems that at the epoch when they emerged, the tragic works did not bring about any corresponding philosophical reflection. I am aware that Nietzsche attempted to establish a close proximity between the Singing of the two tragic poets I just mentioned and the utterances of those "Philosophers of the Tragic Age" (his term), among whom he ranked Heraclitus highest. Still, we cannot avoid noting that in those fragments of Heraclitus available to us, Dionysos may be evoked by name, but that the very word "tragedy" is conspicuously absent.

Second, the concomitance between the epoch and heyday of tragedy and the epoch and heyday of the Athenian isonomic regime (in short, the Periclean Age) is worth noting. Three observations relative to this second fact suggest that the concomitance was more than a mere chronological coincidence. We know—and this is my first observation—that the very tragedy which brought fame upon Aeschylus ("The Persians") was staged and presented to the public under the direct responsibility of Pericles. Aeschylus himself had fought in the Athenian army against the Persians at Marathon in 490 B.C. and at Salamis, ten years later, in a battle that sealed definitively the Athenian victory over the Persians. We know also—and this is my second observation—that Sophocles was a very close friend of Pericles. Finally and most importantly—this is my third observation—the institutional context that promoted the staging of tragic works bears witness to the interest that the isonomic regime had for them. Tragic works were staged twice a year during the Dionysian celebrations, one of which took place in the spring, the other in December. Each time a competition for the best tragic work was organized during three days of the festival. On each of these days, one poet presented three works for competition—three works, that is, a trilogy. But before the spectacle, the City would conduct the election by the assembled citizens of certain magistrates whose task it would be to select poets on account of works which, in the magistrates' view, were worthy of entering the next competition. Once this selection was made, defraying the cost of staging the works was incurred by the wealthiest citizens. Yet, it was expected of all citizens that they would attend the spectacle and those who might be affected by some kind of economic loss because of three days of inactivity received financial compensation from the City. Finally, at the end of those three days, all citizens gathered in an assembly and it was then decided by vote to whom the prize for the best playwright would be awarded.

Quite obviously, this institutional context testifies that tragedy—whatever its religious or, according to Nietzsche, Dionysian origins—concerned the very City and the very mode of life specific to the isonomic regime. In order to bring some light upon what the interest of the isonomic City for tragedy meant, it might be useful to recall the main features of the *bios politikos* such as it had been invented by the isonomic City.

According to historians (e.g., Vernant and Vidal-Naquet), some of the specific features of the Greek City are already foreshadowed in the aristocratic kingdoms whose legend Homer narrates in his epic poems. In such kingdoms, sovereignty was divided into principles that were both rival and complementary: this is why legends relative to the foundation of these kingdoms evoke originary conflicts between brothers seeking assistance from divine powers, which, themselves too, are rival and complementary—such as *Eris*, a power of conflict and rivalry, and *Philia*, a power of friendship and union. Hesiod, the witness of this epoch, notes that rivalry and parity are the two sides of the same coin. The City proper is born exactly when the medium for shared sovereignty and for rivalry within one's peers becomes speech. The birth of *bios politikos* is the emergence of a living in common in which speech plays a decisive role.

This feature of speech as fundamental for *bios politikos* cannot be dissociated from two other ones: *publicness* and *equality*, whose connectedness was reinforced when the oligarchic regime gave way to the properly isonomic one. For this regime is unique in that speaking is shared by means of a public debate between equal interlocutors, who are all deemed capable of judging the persuasive force of each and every debating speech. Moreover, publicness is an essential feature of the City itself, since its laws are written and known by everybody, since its center, the *agora*, is a public place where all citizens meet, since its theater is open to all, and since most of the statues of its gods are visible. Finally, equality means that all citizens—either wealthy or poor—have the same right to speech, that they share to the same extent in the sovereignty of the assembly and that each of them has his share of public service: defense, tax-collection, justice. The Age of the City did invent a number of vocabulary items aiming at designating various aspects of this equality *(isotēs): isonomia, isotimia, isēgoria, isocrateia,* etc.

Such were, then, the major features of the *bios politikos*, consisting in a sharing of *lexis* and *praxis*, of words and deeds, that the Greeks of the City understood this *bios* as an activity for which they also invented a verb, *politeuesthai*. Everything indicates—and Arendt never ceased underscoring this point—that they clearly delineated it in contrast to two other activities: that of labor required for survival and that of production of artifacts. Regarding the first contrast, it can be noted that the invention of the *polis* is accompanied by the relegation of all tasks connected with the survival of the individual and the species to a private sphere, entirely distinct from the public one. Private is the household and the family in the extended sense of patriarchy. The Greeks invented the word *economy* to designate the organization of this private sphere, ruled not by the sharing of deeds and words but by relations of domination, such as that of man over woman, of parents over children, of master over slave. The antithesis of these two types of human relations— sharing and domination—is at the core of the distinction between public and private. More generally speaking, the invention of the *polis* and of its *bios* is concomitant with an overcoming and, therefore, a repression of everything that characterizes the belonging to mere life, *zoē*, with its eternal return of desires, appetites, pleasures, violence, and voluptuousness, also with its cycle of alternating seasons and renewing generations. This whole sphere of *zoē*, which was symbolized by Dionysos, was—as the Greeks of the City fully acknowledged—the indispensable precondition for their *bios*, and they celebrated it in the Dionysian rituals. But they also knew that such a *bios* required the harnessing and the checking of the spontaneous outflow of *zoē*. One can interpret in this double way— acknowledgment and distancing—the emblematic figure of tragedy, if it is true that the word, meaning "song of the He-goat," originally designated the sacrificial ceremony of the scapegoat. Such is the way in which Walter Burkert, the historian of the Greek religion, interprets the origin of tragedy.[3] By means of this sacrificial ritual surrounded by songs of terror and of compassion, the community— so he claims—was taking its distance from its own possibilities of bestiality, which it simultaneously acknowledged. In other words, the community affirmed itself as human while at the same time expressing the fear of ceasing to be so.

But the *bios politikos* also stood equally removed from the activity of production of artifacts and effects and from the specific knowhow *(technē)* that this activity requires. According to the Greeks of the City, there is incompatibility between the condition of citizen and that of *technitēs*, the expert in the wide sense of the term. In the isonomic *polis,* the concern with political affairs could not belong to a limited group of professionals, it belonged to each and every citizen. The isonomic regime seems to have rested upon the conviction that no sooner does the professional mentality of the expert prevail in human affairs than these affairs run the risk of losing what was priceless in their midst: the sharing of deeds and words. One does not argue with experts, one bows to their know-how. That is why when the City needed experts, generals for example, these were elected for short terms. That is why it avoided having professional civil servants, professional judges, professional tax-collectors. Such tasks were assigned by drawing lots. To be sure, the constant debate, the indefinite renewal of the things said and the renewed manner in which different situations appear to each (to their *doxa*), all these affect the *bios politikos* with a considerable load of unpredictability, of variability, of uncertainty, i.e., with fragility and frailty. It is most likely that this fragility and frailty led the isonomic regime to conceive the civic modalities of excellence, *arētē,* not as the strict observation of a determinable ethical rule, but rather as the renewed quest—always in the midst of a situation—of a mean between extremes, a mean called *mesotēs.* It led them to conceive, among other things, courage as a frail measure between cowardice and temerity; to conceive distributive justice as the frail measure—and this was a view previously formulated by Solon—between an excess of wealth which generates indolence and selfishness and an excess of poverty which generates a slackened mind and hatred; to conceive retributive justice as a frail measure between vengeance and the excess of magnanimity; to conceive prudence as a frail measure between procrastination and precipitation. It is, to summarize it all, this mean that was expressed in the Apollonian maxims from Delphi: *gnōthi seauton, mēden agan,* know thyself, nothing in excess.

No one, in my view, has been more clear-sighted and convincing than Hannah Arendt in presenting the anthropological foundations of the various delineations I just made: *zoē-bios;* private-public; expert-citizen. At the risk of repeating myself, I would like to recall briefly what she taught concerning the anthropological foundation of the distinction between the expert and the citizen. This foundation resides in the difference, underscored in the wake of *Nicomachean Ethics,* between the activity of production *(poiēsis)* and the activity of action proper *(praxis).* It might be useful here to recall certain features of this difference because it is concerning the status of *poiēsis* and *praxis* that the views of Plato and Aristotle diverge most characteristically with respect to the account each gives of tragedy.

Strictly speaking, the constitutive factors of the activity of fabrication or of the production of effects can be defined in a univocal manner. This univocity applies to the beginning: model or plan; to the means: specific materials and tools; to the end: defined product or result; to the required know-how: the *technē* of the expert.

By contrast, action is strictly speaking withdrawn from claims of univocity and is characterized by ambiguousness. Its beginning escapes univocity because it inscribes itself in a preexisting, inherited, network of human interactions and interlocutions. Its process also escapes it because it cannot be dissociated from an indefinite overlapping of the various perspectives, the ones over the others. Its end escapes it no less, because this very overlapping is renewed at the appearing of newcomers. The knowledge that action requires is not expertise, but rather availability to the unpredictable and the unknown.

As a result of the definite character of the activity, the agent committed to fabrication stands in a position of mastery, dominating the nature he transforms and those subordinates of his or hers who have to obey him or her.

By contrast, as a result of the ambiguousness of action, the acting individual never stands in the position of mastery, he is always a patient as much as an agent, he is an actor, never author.

Opposed to the predictability of fabrication, the unpredictability of action entails an unsurpassable mixture of knowledge and impossibility to know.

Moreover, inasmuch as it presupposes mastery and domination, the activity of fabrication is reversible. It can erase its failures and start all over again. By contrast, action, as a result of its ambiguousness and of the fact that it is involved with human beings rather than nature or things, is loaded with a non-reducible non-reversibility, which only promising and forgiving can remedy.

Finally, in the activity of fabrication, the agent does not have to appear as a singular individual but as the generic representative of a specific capacity or as an exemplar, which could be multiplied, of a certain type. By contrast, action is fundamentally individuated. However, it is so not in spite of human plurality, but by virtue of this very plurality. The antithetical notions of the one and the many, of the same and the other cannot be applied here because the plurality in which action is inscribed is a condition such that all acting individuals are both similar and different, they are all capable of interacting and understanding each other (because they are similar—and, by their actions and self-expression, they cannot avoid declaring who they are—because they are all different.

One can think with Arendt that the isonomic City, the enemy of experts, aimed at giving right to these specific features of action and at preserving all of its ambiguousness, all of its fragility, by means of instituting a public realm for the sharing of deeds and words (not by erecting a monopoly of violence since violence is connected with the domination characteristic of fabrication); this realm would be entrusted with conjuring away what threatens *praxis*, that is, what risks covering over the tensions of which it lives: for tensions are inescapable, such as the opposition of perspectives, the tension between generations, the tension with an indispensable *poiēsis* (and its claims to mastery, prediction, and the knowledge of an ultimate norm), the necessary tension with the indispensable *zoē*, the tension between public and private, between husband and wife, between one's city and the cities of others, between war and peace. This ambiguousness was underscored by Arendt who liked to repeat those words of Pericles to the Athenians: "We have made ourselves memorable on account of the good as well as the bad" (Thucydides).

This presentation is perhaps sufficient for me to shed some light on the interest the isonomic City had for tragedy. Arendt merely speaks of tragedy by allusions, but they always insist on the link that the tragic work contains with the various aspects of *praxis* understood in the context of the City. It is in this sense that at the end of her essay *On Revolution* she evokes *Oedipus at Colonus* concerning the close connection between tragedy and the City. And she shows also in the first book of *The Life of the Mind* that before the Platonic invention of *bios theōrētikos*, the only *theōria* corresponding to the isonomic City consisted in the gaze of the spectators at the theater: the spectators attending a performance could cast their gaze upon human affairs not in order to detach themselves from the world of appearing so as to reach a higher region of contemplation but rather in order to find the means of judging in the company of others, at the heart of plurality. As for the spectacle itself—and this will be my last consideration in this too long, yet too schematic introduction—I will draw upon a recent book on Greek tragedy which in my view concurs with Arendt's analyses inasmuch as it focuses on the fragility of *praxis*. I have in mind the remarkable study by Martha Nussbaum on *The Fragility of Goodness*.[4] In very fine analyses of Aeschylus' *Oresteia* and also Sophocles' *Antigone* Nussbaum successfully shows, by taking her bearings in the very text of the works and in particular in the speeches of choruses, that one may overcome those simplistic readings that traditionally oppose *mythos* and *logos* and merely see in tragedy the expression of an archaic ethics and the staging of insoluble conflicts between ethical characters vying for the protection of incompatible divinities. Nussbaum shows, instead, that the spring of tragedy—fate being triggered to unleash destruction upon heroes—lies in the decision they made to dismiss the conflicts inherent in their respective causes. In this, she says, there is a deathly strategy of oversimplification of a complex situation. Creon oversimplifies the realm of the political by reducing it to mere patriotism. Antigone also subjects the situation to an oversimplifying reduction when she exclusively restricts the non-written laws to fidelity to the dead. Everything happens as though the *hubris* of the protagonists—which needs reparation and over which the chorus laments, while promoting against it the measure and mean of *phronein*, or the *metron to beltiston* as in the chorus of Aeschylus' *Agamemnon*—results from the stubbornness with which the hero covers over the ambiguousness and intrinsically conflictual nature of the practical situations he or she faces. It is because of this stubbornness that a hero poses as one entrusted with a divine mission, whereas the chorus reminds the listeners that capacities of foresight and foretelling, which are the lot of divinities, are not shared by humans. One is tempted to paraphrase these considerations in Arendt's language and to say that tragedy teaches that the fragility and the manifold ambiguousness of *praxis* forbid anybody putting himself or herself in a position of mastery and never allows them to anticipate an entire process of events and subject interhuman enterprises to the indisputable norms legitimately prevailing in the realm of *poiēsis*. One is consequently tempted to say that if the *theōria* involving the theater spectator is, indeed, tantamount to judgment in the sense of *phronēsis*, it is because, in the words of Paul Ricoeur[5] commenting on Nussbaum's reading of *Antigone*, "an appeal to 'deliberate well' *(euboulia)* stubbornly winds through the play, as though 'thinking justly' were the answer to 'suffering the terrible' *(pathein to deinon)* (line 96)." Or later: "By refusing to contribute a 'solution' to the conflicts made insoluble by fiction, tragedy, after disorienting the gaze, condemns the person of *praxis* to reorient action, at his or her own risk, in the sense of a practical wisdom in situation that best *responds* to tragic wisdom."

I am finally able to turn to the philosophical reception of tragedy as it is first articulated in Plato's *Republic*. I have already stated at the outset that it is in terms of *mimēsis* that Plato approaches tragedy. But the aiming that determines his use of that notion is focused on the celebration of a totally new *bios,* the *bios theōrētikos,* the contemplative mode of life of a man of a certain type, of which the isonomic City had hardly any notion; for, if it is true that in the famous Funeral Speech recounted by Thucydides Pericles evokes not without pride for his fellow citizens the motto *"philosophoumen aneu malakias"* (we philosophize without indolence), we surmise that by this search for wisdom he aims at the measure characteristic of the excellence of *bios politikos.* In book 10 of *The Republic* Plato claims that just as a mirror can reflect and henceforth imitate all visible things directly accessible to the common gaze, likewise the artist—the painter, musician, or tragic poet—can imitate all things. But the artist does so without paying attention to what they are truly and by being exclusively involved in the way in which they appear. This way of presenting matters gives Plato the opportunity of praising the merits of the experts, of whom I pointed out that the City is wary. The expert, whatever his know-how, is one who, from the inception of his productive activity, detaches himself from the common perception of appearances and takes into consideration the pure form of the work he will bring into the world. He is, therefore, in relation with Ideas, whereas the artist only cares for semblance. That is why Plato grants the expert a mediating position between those who are attached to the ordinary appearances of things and those who devote themselves to *theōria* in the new sense, the pure seeing of what beings are in their truth. If we agree to call speculation this contemplative view of beings in their totality and as such, we can say that it is with respect to speculation that Plato depreciates all artists, including the tragic poets, and celebrates the expert. With respect to the ontological structure of beings, the activity of the artist leads astray. Whereas it is the brightness of the world of Ideas that requires the adjustment of the gaze, the artist makes us believe—erroneously according to Plato— that only appearances are worthy of being contemplated. But, by considering the activity of the expert, we are invited to raise our gaze above appearances. As an imitator of Ideas, the expert deserves every praise; by contrast as an imitator of appearances, the artist deserves nothing but scorn. Moreover, it is because the artist limits himself to appearances that he is capable of imitating all things: gods and human beings, everything that is part and parcel of nature and all artifacts, whereas the true expert, precisely because he must submit himself to an ascetic contemplation of determined forms, cannot be a polymath expert: the good cobbler cannot also be a good carpenter, the good doctor a good general.

For Plato, the true poet is the craftsman, the artisan. The Greek language used the same word *poiēsis* to designate productions owed both to artisans and to painters, sculptors, poets; it used the same word *technē* to designate the know-how of both the expert and the artist. Plato, so to speak, purifies this usage by restricting to specialists only the prerogatives of *poiēsis* and *technē*, which emerge from a *theōria* very different from the gaze of the citizens of the *polis* assembled in the theater to see tragedies. For it is against the former theater—the theater of Aeschylus and Sophocles in which the average person was a judge—that Plato directs the famous narrative of the Cave, a commanding part of his *Republic*. At issue is the task of making liable of expulsion the uncertain light and ambiguousness of ancient theatrical plots in order to gain access to another stage, no longer *praxis* but instead the onto-theological order of Ideas. This order of Ideas never calls for the frail measure of *phronein*, always individuated and committed to a situation inscribed within plurality (*Dicha d'allon monophrēn eimi*, said the chorus of Aeschylus' *Agamemnon*), but rather for the clarity of a *noēsis*, purified and solitary, from which emerges a claim to self-sufficiency. Whereas the theoretician in the sense of the City, i.e., the spectator in the theater, was the judge of the ambiguities of the *praxis* of mortals, ambiguities brought to poetic celebration, the theoretician in the new sense makes himself the spectator of a transcendent order, an order which is devoid of ambiguities and involves forms which always were and always will be. From this considerable metamorphosis of the very nature of *theōria* and from the fact that the latter from now on aspires to bear on the onto-theological structure of beings in their totality, what was formerly hailed by the City having *praxis* in mind is now depreciated by Plato having speculation in mind.

Whereas the City put a high educational value on *mythoi*, narratives in general, and more precisely intrigues from Homeric times as well as the tales inspiring tragedies, Plato says and repeats that the first philosophical gesture consists in losing interest for narratives.

Whereas tragedy allowed citizens in the Periclean age to remain awake to the ambiguities of *praxis*, Plato depreciates the tragic poems precisely because of their ambiguousness. All the examples by which Plato in *The Republic* attempts to prove that the language of poets is misleading bear testimony to the rift between speculation and *praxis*. When the poet says, for example, that Zeus dispenses both evil and good things to the mortals, one can presume that the City has nothing to object inasmuch as, with respect to *praxis*, such words signify that mortals are not masters of their destinies and that, in human interaction, no one reaches an ultimate knowledge of the good for the simple reason that judgment is always situation-bound. Inscribed in tragic Singing, these ambiguous words teach one—and this teaching had been detected by Hölderlin with extraordinary acuity—how to purify oneself from the infinite temptation to confuse mortals with deities. One may think that this teaching had a practical aspect, if it is true that the *bios politikos* had no interest in defining the Divine theologically, but rather in acknowledging the finitude and intrinsic frailty of *praxis*. But from the perspective of the new *theōria*, the ambiguousness within which the poet moves is to be discredited because at issue now is the question of defining the Divine in its simple unalloyed nature.

Likewise, when Plato rejects as unacceptable the dark theogony recounted by Hesiod—which forms the fertile ground from which Aeschylus' trilogy *Prometheus* emerged, specifically against the backdrop of the vengeance of Chronos against his father Ouranos, and the vengeance of Zeus against his father Chronos—we may suspect that this rejection aims at tales to which the City would indeed have granted educational value with respect to *praxis*. Obviously, for the City and for Aeschylus who is so to speak its mouthpiece, Zeus is the epitome of justice, of *dikē*. Considered from the perspective of *praxis*, the frightful titanic genealogy of Zeus taught that, in the final analysis, the highest principle of order and harmony is not without affinity with a chaos and a primitive violence from which it arose and which it managed to repress and curb.

Likewise, when Plato opposes the idea that divinities might blind mortals and be the source of the punishment of acts humans believe sanctioned by gods, we may wonder whether his theological option in favor of an unalloyed Good and the ethical division he sanctions—between virtuous and reprobate, those with knowledge and those holding a shadow of it—is not tantamount to dismissing the ambiguousness of *praxis*, which is an unsurpassable mixture of inheritance and initiative, acting and suffering, knowledge and ignorance.

Now is the time to note that, from the perspective of this speculation, the very notion of excellence *(arētē)* changes its meaning. Whereas for *bios politikos* it consisted in searching for a frail measure between extremes, Plato now defines it as the strict observation of a univocal principle. Here the preponderance of the paradigm of *poiēsis* reappears and I have previously argued that this takes place in connection with the privileging of speculation.

Treating *arētē* in book 3 of *The Republic*, the Platonic Socrates takes for model the excellence of the tool. In the same fashion, he claims, as there is excellence in the tool when, as a means, it is perfectly adapted to a determinate goal, likewise excellence in the expert *(technitēs)* resides in his or her aptitude to imitate a preordained model. In such conditions, the virtue of warriors, i.e., courage, has to conform to a pre-established pattern. For the City, courage was a measure, a mean, between two extremes, cowardice and temerity, that is, mastery of fear, in particular fear of death. For Plato, by contrast, it consists in ignorance pure and simple of fear, in particular fear of death. Moreover, whereas in *bios politikos* excellence was connected with competition in the midst of plurality, its peak is now characterized by Plato in terms of self-sufficiency: "The virtuous man is sufficient unto himself to live well, and he is the one the least in need of others" (387d).

In accordance with the paradigm of *poiēsis*, the ideal City is defined as a sort of large workshop in which everybody accomplishes a specific task. It is impossible for a man, says Socrates in book 2, to accomplish good work in several arts, thereby objecting against the democratic principle that every citizen is capable of discharging whatever public function. Therefore, dialogue characterizes the best regime in terms of *poiēsis* by contrast to the ambiguousness and the plurality inherent in *praxis*. In book 4, Socrates says: "We wanted to show that all citizens must, each one individually, be concerned with one task, also individual, the one to which each person's nature destines him, so that each one, discharging one single task, the one most proper his, does not risk becoming several human beings at once, but is only one and so that the *polis* as a whole develops as one single being and not as several" (423d). For Plato, the political demarcation between *praxis* and *poiēsis* should be abolished and, furthermore, no demarcation should exist between public and private, since the Platonic City with the famous injunction of having all wives in common can be conceived as a sort of extended family ideally subjected to the government of a single one.

Everyone knows that Aristotle, to whom it is time that I turn now, reacts against these speculative views in matters of politics and art. It is not perhaps exaggerated to say that, to a large extent, his reaction consisted in dismissing Plato's pretension of subjecting both domains to speculation, in restoring *praxis* to its fundamental ambiguousness, and consequently in rehabilitating the *mesotēs* and, in particular, the noetic measure of which *phronēsis* consists.

Concerning tragedy, the key text is obviously the *Poetics* of which various commentators (Gerald F. Else in his magnificent commentary[6] and, after him, Paul Ricoeur in *Time and Narrative*) were justified in writing that its central concept is *mimēsis*. But this concept no longer plays the role it formerly did in the Platonic evaluation of the arts in general and tragedy in particular: Plato was using the metaphor of the mirror to define *mimēsis* as passive reflection; by contrast, Aristotle views *mimēsis* as an active process of composition. Whereas for Plato tragic *mimēsis* is exclusively slave to mere appearances and thus leads astray from onto-theology, it is toward *praxis* that the *mimēsis* evoked by Aristotle is oriented. Tragedy is *mimēsis praxeōs*. It consists in bringing together actions so that they make a plot. In this bringing together, the essential thing is not to put on stage individuals as they appear at first glance and also not to focus on the qualities of their specific character:

> Tragedy is an imitation, not of human beings as such, but of an action, of an existence *(bios)*, of one *eudaimonia*, and its goal is a certain action, not a quality. Dramatic heroes have certain qualities in connection with their character *(ēthos)*, but it is in connection with their *praxis* that they are, or are not, *eudaimones*. They do not act therefore in order to represent their characters; rather, they receive it from action itself. Thus the course of actions and the plot are the goal of tragedy, and the goal is what is most important. (50a15)

This underscoring of *praxis* and *mythos* as plot, hence conceived in terms of the interaction through which the individuals reveal who they are, the insistence with which Aristotle refers to the plot as the *archē*, the *telos*, and the *psychē* of tragedy (50a38) indicate how far apart his views are from the Platonic ones. By assigning an overwhelming importance to the plot and claiming that it is with reference to it that the protagonists of the drama reach or miss *eudaimonia*, i.e., authentic individuation, Aristotle highlights the distance of his position from Plato's; for Plato insists in *The Sophist* (242c) that the first philosophical step is the rejection of plots and claims in *The Republic* that ultimately only in the dialogue of the soul with itself and under the auspices of the Ideas is *eudaimonia* reached—as if only the activity of the thinker were the principle of individuation. Moreover, whereas not a single masterpiece of Greek theater meets with Plato's approval, concerning Aristotle it is as though he grants them all an educational validity. Whereas Plato maintains that artistic *mimēsis* in general and tragic *mimēsis* in particular are closely confined with shimmering factual and singular appearances—hence ever ambiguous and void of any philosophical meaning for speculative *theōria*—Aristotle emphasizes that the poet is more interested in what is possible, plausible, and necessary than in what is factual. That is why his Singing has a universal value, whereas the narratives of the historian only tell of particulars. That is why, says Aristotle, the writing of the poet is "a philosophical activity" (51a36–b15), which deserves being taken seriously.

One may think that the issue in this rehabilitation of the tragic is not speculation at all but practical *phronēsis*, which various commentators (from Pierre Aubenque,[7] and more recently Martha Nussbaum, followed by Paul Ricoeur) have stressed that its source is tragic wisdom. Aristotle underscores in his *Poetics* (Chapter 13) the various features of tragedy: a tragedy can show neither good persons being tumbled from happiness into wretchedness nor bad persons elevated by crime to prosperity, nor perverse ones moving from happiness to misfortune; and he points out that tragedies show persons similar to ourselves, people akin to us, perhaps slightly better instead of worse than ourselves, who are being tumbled into misfortune as a result of one mistake; tragedy arouses our pity for their misfortune and our fear because they are our kin. In these features it is indeed the fragility of *praxis* and its plurality that is in view. This fragility—not some ideal model for existence— is under consideration when Aristotle asks what distinguishes a good tragic work from defective ones. Everything happens as if his gaze was in close proximity with that of the citizen spectators, upon whom lay the injunction to name the best trilogy.

When he writes that "because the plot imitates a *praxis*, it must imitate an action that is unified and forms a whole, whose elements are so arranged that, should one of them be assigned to another location or removed, the whole is disjointed and dislocated" (51a30–35), reference is made not to the contemplation of an Idea, but to the sense of measure and proportion enjoined by the maxims of Delphi and inherent in the civic *phronēsis* of the isonomic City. When in the same context he underscores that a totality of this kind is "what has a beginning, a middle, and an end" and notes that these moments do not occur at random but are significant events (because organized according to the requirements of verisimilitude or necessity), he suggests by the same token that the plot metamorphoses the contingencies of life into a sequence loaded with universality; again, reference to practical wisdom is intimated because it is one of the functions of *phronēsis* to consider the particular situations of *praxis* in the light of universals that can never be dissociated from a situation. The same reference is intimated when Aristotle stresses that "the beauty of the composition has for its conditions a certain magnitude and some order, for the same reason that an animal cannot be beautiful if it is extremely small [for then our sight, *theōria*, is blurred when approaching the moment at which perceptibility ceases] and even more so if it is enormously big [for then our sight does not apprehend a whole]" (50b34, ff.). Obviously, the *theōria* evoked here is not at all that of speculation; it is the apprehension, in the midst of a common world of appearances, of a mean, *mesotēs*, between two extremes. The beautiful is not at all the intelligible Idea, but a sensible appearing offered to judgment.

But perhaps the contrast between the Aristotelian approach to tragedy conceived as *mimēsis praxeōs* and its Platonic depreciation as *mimēsis mē ontos* is even more marked when Aristotle characterizes tragedy as *katharsis* of pity and fear. It must be noted first that such emotions arise from the plot itself, from verisimilitude and necessity and not at all the monstrous irruption of a *deus ex machina*. Aristotle's rejection of *deus ex machina* does not give rise, as in Plato, to considerations of rational theology; it opens up, at the most, the possibility for a sketch of a strictly practical theodicy. Aristotle argues: "The gods intervene for what has happened antecedently to the drama and for what humans cannot know or for those subsequent events, which it is necessary to predict or announce, for we grant gods the possibility of seeing all *(kapanta horan)*" *(Poetics,* 37/54b6). What is at stake here is the ignorance inherent in *praxis* on its two chronological sides—the anterior network of deeds and words within which it inscribes itself and the unpredictable future to which it opens. One will note, furthermore, that the very notion of *katharsis* of the *pathēmata* (passions) of fear and pity is not at all a purging—tantamount to eliminating them, which would be a Platonic gesture—but rather their transformation into *mathēmata*, into a teaching. In other words, *katharsis* is the equivalent of a veritable refutation of the various dualisms (sensible-intelligible, perishable-eternal, soul-body) which found the Platonic *theōria* of *mimēsis*. Indeed, for the Platonic *theōria*, the only conceivable *mathēmata* are the Ideas, whose access is conditioned upon the exclusion of every passion, except *thaumazein*. Finally, we will note that although pity and fear are susceptible of meta-morphosing into *mathēmata*, this is so only inasmuch as they play a decisive role in *praxis* and, more generally speaking, in political interaction. The person who would never experience pity is alone in the world and, should he come to rule over human affairs, could not but be a tyrant and destroy every sharing of words and deeds. Conversely, the one submerged by pity or fear cannot set out to at-tempt anything. As for the one who would never experience fear, he does not belong to the world of humans: in him there would be nothing but recklessness (as in the automaton or the wild animal) or the indifference of a god. In either case, he would be apolitical.

In light of these distinctions, it is not surprising that Aristotle's political texts should testify to a resistance against Plato's efforts to submit the City to the univocal norms of the activity of produc-tion, as these norms are themselves subjected to the order of specu-lation. Where Plato claims that rectitude, including in political af-fairs, is a matter for One alone and asserts that it will never be possible for a plurality to govern rationally a *polis*, Aristotle main-tains that by nature the City is a plurality, that it will perish if it is to unite in the manner of a single family and, even more so, of a unique individual, for it needs differences between its members and resists the possibility of being made up of entirely identical individ-uals. Whereas Plato tends to subordinate *praxis* to the univocity of the *poiēsis* of the *technitēs*, Aristotle by contrast dissociates the first from the second and, higher than *technē*, he ranks *phronēsis*, the practical wisdom always in situation and aspiring to a mean be-tween extremes.

Keeping in mind this antinomic picture, I should like—before re-turning to Heidegger—to question two of the most famous recep-tions of Greek tragedy by the moderns, namely Hegel and Nietz-sche, and determine whether they are set in motion by speculation and *poiēsis* or by *phronēsis* and *praxis*. A few remarks are therefore in order concerning those pages of *The Phenomenology of Spirit* de-voted to tragedy and concerning *The Birth of Tragedy*.

The fact that Hegel celebrates the isonomic City seems to stand as evident. No less obvious is the fact that he perceives the link tragedy had with the regime whose accomplishments he praises, since it is in the light of Sophocles' *Antigone* that he describes the spiritual level achieved by the Greek City, the level of the beautiful *Sittlichkeit* (ethical life). He seems, therefore, very removed from the Platonic depreciation of tragedy. But we would be wrong to infer from this that neither the privileging of speculation nor its corollary, the privileging of *poiēsis*, guides his interpretation of the Greek City. In an effort to dismiss this inference, let me limit myself to some pages that precede the section called "True Spirit, Ethical Life." I will retain four notions that bear witness to the recurrence of two themes whose Platonic origin I have tried to establish.

First, the very definition of Spirit as higher court to which the ethical life of the Greek City gives accounts is speculative in the sense of a contemplation of the Being of beings in their totality, of an onto-theological contemplation. "Reason is spirit when its certainty of being *all reality* has been raised to truth and it is conscious of itself as its own world and of the world as itself" (Hegel, *The Phenomenology of Spirit*, trans. A. V. Miller, Oxford University Press, 263). Or: "But essence that is *in* and *for itself* and which is at the same time actual as consciousness and represents itself to itself, is *Spirit*" (*ibid.*, mod.). This self-presentation of the essence denotes that it is a *theōria* in the speculative sense, i.e., a gaze aiming at the totality of reality and at what it is in itself. This is a return of the Platonic Idea except that it bears no longer on an object external to the mind but rather on an object-subject. We witness here the privileging of speculation.

But there is also a privileging of *poiēsis*. For this ethical life of the Greek City is described by Hegel not in terms of a sharing of *praxis* and *lexis*, but rather of the production of a work, *Werk*, to which everybody finds himself summoned and for whose elaboration he plays a part. Hegel says that this spirit, being as ethical effectiveness "the *substance* and the universal, self-identical and abiding essence, is the assured solid *ground* and starting point for the action of all, and it is their purpose and goal, the in-itself of every self-consciousness expressed in thought. This substance is equally the universal work produced by the action of all and each as their unity and identity for it is the being-for-self, the Self, action" (*ibid.*, 264). From there results the third point, Hegel's obliteration of *plurality*. The Greek individual is not the one whom you and I may think of, the citizen who searches for the *mesotēs* in every modality of excellence and exercises his own judgment in the midst of other individuals. For Hegel, the Greek individual is the people. "The spirit is the ethical life of one *people*, inasmuch as it is immediate truth, the individual that is a world" (*ibid.*, 264).

Finally, this ethical life of the City, speculatively conceived in terms of *poiēsis*, not *praxis*, and as a homogeneous people not plurality, is relegated by Hegel—at the same time as he praises its beauty—to the benefit of a higher life, higher because more purely speculative. Such a relegation is a speculative gesture akin to a Platonic one. The Spirit "must advance to the consciousness of what it is immediately, must leave behind it the beauty of ethical life, and by passing through a series of shapes attain the knowledge of itself" (ibid., 265). Bios politikos is no more than the antechamber to bios theōrētikos.

It is necessary, of course, and in line with good speculative logic, that the necessity of this overcoming should have been demonstrated already by the Greek City itself considered in its ethical life. Such a proof Hegel finds in Sophocles' Antigone, in light of which he describes the structure, the movement, but also what he takes to be the intrinsic contradiction of the Greek bios politikos. The structure is found by Hegel in the equilibrium of two laws—the human law of the City, masculine and diurnal, contrasted with the divine law of the family, feminine and nocturnal. The movement is found by Hegel in the confirmation of each law by the other one in regard to death which is the point of intersection. By confronting its own members to the risk of death brought about by war, the City reminds the citizens that they belong to it. And the worship of its dead, of its departed kin, is what cements the family and comforts it. As for the intrinsic contradiction of this bios politikos, Hegel finds it in the setting-into-work of these two laws. Ethical action is the action of a consciousness that feels itself obligated in its very being—being male or being female. By means of the speculative concept of ethical life I have just evoked, such an action should merely attest effectively that the acting consciousness recognizes itself in its own world and knows itself in it. Yet man and woman, each acting according to the relevant law, clash against each other and find in the other that which resists and opposes his or her knowledge. Clarity, which should be penetrating everything in the action of each side, clashes against the obscurity shrouding the reaction coming from the other side. What creates a conflict is the fact that each protagonist assumes he or she knows the totality but turns out to have merely a partial knowledge of it.

No one can possibly deny the power of this analysis. But it is striking to note its speculative bias. Everything happens as though the bios politikos of the Greeks is conflictual because, in this bios, a partial knowledge claims to be a knowledge of the whole. Everything happens, therefore, as though this bios expects the emergence of a spiritual figure in which such partiality would be overcome and, by the same token, conflict disappear and be resolved. In other words, everything happens as though, in such a *bios*, blindness is owed to the necessarily partial character of the knowledge held by the protagonists. But what tragedy, it seems to me, teaches in its connection to the world of *praxis* and not speculation, is rather, first, that blindness, or *hubris*, results from strategies for avoiding a conflict that is perceptible; second, that the conflictual nature of the human interaction far from being a contradiction to be solved is unsurpassable because inherent in *praxis*; third, that we may call for not a solution to, and a superior synthesis of, contraries but merely a frail *mesotēs* between an excess and a default.

Mesotēs s and therefore *phronēsis* are obstinately ignored by the Hegelian analysis. I find confirmation of this in the fact that, when later in the *Phenomenology*, i.e., in the chapter on the Religion of Art, Hegel treats tragedy as a work of art, he puts the chorus on a level of consciousness inferior to the stage. The chorus is alleged to be prisoner of a mere *Vorstellung*, a thoughtless imaginative consciousness, while the stage is deemed to show already, inchoately, the absolute movement of the Concept. Yet, if in tragedy there is a location in which *phronein*, or judgment, responds to *hubris*, it is no doubt the chorus.

One more word on Nietzsche. Should one inscribe *The Birth of Tragedy* in the speculative legacy of Plato or in the praxeological legacy of Aristotle, who obviously accepted teachings from tragedy? No sooner is this question asked than one faces the emergence of a certain number of paradoxes. The fact that Nietzsche claims to be on the side of tragedy against Platonism is manifest.

That an insurmountable ambiguity is the most insistent theme of his reading, is no less manifest, in spite of the fact that the schemas with which he operates—predominantly the Apollonian and the Dionysian—are often projected upon dualistic structures inherited from Schopenhauer, who in *The World as Will and Representation* claimed that he was doing nothing but reappropriating Plato.

But from the fact that tragic ambiguity, unbearable to Plato, is rehabilitated by Nietzsche there does not result that he designates its proper domain, which is *praxis*. Instead, it is inscribed within a metaphysical framework, that of a metaphysics of artists. In such a metaphysics, a certain *theōrein*, the gaze of a certain *Schauen* is essential and, far from being focused on *praxis*, it bears on the Being of beings, i.e., on nature in its totality, whose essence is will, and on the relation between nature in itself and nature as phenomenon. To this extent, in spite of his imprecations against Platonism,

Nietzsche's first book shares with the Platonic approach to tragedy the privileging of *bios theōrētikos* as a matter of principle. The ancient spectator of the Greek theater is in no way for Nietzsche a citizen called upon to judge on the ambiguities of *praxis* and what risks covering them over. He is a "Dionysian man" called upon, as he says in section 7, to "cast a true glance into the bottom of the essence of things," or in section 9, "to cast his glance in the terrifying abyss of nature."

The stress put on *seeing* what Nietzsche calls the "truth of nature in all its force" (sec. 8) is such that the tragic plot proper is hardly analyzed by Nietzsche and occupies a minor place in his book. A mere five pages, in a hundred and fifty, are devoted to the topic.

This quasi marginalizing of the plot which unfolds on the stage can, of course, be explained by the preponderance Nietzsche grants to the chorus, which according to him is Dionysian, whereas the plot is Apollonian. This amounts to an inversion of the Hegelian views. But this very inversion does not affect the maintaining of a speculative bias. The chorus is celebrated because it perceives a fundamental ontological ambiguity, because it comes to see in the abyss of Being that creation and destruction, order and chaos are one and the same thing. From this it results that everything which in the language of the chorus is called measure and a reply to *hubris* is covered over by Nietzsche in silence.

Moreover, the very use Nietzsche makes of the notion of *mimēsis* is entirely metaphysical and in no way praxeological. The Apollonian artist, he says, imitates the ontological process by which nature produces appearances in the attempt to enjoy itself. The Dionysian artist imitates the process by which nature attests to its inexhaustible force by feeling joy in the annihilation of appearances. The tragic artist, both Apollonian and Dionysian, associates these two ontological dimensions. It is in an exclusively metaphysical context that the tragic *mythos* is evoked by Nietzsche in terms that have hardly anything praxeological:

> The *tragic myth* is to be understood only as a symbolization of Dionysian wisdom through Apollonian artifices. The myth leads the world of phenomena to its limits where it denies itself and seeks to flee back into the womb of the true and only reality, where it then seems to commence its metaphysical swansong, like Isolde:
>
>> "In the rapture ocean's
>> billowing roll,

> in the fragrance waves'
> ringing sound,
> in the world breath's
> wafting whole—
> to drown, to sink—
> unconscious—highest joy!"
> (*The Birth of Tragedy*, trans. Walter Kaufmann,
> New York: Vintage Books, 1967, sec. 22)

It is doubtful that citizen Pericles, a friend of the tragic poets, would have agreed with such views.

It is well known that Nietzsche did not remain on this position and soon thereafter qualified his first book as "impossible," precisely because it had espoused the metaphysical aiming at some otherworldly realm. And perhaps one should say that his self-critique led him to reactivate against this speculative propensity a praxeological approach to tragedy. It appears to me significant in this respect that the first page of *Thus Spoke Zarathustra*—a work which, among other things, denounces the metaphysical doubling of the world, celebrates appearances, fustigates both the invention of happiness by *homo laborans* and of utilitarianism by *homo faber,* and attempts to reinvigorate the agonistic *aristeuein* of the Ancients in dealing with the interaction of mortals—should have appeared in *The Gay Science* under the title *Incipit tragoedia*.

What about Heidegger in facing this legacy? At the time of the genesis of fundamental ontology, the tragic poets hardly seem to have solicited his reflections and his lecture courses on Aristotle pay no attention to the *Poetics*. Everything changes when, in 1933, the *Dasein* of a people and no longer of the single individual moves to the center of the metaphysical questioning. We have noted earlier that this expanded *Dasein* mobilizes not at all a plural *praxis* but a high-ranking *poiēsis* connected to an eminent know-how *(technē)* with three fundamental modalities: artistic, philosophical, political. Hence the lecture course *An Introduction to Metaphysics* (1935) contains the following: "Unconcealment occurs only when it is achieved by work: the work of the word in poetry, the work of stone in temple and statue, the work of the word in thought, the work of the *polis* as the historical place in which all this is grounded and preserved."[8] In this context tragedy becomes worthy of attention to the same degree as the works of speech of founding thinkers such as Parmenides and Heraclitus. But precisely, it is in close parallelism with writings dealing with *physis* now understood as the uncovering of beings in their totality that tragedy turns out to be worthy of attention. Its reception takes place, therefore once more, in connection with speculation and *poiēsis*. A privilege is again granted to speculation in the sense that what is at stake in tragedy for Heidegger is *bios theōrētikos* understood as the mode of existing committed to the unveiling of Being. To be sure, given the fact that this very unveiling is conceived as ontological *polemos*, it is less Plato that inspires it than Parmenides and Heraclitus. And it is precisely with reference to this ontological *polemos*, to which previously the Greek people, and now the German *Volk*, are deemed to respond, that a certain type of *poiēsis*, specific to the thinker, or the poet, or the founder of state, is granted the instituting role of setting-into-work *alētheia*, whereas at the time of *Being and Time*, *poiēsis* was ranked lowest along with the concern for everyday fallenness. Whatever these metamorphoses of fundamental ontology, it is indeed the conjunction of speculation and *poiēsis* that determines the manner in which Heidegger approaches tragic Singing, as is shown in the first text that to my knowledge makes a reference to Aeschylus, the famous "Rectorial Address." In it Heidegger claims that Prometheus was the first philosopher and recalls the line from *Prometheus:* "*technē d'anankēs asthenestera makrō*" (verse 514). He translates: "Knowing, however, is much weaker than necessity," and comments as follows: "This means: all knowledge concerning things is first of all delivered to the overpower of destiny and falters in front of such overpower. That is precisely why, if it is truly to falter, knowledge must display its highest challenge, in front of which only the power of concealment of beings is erected" (11). In other words, philosophy, as an eminent modality of the challenge which wrests beings from their concealment in order to know them in their Being, is both *theōria* (and in this respect it stands highest in the rank of *praxis*) and *technē*, as this word—quite obviously—can only designate a discovering adapted to a setting-into-work, a *poiēsis*, regulated by it. It is, in the last analysis, the same conjunction of *theōria* and *poiēsis* that was expressed according to the *Introduction to Metaphysics* in *Antigone*'s chorus, "*polla ta deina*." Heidegger interprets these stanzas by Sophocles in a section whose very title, "Being and Thought" designates unequivocally the axis of his reading. It can be summarized thus: "Being-human defines itself from out of a relation to *beings as a whole*. The human essence shows itself here to be the relation which first opens up Being to man. Being human, as the need to grasp and gather, is forced into freedom, which consists in undergoing *technē*, the setting-into-work of Being. Such is history" (*An Introduction to Metaphysics*, p. 170, mod., stress added). Since this *technē* and this setting-into-work proceed in the element of challenge and violence, one might as well say that tragedy was a celebration of speculative *hubris*.

This reading, no matter how attentive it might be to the ambiguity of Being, remains deliberately blind to the ambiguities of the sharing of deeds and words essential for action, as is indicated in the fact that the only decision *(Entscheidung)* for which Heidegger calls then, far from involving *euboulia*, the *mesotēs*, and *phronēsis*, is merely a "sundering within the ensemble formed by Being, unconcealing, appearing, and non-Being" (*Einführung in die Metaphysik*, p. 84). And this decision, of course, is the affair of the one who has devoted himself to *bios theōrētikos*.

NOTES

1. H.-G. Gadamer, "Erinnerungen an Martin Heideggers Anfange" (Remembrances of Martin Heidegger's Beginnings), in *Dilthey Jahrbuch*, 1986–87, 4: 23.
2. H.-G. Gadamer, "Heideggers theologische Jugendschrift" in *Dilthey Jahrbuch*, 1988, 6.
3. Walter Burkert, *Homo Necans*, trans. Peter Bing, Berkeley: University of California Press, 1983.
4. Martha Nussbaum, *The Fragility of Goodness*, Cambridge: Cambridge University Press, 1986.
5. Paul Ricoeur, *Soi-même comme un autre*, Paris: Le Seuil, 1990, pp. 287–88; see *Oneself as Another*, trans. Kathleen Blamey, Chicago: University of Chicago Press, pp. 246–47, mod.
6. Gerald F. Else, *Aristotle's Poetics—The Argument*, Cambridge: Harvard University Press, 1967.
7. Pierre Aubenque, *La Prudence chez Aristote* (Prudence in Aristotle), Paris: P.U.F., 1963.
8. *An Introduction to Metaphysics*, trans. Ralph Manheim, New Haven: Yale University Press, 1959, p. 191.

FOUR

The Paradox of Belonging and Withdrawal

Hannah Arendt refused considering herself a "philosopher" of the political.[1] She justified this refusal by arguing that, starting with Plato, the philosophers of the political had founded their approach upon a depreciation, and therefore an obliteration, of action and action's constitutive features. In their bias for thought—more precisely for a mode of living entirely devoted to thinking, i.e., the *bios theōrētikos* they invented—they asserted its excellence and, in its name, denounced the insufficiencies of *bios politikos*, i.e., the mode of life considered highest by the Greeks of the city. The mode of appearing of the objects in *theōria* is infinitely superior, so the philosophers claimed, to the mode of appearing of human affairs. By virtue of which Plato argued that familiarity with Ideas was what justifies that the philosopher should rule over cities or be the counselor of a tyrant on the basic principle that plurality is unreasonable and that "only to the One does rectitude belong" *(Statesman)*. Convinced as she was of the contrary, i.e., "that plurality is the law of the world" and that philosophies of the political since Plato have been infected with Platonism, Arendt declined the title of "philosopher" of the political. She would on occasion, however, present herself as "a sort of phenomenologist." Furthermore, in one of those relatively few pages in which she was willing to define her approach she declared that she had "clearly joined the ranks of those who for some time now have been attempting to dismantle metaphysics, and philosophy with all its categories, as we have known them from the beginning in Greece until today" *(L.M.,* 1: 212)

I propose here to elucidate the unique features and specificity of the dismantling she practiced, in particular concerning the thinking activity. Since she called herself "a sort of phenomenologist"— a qualification that would be meaningless if it did not intend some attachment to the phenomena—we may presume that her dismantling is in keeping with that attachment. At issue is not some breaking down to pieces and a shattering, but rather a showing and manifesting. In what sense are the dismantling of metaphysical categories and the manifesting of phenomena mutually connected? Such is the general question that directs my investigation.

Before attempting to highlight this link through some selected gestures of dismantling let us bear in mind that Arendt herself underscored it with sufficient clarity when on occasion she provided a few reflections on her approach. The context of the sentence quoted above provides the following clarifications. There exists a prior condition for the dismantling: It is "possible only on the assumption that the thread of the tradition is broken and that we shall not be able to renew it" *(ibid.)*. The break is that of the triad, which is of Roman origin: religion-authority-tradition. This triad has disappeared. Upon it rested the metaphysics of the Christian era. Far from being tantamount to the disappearance pure and simple of the legacy of the past, the disappearance of the binding connection between the three terms of the triad only means that the heritage is "preceded by no testament" or by no agreed upon or imposed mode of use. But this very situation allows us "to look on the past with new eyes, unburdened and unguided by any traditions" (1: 12). The condition for dismantling—or the rupture in the tradition within which metaphysics was inscribed—is thus something that frees our eyes. And this rupture is all the more conducive to freeing our eyes as it is associated to abolishing the privileges of the specialists, more precisely the devaluation of the distinction between the many and the "professional thinkers"—whom Plato used to consider elect by the gods. Certain phenomena, however, are accessible to a gaze only through the dismantling of metaphysics. In the introduction to *The Life of the Mind* Arendt sketches the genesis of her current work and points out that her previous book on *vita activa* had to oppose the leveling of the phenomenal articulations specific to the degrees of *vita activa*, a leveling which had resulted in metaphysics privileging *vita contemplativa* as a way of life supposedly leading to absolute quietude. But she also draws attention to the fact that, in its final pages, her previous book contained a sort of suspicion directed at the so-called contemplative quietude and passivity of thinking. This suspicion imposed itself to her in the wake of Cato's statement, as it was reported by Cicero in *De Republica* (1: 17) "Never is a man more active than when he does nothing, never is he less alone than when he is by himself" (1: 7–8). The dismantling, therefore, concerns not merely the screens metaphysics sets up in front of what it spurns (namely, action), but those walls it erects in front of what it honors, *thinking first and foremost*. These obstacles are the specious arguments—or fallacies—in which metaphysics wraps up the thinking activity. But the paradox of those arguments is that in no way do they limit themselves to being arbitrary masks hiding that activity; she insists that "on the contrary, the metaphysical fallacies contain the only clues we have to what thinking means to those who engage in it" (1: 13). Concerning action, which metaphysics spurns, it is possible to seek its articulations in texts that do not originate in philosophers: Homer, Thucydides, Machiavelli, the American Founding Fathers, de Tocqueville. Concerning thinking, however, no other access is possible but the specious arguments of metaphysics, which therefore function both as masks and indispensable revealing agents. In addition, Arendt claims to be able to perform this dismantling of metaphysics— whose precondition is that it has ceased being credible in its categories, methods, doctrines, and claims to safeguard thought only for the benefit of a few elect ones, yet has not ceased deserving being remembered because it is the only testimony to what thinking is— only from one *location*. In reporting the sentence that Cicero attributes to Cato, she adds: "Assuming Cato was right, the questions are obvious: What are we 'doing' when we do nothing but think? Where are we when we, normally surrounded by our fellow-men, are together with no one but ourselves" (1: 8). The dismantling is therefore conducted from the location of the common world, of which plurality is the law and in which it is also the condition for action, by contrast to what is the case for labor and the production of artifacts. Hence dismantling the specious arguments of metaphysics, considered both as masks and revealing agents of the thinking activity, amounts to situating this activity with respect to action and its world.

Finally, this dismantling has a goal. Eichmann's trial in Jerusalem had imposed upon Arendt a notion that she knew ran against traditional thinking: the banality of evil. Eichmann was not a satanic figure; he didn't harbor a desire to be evil. Nor was he stupid or unintelligent. Simply, he was not thinking, and what made him ridiculous were the clichés cluttering his statements, his inaptitude for any thinking whatsoever, and his robotized gait. Miles apart from some recent apocalyptic questions (such as: Can one still think after Auschwitz?), which she would have thought still entail the Hegelian trap of an end of history, her observation evokes a *quaestio juris* remarkable for its sobriety: Would it be legitimate to use a notion such as the "banality of evil" if it could not be shown that the aptitude to discern good from evil is related to the thinking activity.

After recalling the most characteristic features of her dismantling, let me consider how she concretely shows that the specious arguments of metaphysics have the double function of mask and revealing agent. In a first approximation, it could be said that these specious arguments mask the belonging of the thinker to the world of appearances. What they reveal is the essential escape of that activity from the world of appearances. Concerning these arguments, she writes that "the only relevant question is whether the semblances are inauthentic or authentic ones, whether they are caused by dogmatic beliefs and arbitrary assumptions, mere mirages that disappear upon closer inspection, or whether they are inherent in the paradoxical condition of a living being that, though itself part of the world of appearances, is in possession of a faculty, the ability to think, that permits the mind to withdraw from the world without ever being able to leave it or transcendent it" (1: 45). For Arendt it is the second part of the alternative that is valid.

The specious arguments of metaphysics have the double function of masking and revealing because they are in keeping with the paradoxical condition of *belonging* and *withdrawal* with respect to the world of phenomena. And since we face a paradox the formulation just given must be immediately corrected because it is too dualistic. It is not sufficient to say that specious arguments mask the belonging of the thinking activity to the world of appearances; we must add immediately that they mask this belonging unsuccessfully. And it is not sufficient to say that they bear witness to the essential withdrawal of thought from the world of phenomena; we must add that this withdrawal is caught up in what it tries to disengage itself from.

I would like to follow a few of the analyses along which the dismantling by Arendt of specious metaphysical arguments allows us to heed the paradox, which is entirely comprised when considering Cato's statement: "Never is a man more active than when he does nothing, never is he less lonely than when he is by himself." To deconstruct a metaphysical argument or category amounts each time for Arendt to exhibiting a figure of this paradox.

And since, first, this deconstruction contains as an exergue a few sentences from Heidegger's *What Is Called Thinking?*

> Thinking does not bring knowledge as do the sciences.
> Thinking does not produce usable practical wisdom.

> Thinking does not solve the riddles of the universe.
> Thinking does not endow us directly with the power to act.

and since, second, she often quotes Heidegger with no apparent critical reservation—which might give a hurried reader the impression that their two approaches are in profound agreement—I would like, as a counterpoint to my investigation of the figures of the paradox, to detect along the way certain signs of various deep-seated divergences between these two deconstructions of metaphysics.

In my eyes the divergence is patent as early as the Introduction. Treating the famous "modern 'deaths'—of God, metaphysics, philosophy, and by implication, positivism" she writes the following:

> However seriously our ways of thinking may be involved in this crisis, our *ability* to think is not at stake; we are what men have always been—thinking beings. By this I mean no more than that men have an inclination, perhaps a need, to think beyond the limitations of knowledge, to do more with this ability than use it as an instrument for knowing and doing. To talk about nihilism in this context is perhaps unwillingness to part company with concepts and thought-trains that actually died quite some time ago, though their demise has been acknowledged only recently. (1: 11–12)

We cannot but notice that these assertions are frontally opposed, term for term, to ones issued by Heidegger, since for him the death of metaphysics means its abolition in the realm of technology, which seals the densest obscuring of the ontological difference and therefore the advent of *nihilism*—because now Being is Nothing, because there is nothing but ready-to-hand and calculable entities and because a threat is posed to thought, inasmuch as thinking has no other resource but being attuned to the ontological difference. This term-for-term opposition seems to me to suggest that in Arendt's view the Heideggerian approach could very well be fraught with traps set by what she calls the fallacies of metaphysics, because the pitfalls of Platonic dualisms may gain the ascendancy over the paradox of belonging and withdrawal.

But let us consider the fallacy contained in the two-world theory. It consists in affirming under various modalities the superiority of the foundation over the surface, of Being over Appearance, of the cause over the effect. Now, in the world where our existence unravels between birth and death, this distinction has no legitimate applicability. In this world of ours, Being and Appearing do not form

hierarchical degrees, they coincide; and precisely because they coincide, nothing of what is, i.e., of what appears, is strictly singular:
instead, it remains offered to the gaze of several spectators. And
those spectators in the plural are also offered as a spectacle—they
are at the same time perceiving and perceived. *Instead of being in
the world, they are of the world.* Their identity is therefore strictly
relative to a common scene upon which they come to appearance.
And because this production is offered to a plurality of perspectives
or points of view, that difference in the points of view is no obstacle
to the identity of emerging spectators, it is constitutive of it. This
also means that appearing is always a *dokei moi*—or an "it seems to
me from a given perspective" and entailing a "side" which is being
offered and presented—which conjoins both manifestation and dis-
simulation. A profile, Husserl used to say, both announces and
hides other profiles.

To these overlappings which characterize what Arendt used to
call the "phenomenal nature of the world," metaphysics opposes
the two-world theory of the true and the apparent worlds, of Being
and mere Appearance. Deconstructing this doubling amounts to revealing the paradox that is inherent in it. The paradox is that at the
very same time as the philosopher asserts in thought the supremacy of thought over the apparent world, it is in the apparent
world that he seeks a red thread that will supposedly take him into
the true world, and by the same token he asserts the supremacy of
the apparent world. For this true world—which relegates the common world down to the level of mere appearance—is also deemed
capable of appearing; and the distinction between simulacrum and
true being, which separates these two worlds, is first experienced
by the thinker in the world of appearances, because it is specifically
characteristic of the common phenomenal world to dissimulate as
much as reveal and to allow constantly that certain appearances
will be shattered for the benefit of others.

The fact that this deconstruction is inspired by the later work of
Merleau-Ponty is beyond doubt. That Heidegger should be counted
among its targets is not explicitly affirmed by Arendt in the first
volume of *The Life of the Mind*.

I believe, however, that her underscoring that we are of the world
and not simply in the world, that we belong to a common world
and that it is in its midst that our personal identity and individuation is constituted goes counter to views held in *Being and Time*
and the division maintained by Heidegger between on the one hand
a common everyday world (in which individuation is not possible

because of the ascendancy of the "they") and on the other the world in the authentic sense (in which individuation escapes appearances simply because it consists in *Dasein* facing up to the indeterminate certainty of its demise). In addition, Heidegger expresses this distinction between the everyday and the ownmost world in the old language of Being and Appearance, thereby espousing "the old prejudice of Being's supremacy over appearance" (1: 27).

It is another prejudice and another specious argument to believe that our "'inner life' is more relevant to what we 'are' than what appears on the outside" (1: 30). What is at issue in the dismantling conducted by Arendt of different variations on this fallacy is a certain idea of individuation, supposedly removed from the world of appearances. There is a reason why Arendt asserts in such massive fashion that the moods—emotions, feelings, affects—are identical in all individuals just as much as the organs of the body are identical and why she claims allegiance to the Aristotelian distinction between *psychē,* closely associated with the body, whose expressions are neither metaphorical nor individuated, and *nous,* which is not at all the other side of the activity of the body and whose activity requires the metaphors of discourse. What she wants to emphasize is, first, that individuation consists in someone presenting himself or herself to others by words and deeds, in showing them how the individual intends to come to appearance and what this individual also deems worthy of being seen by them. "Obviously, self-presentation and the sheer thereness of existence are not the same" (1: 37). She adds immediately afterwards that "choice, as the decisive factor in self-presentation, has to do with appearances." Here too as in the case of the previous specious argument, we may wonder whether, although Heidegger is not named, he is not implicitly aimed as a target, inasmuch as in his analyses of choice the ultimately nonrelational *(unbezüglich)* character of resolution, or *Entschlossenheit,* is what comes to the forefront.

Another specious figure is that of *solipsism,* whose variations are manifold: they are owed to Descartes, Hume, Husserl, Heidegger himself and his existential solipsism.

Dismantling this specious figure is to manifest the paradox upon which it rests and which consists in the fact that the individual given over to thinking belongs to the sphere of appearing at the same time as he or she withdraws from it. The pertinent phenomenal foundation of solipsism is the fact that one cannot think without withdrawing from a world of common appearances, whose law is plurality. When someone thinks, in a sense he or she is no longer among others, that person is alone in the world. But this withdrawal continues to presuppose that from which it is taking leave, namely his or her belonging to appearances. It is this appearing which the various formulae of solipsism cover over. In the Cartesian version, only the proposition *I think–I am* is true, and it is so only as long as I am thinking. In the Husserlian version, only the reduced *ego* is endowed with absolute existence. In its Heideggerian version, in his fundamental ontology, *Dasein* exists for the sake of itself, and this existing is the key to the meanings of Being. What all these versions say is that only the thinking activity is in touch with Being. What they mask is that, left to its own, this activity could not convince anyone of any reality and that the Being of which they speak—overlapped as it is by appearing—could summon a meaning for the authors of such formulae only after being initially equated with Appearing. Arendt writes:

> It never occurred to [Descartes' mind] that no *cogitatio* and no *cogito me cogitare*, no consciousness of an acting self that has suspended all faith in the reality of its intentional objects, would ever have been able to convince him of his own reality had he actually been born in a desert, without a body and its senses to perceive "material" things and without fellow-creatures to assure him that what he perceived was perceived by them too. The Cartesian *res cogitans*, this fictitious creature, bodiless, senseless, and forsaken, would not even know that there is such a thing as reality and a possible distinction between the real and the unreal, between the common world of waking life and the private non-world of our dreams. What Merleau-Ponty has to say against Descartes is brilliantly right: "To reduce perception to the thought of perceiving . . . is to take out an insurance against doubt whose premiums are more onerous than the loss for which it is to indemnify us: for it is to move to a type of certitude that will never restore to us the 'there is' of the world." (1: 48–49)

Having truck with Being therefore does not require that we take leave of common appearing. It lies at the heart of our relationship to common appearing. She writes: "Although everything that appears is perceived in the mode of it-seems-to-me, hence open to error and illusion, appearance as such carries with it a prior indication of *realness*" (1: 49). The correlate in each one of us of this quality of the real is the *sensus communis*, the sense of the real, which is the point of encounter of a "threefold commonness" that Arendt expresses as follows: "The three senses, utterly different from each other, have the same object in *common*; members of the same species have the same context in *common* that endows every single object with its particular meaning; and all other sense endowed beings, though perceiving this object from utterly different perspectives, *agree* on its identity" (1: 50, stress added).

The withdrawal of thought with respect to phenomena, with respect to the coinciding of Being and Appearing thus results in the loss of the sense of realness, which *sensus communis* brings along. Is this tantamount to saying that in order to obviate that loss one might and should content oneself with a reasoning grounded upon this good sense, which constantly is adjusted to what appears, which corrects illusions, denounces past evidences for the benefit of new ones, segregates true and false on the basis of a renewed effort? This demand would be tantamount to claiming that there is no other object of thought than that upon which a given community is in agreement. This demand would also be tantamount to claiming that the task of thought is restricted to separating the false from the true, i.e., to the activity of knowledge.

But thinking, Arendt stresses, is not knowing. Cognition aims at truth. Thought aims at meaning.

The problem, however, is that those who are given over to the thinking activity are the first to cover over this distinction by passing their approach for the acquiring of a knowledge superior to everyday knowledge and that of the scientists. It is therefore appropriate to dismantle this *fallacy* by means of which the professional thinkers pass the aiming at meaning for the conquest of truth and a work of science. Here too what seems to me at issue in this dismantling—or what this dismantling aims at showing—is the paradox of belonging to and withdrawal from the phenomena.

Science as such, according to Arendt, is nothing but "an enormously refined prolongation of common-sense reasoning in which sense illusions are constantly dissipated as errors in science are corrected" (1: 54). She stresses that "all science still moves within the realm of common sense experience, subject to correctable errors and deception" *(ibid.)*. It is the world of appearances and its correlate, *sensus communis*, that form a necessary cradle for truth. It is to this world that science remains bound. Because of its ever renewed pursuit of a dispelling of error, because of its appetite for seeing, science is for Arendt "the refinement [of common sense]" (1: 58). More generally speaking, cognition "whose highest criterion is truth, derives that criterion from the world of appearances in which we take our bearings through sense perceptions, whose testimony is self-evident, that is, unshakable by argument and replaceable only by other evidence" (1: 57).

By contrast, the faculty of thinking, or *Vernunft* in the Kantian sense, which is distinct from the understanding as the faculty of knowledge, asks questions of meaning that escape *sensus communis* and science and for which these two have no interest. Science and common sense endlessly reawaken questions *"an sit"* (whether it is) and *"quid sit"* (what it is); never do they ask what it *means* for something to be and to be as it is.

Yet, the same people who, like Kant, may insist on the distinction between thinking and knowing and argue that "the need of reason" is other than "the need of cognition" succumb to the temptation of equating them. To know is to use thought as a means toward a determined end—the acquisition of a cognition which, once it is given, can be counted upon in the world of phenomena. Thought, by contrast, is an activity that is not slave to a goal, that is not guided by determined intentions, as is the case with cognition or productive activity in *vita activa*, but rather that is "done for its own sake" (1: 64) and whose concepts—"heuristic" and not "ostensive"—are as Arendt says "tentative: they do not demonstrate or show anything" *(ibid.)*; in other words, the questions of thought are raised without the expectancy of a response. And yet Kant speaks of knowledge attained by pure reason, of a final unity of things and of the pursuit by reason of determined ends, thus hinting that he nonetheless considers the thinking activity on the model of the cognitive one.

This sort of confusion is what constitutes, according to Arendt, the "basic fallacy." She writes: "The basic fallacy, taking precedence over all specific metaphysical fallacies, is to interpret meaning on the model of truth" (1: 15).

The paradox upon which this fallacy rests consists, perhaps in reverse of the fallacious figures that I have evoked so far, in giving ultimate superiority to the world of common sense over the withdrawal from it which is required in order to think. Arendt, in this context, evokes Heidegger, whom this time she criticizes: "'The latest and in some respect most striking instance of this [fallacy] occurs in Heidegger's *Being and Time*, which starts out by 'raising anew the question of the meaning of Being.'" Heidegger himself, in a later interpretation of his initial question, says explicitly: "'Meaning of Being' and 'Truth of Being' say the same" (1: 15). To be sure, this way of presenting things is a bit cavalier inasmuch as it makes short shrift of the fact that "the truth of Being," precisely in Heidegger's rereading of his initial question, doesn't mean at all that

Being is an object of knowledge, or is open to cognition. It remains nonetheless true that *Being and Time* was inscribed in a project, that of fundamental ontology, which aimed at the completion of metaphysics as the *science of Being* and assigned to the destruction of the history of ontology the task of showing that the ontological categories of the metaphysical tradition have their ultimate key of intelligibility in a unique center, which is *Dasein*'s mode of being.

This superiority of the phenomenal world of common sense over the withdrawal from it is detected by Arendt, so it seems to me, on the backdrop of another fallacy, the one affecting the discourse of "professional thinkers" about death.

But before continuing, I find it useful, for fear of not having made my case clearly enough, to underscore that Arendt's denunciation of what she calls the "metaphysical fallacies" does not consist at all in denouncing the paradox of belonging to and withdrawing from appearances, but quite on the contrary in putting value upon it and assuming it. There is a fallacy when the paradox, far from being recognized as such, is covered over. This paradox is that of the human condition, which in part belongs to appearances and in part also must withdraw from them so as to think, will, and judge. It is in this world of appearances that the levels of active life are inscribed: first, the level of life with its necessities and cycles of labor and pleasures; second, that of the fabricating activity by means of which the dwelling of the world is established and maintained; and third, that of action thanks to which individuated existing beings present and reveal themselves to others. At each level appearing is involved, first in the living being, second in the bearer of fabricating capacities, third as individual proper. To this ensemble of appearing our *sensus communis* is adjusted. Yet thinking enacted by someone belonging to this totality is tantamount to withdrawing from it. Whereas *vita activa* is conditioned upon life, the world, and plurality, the thinking activity escapes those conditions, it transcends them. At no point does Arendt doubt the importance of this withdrawal. Rather, she is convinced that "the principles by which we act and the criteria by which we judge and conduct our lives depend ultimately on the life of the mind" (1: 71). But she is also convinced that "in our world there is no clearer or more radical *opposition* than that between thinking and doing" (1: 71). Such is the paradox. There is no doubt that the fallacies she denounces consist, in the last analysis, in denying this opposition. The professional philosopher, toward whom Arendt's dismissive attitude is directed following the Thracian maid's mocking of Thales, is the individual who by devoting himself totally to the thinking activity has elevated this human aptitude—which is only one among others—to the rank of absolute.

Every fallacy, in her eyes, consisted in blurring necessary distinctions. Metaphysical fallacies consist in blurring the differences between thinking and doing, in masking their opposition or inevitable internal warfare, and even in resolving doing into thinking. And because the one who thinks is also one who belongs to the world of phenomena in which action is inscribed, this resolving consists in his crediting the thinking activity with the very themes usually objected against it by *sensus communis* in general, including of course his own common sense.

Such is the metaphysical fallacy that Arendt detects in the diverse variations on the affirmation by the professional thinkers of a specific affinity between the thinking activity and death. Plato, Hegel, Schopenhauer and Heidegger are obviously in the ranks. "The very fact that there have always—at least since Parmenides—been men who chose this way of life deliberately without being candidates for suicide shows that this sense of an affinity with death does not come from the thinking activity and the experiences of the thinking ego itself" (1: 80). On this point, the essential clue comes from Plato who reveals in *Phaedo* that it is to those who do not philosophize that the philosopher withdrawing from the world of appearances seems to be uniquely concerned with the pursuit of death. It is for *sensus communis* and with respect to the common world of appearances that the most radical disappearance is death and a withdrawal from phenomena is tantamount to a sort of dying. Generally speaking,

> it is the philosopher's own common sense—his being a "man like you and me"—that makes him aware of being "out of order" while engaged in thinking. He is not immune from common opinion, because he shares after all, in the "common-ness" of all men, and it is his own sense of realness that makes him suspect the thinking activity. And since thinking itself is helpless against the arguments of common-sense reasoning and the insistence on the "meaninglessness" of its quest for meaning, the philosopher is prone to answer in common-sense terms, which he simply turns upside down for the purpose. (1: 80)

If common sense says that death is the greatest of evils, the philosopher, Plato first on the list, will make heeding it a condition favorable to the thinking activity.

This specious reversal or metaphysical fallacy is something Arendt sees enacted in *Being and Time*, which allows her to put Heidegger and Plato back to back. She writes:

> Even the younger Heidegger of *Being and Time* still treated the anticipation of death as the decisive experience through which man can attain an authentic self and be liberated from the inauthenticity of the They, quite unaware of the extent to which this doctrine actually sprang, as Plato has pointed out, from the opinion of the many. (1: 79–80)

It would be possible from this point to multiply examples of that specious reversal in which Arendt detects the obliteration of a paradox (the "internal warfare"), which results from our condition, characterized both by belonging to the phenomena and by the need to withdraw from them in order to aim at a meaning.

Whereas the thinking activity entails a quieting and forgetting of the phenomenal realm because of its withdrawal from the common realm of phenomena, the professional thinker, by contrast, accuses the phenomenal sphere of being forgetful of Ideas, or Spirit, or Being.

Likewise, whereas the thinking activity, which is solitary in this very retreat, withdraws the thinking ego from the phenomenal plurality, which is the only medium allowing individuation for a specific existing being, by contrast the thinker accuses this plurality of being anonymous multiplicity (*hoi polloi* in Plato, the They in Heidegger) and turns the thinking activity into the sole veritable principle of individuation. This reduction was also enacted by Heidegger during the Marburg period, because although on the one hand he recognized that a thinker totally devoted to the thinking activity is without individual history (Heidegger used to summarize Aristotle's life thus: He was born, he worked, he died), he also maintained on the other hand that only metaphysics—not as doctrinal body, but as *bios* or mode of life—insured the full concretion of existence.

In the same fashion, finally, whereas action is only meaningful at the heart of plurality and whereas thought extracts itself from both, the professional thinker guarantees that only thought is authentic action, a claim that is made in texts both of Hegel and Heidegger, namely in Hegel's *Phenomenology* and in Heidegger's fundamental ontology, "Rectorial Address" and even "Letter on Humanism."

In all three cases, according to Arendt, the trouble taken in justifying these reversals does not emanate from thought. It is common sense that imposes it upon the professional philosophers. Because of this trouble they turn out to be unfaithful to both thought and common sense. They are unfaithful to common sense because they accuse it of fallenness. They are also unfaithful to thought because they attribute to it the privilege of either acting in the world (which it does not do) or seeing and hearing (whereas the aimed meaning is invisible as much as inaudible) or even reaching goals (whereas the work of thought is a Penelope's work, or if one prefers a finality without end). Thinking is therefore not, contrary to what the professional thinker claims, to put oneself in the position of privileged spectator and seer. Rigorously speaking, a spectator is one who does not put himself in a position of complete withdrawal with respect to the common world. Spectatorship is fitting for one who, to be sure, takes his distances from the world in which phenomena and events are manifold, new, particular in order not however to abolish that particularity, but to judge it in an approach which, as Kant notes in his analysis of reflecting judgment, comports both personal responsibility and the taking into account of others. Such a spectatorship exists only in the plural, it is bound to plurality. By contrast, the self-proclaimed speculative gaze of the professional thinker only exists in the singular. As a result, he may issue the claim that it is the history of the world that is the judgment of the world.

At this juncture, it is possible to wonder what this dismantling is bringing to the question that had set it into motion, namely that of knowing what link there is between the aptitude to discern good from evil and the activity of thinking. It is regarding this issue that an ultimate fallacy emerges.

Regarding the question of what makes us think, Plato, the prototype of the professional thinker at the same time as an authentic thinker, responded in *Theaetetus* that it is wonder, or *thaumazein*. From the course of her analyses of the reverberating echoes this question had in the history of philosophy (which is not to be confused, she urges, with the history of thought) I shall retain the following. First, this wonder is a *pathos* which consists in being forced to admire. Next, the admirative wonder to which the philosopher is subjected can in no way concern something particular, but is always aroused by the totality, which unlike the totality of beings is never manifest. This is, she says, Heraclitus' "invisible harmony" (1: 143). Finally, there is this sentence, which in my view is crucial:

> Admirative wonder conceived as the starting point of philosophy leaves no place for the factual existence of disharmony, of ugliness, and finally of evil. (1: 150)

In other words, there is in the very activity of thinking—inasmuch as it radicalizes its withdrawal from the phenomena, inasmuch as it takes itself for a cognition, inasmuch as it takes itself for a seeing of the invisible, in short inasmuch as it obliterates the internal warfare between thought and common sense instead of assuming the paradox—a tendency to blindness vis-à-vis the distinction between good and evil, a tendency to avoid judging. This is a tendency symmetrical to the one that had struck Arendt so much in her assessment of Eichmann, a man who never thought and never judged. In addition to Heraclitus, Arendt evokes Nietzsche and Hegel in the same context.[2] She alludes briefly to Heidegger's *Denken ist Danken*. With greater benefit she could have evoked—but she did not know them—Heidegger's lecture courses during the Nazi rule, especially the first lecture course on Hölderlin dating from 1934–35 in which one finds pellmell the Platonic theme of the solitary philosopher and demi-god, the Heraclitean theme of invisible harmony, and proclamations of his own thinking proximity with Nietzsche and Hegel. In that lecture course Heidegger takes great care to dismiss into the sphere of everyday inauthenticity such things as: racism, mass organization, brutality, and the normalization of the universities. After which, the inevitable tension between Appearance and Being prompts him to conclude in a Heraclitean gesture:

> In facing such a devastation of every authentic thought, only one who does not understand what authentic is would raise objections. Astonishment and horror are just as misplaced here as they would be in front of a beautiful farmstead if someone complained the courtyard contains an imposing heap of manure! Can one imagine a farm without manure? (*GA*, 39: 42)

In specious figures of that sort it could very well be once more that it is common sense that plays tricks upon the professional thinker since the adjustment of that sense of realness to the world seems to be expressed here by something akin to an expostulation—"Here we are!" Don't raise an eyebrow! (1: 59).

Is this tantamount to claiming that the thinking activity is as detrimental as its absence for discerning good from evil? Not at all, of course. But in all the different variations of the admirative *pathos*, which places itself beyond good and evil, the thinking activity gives way to metaphysical imposture, it does not think any more, it claims to see or act, it comes up with a pact with common sense at the very moment when it publicly displays scorn for it.

One might as well say that the thinking activity avoids fallacies only if it fully assumes the paradox of appearance and withdrawal. Is there a model for such a capacity? We know that Arendt found it in Socrates, "the thinker who was not a professional, who in his person unified two apparently contradictory passions, for thinking and for acting" (1: 167), "a man who counted himself neither among the many nor among the few . . . , who had no aspiration to be a ruler of men, no claim even to be particularly well-fitted by his superior wisdom to act in an advisory capacity to those in power, but not a man who submitted meekly to being ruled either" *(ibid.)*, a thinker without a doctrine, whose arguments are strictly aporetic, do not lead anywhere or go in circles, and who merely claims the right to reflect on the opinions of others by asking them to do likewise. He was a thinker who as Heidegger says—and for once Arendt is in full agreement—"throughout his life and up to his very death did nothing other than place himself in this draft, this current of thinking, and maintain himself in it. This is why he is the purest of the West. This is why he wrote nothing" (1: 174).

Among the rare assertions attributed to Socrates Arendt retains two propositions from *Gorgias* (1: 181). The first says: "It is better to be wronged than to do wrong" (474b); and the second: "It would be better for me . . . that multitudes of men should disagree with me rather than that I, *being one,* should be out of harmony with myself and contradict me" (482c). Neither statement is the outcome of an investigation, the fulfillment of a cognitive intention. Likewise, neither statement consists of a moral maxim. But those statements do not emanate either from the man of action, from the *citizen,* since for a Greek to suffer injustice is not expected from a citizen and is considered characteristic of the position of the slave and since—more importantly, assessing matters from the point of view of the city in the case of a transgression—it is transgression itself or injustice as such that requires punishment, without concern for the question of who benefits from it, the victim or the perpetrator. But it is rather from the very experience of thinking that both propositions emerge, not as a result but as a glimpse of its movement. In the first statement, Socrates tells Callicles, who is opposed to it: If you were as I am searching after meaning, if you were ceaselessly inquiring into Justice, Beauty, Wisdom, you would understand what I am saying. Yet the first proposition is conditioned upon the second, which is that upon which Arendt's remarkable reading rests. She says that the second proposition is strange because, by saying that he is one, Socrates seems to imply in good logic that he could be neither in tune nor out of tune with himself. Actually, what the sentence expresses is the very movement of thought: being oneself and simultaneously being for oneself, being two-in-one, keeping oneself company. The thinking activity sets in motion a duality of myself with myself. "Nothing perhaps indicates more strongly that man exists *essentially* in the plural than that this solitude actualizes his merely being conscious of himself . . . into a duality in the thinking activity" (1: 184). In this company that one keeps with oneself plurality, the law of the common world, is implied, as well as the sense of what is evil. To think, is to act in such a way that the interlocutors of the two-in-one come to an agreement and are *friends*. For who would be the friend of a murderer? What does Kant's categorical imperative lay a claim to, if not the agreement of oneself with oneself? Such an accord, according to Arendt, presupposes the thinking activity. The banality of evil is connected with the fact that those who slip into it care neither to agree with themselves nor to disagree, because they are incapable of keeping themselves company.

> A person who does not know that silent intercourse (in which we examine what we say and what we do) will not mind contradicting himself, and this means he will never be either able or willing to account for what he says or does; nor will he mind committing any crime, since he can count on its being forgotten the next moment. Bad people—Aristotle to the contrary notwithstanding—are *not* "full of regrets." (1: 191)

How, then, is the paradox of belonging and withdrawal relevant in the case of Socrates? Socrates fully takes it upon himself and avoids its metaphysical garbling. The reason is that, first, he holds that the life of someone, which by definition is individuated in the midst of plurality, is not worth living if the person does not reflect upon it, does not ask what it is to live well, what virtue is, and beauty, and wisdom. But, second, the infinitely reiterated meditation on these themes does not take him into the solitary contemplation of an invisible order (e.g., that of *physis*) claimed possible by the physiologists (he detested them). For the meditation on these themes, infinite though it is, opens up a return to appearances because ultimately it is always *hic et nunc*, in a particular situation concerning a singular destiny facing others, that each of us has to decide, and this means to judge, what is wise, what good, and what beautiful.

NOTES

1. This text is the revised version of a study published in *Ontologie et politique*, Paris: Tierce, pp. 85–99, a collection of papers on Hannah Arendt, given in Paris at the Collège international de philosophie (14–16 April 1988).

2. See my book *Heidegger and the Project of Fundamental Ontology*, trans. Michael Gendre, Albany: State University of New York Press, 1990, chap. 7.

FIVE

The *Kehre* and the Conflict between Thinking and Willing

E xcept for the text of homage to Heidegger for his eightieth birthday, it is in the second volume of *The Life of the Mind*, "Willing," that Arendt brings the most sustained focus on him. These pages deserve our attention.

Inasmuch as they are to be found in the conclusion of the volume, it is essential in our attempt to bring light upon them not to dissociate them from the inquiry leading up to them. Dissociating a consideration of Heidegger from that inquiry would certainly simplify things but would miss a great deal because although Heidegger is not named directly or is evoked merely in allusions, he is far from being absent in it. The inquiry follows the deconstructive precept adopted in the first volume of the work, which is to extract the phenomenon from a layer of ossified theses that amalgamate what should be distinguished. This deconstruction claims to be "phenomenological" through and through and we witness the recurring emergence in the text of that adjective. It aims at saving the phenomena, according to the Aristotelian motto which Heidegger used to be fond of mentioning. The irony, however, was that it did happen not only that he overlooked them and that he confused *poiēsis* and *praxis* but also—concerning the very activity to which he had devoted his life, namely thinking—that he either equated it with knowing or absorbed into it the entire field of *praxis*.

But precisely because she aims at extracting phenomena from the conceptual fallacies and confusions regarding each kind of activity that covers them over, deconstructive irony is not a refutation. It is rather an appeal to lucidity, an injunction of caution with respect to what lowers our attention to the phenomena. It is quite obvious from the inquiry on willing that in spite of her irony Arendt was in no way tempted to refuse Heidegger the title of phenomenologist.

In the Introduction she cautions that "it is in the nature of every critical examination of the faculty of the Will that it should be undertaken by 'professional thinkers' (Kant's *Denker von Gewerbe*), and this gives rise to the suspicion that the denunciations of the Will as a mere illusion of consciousness and the refutation of its very existence, which we find supported by almost identical arguments in philosophers of widely differing assumptions, might be due to a basic conflict between the experiences of the thinking ego and those of the willing ego" (2: 4).

Do these words aim Heidegger, and how? It would be cavalier to answer this question without first considering the leading theme and the specific contour of the emerging deconstructive inquiry, that is before determining what in Arendt's eyes the phenomenal features of willing are.

The leading theme of her inquiry is time. This theme is undoubtedly Heideggerian. Paul Ricoeur notes in the French preface to *The Human Condition*[1] that the categories of active life considered in that book—labor, work, action—are tantamount to "specific responses to specific questions posed by the temporal condition of 'mortal' beings" (*La Condition de l'homme moderne*, p. 17). The same thing could be said of the categories of mental activity considered in *The Life of the Mind*, as is already stated in the title of the first section of that work, "Time and the mental activities." Arendt evokes here again the considerations of time upon which she had just concluded her investigation of the thinking activity. For she had noted then that the question of a *topos noētos* is without pertinence. Instead, it was appropriate, she suggested, to assert with Paul Valéry, "Tantôt je pense, tantôt je suis" (At one time I think, at another time I am), for the one who thinks has withdrawn from phenomena, from his body and finally from his Self, "phenomenon among phenomena." I attempted to show earlier, along this line, that speculative individuation in the sense of Heidegger's fundamental ontology has purified itself of belonging to the phenomena, to such an extent that it is no longer the individuation of someone. By contrast, if this thinking activity has withdrawn from the space of appearances, it nevertheless has some connection with time. First, it is memory that sustains and inspires thought. From Plato's *anamnesis* to the Heideggerian attempt to overcome the forgetfulness of Being, various thinkers have underscored the affinity of their activity with remembering. Sustained by memory, this activity consists, Arendt says, in struggling against "the inherent futility of everything that is subject to change" (2: 12) and in "salvaging" it from "oblivion" (*ibid.*). She adds:

The time region in which this salvag[ing] takes place is the Present of the thinking ego, a kind of lasting "todayness" (*hodiernus*, "of this day," Augustine's called God's eternity), the "standing now" *(nunc stans)* of medieval meditation, and "enduring present" (Bergson's *présent qui dure*), or the "gap between past and future," as we called it in explicating Kafka's time parable. (2: 12)

She could have added—inasmuch as such the topic was familiar to her—*Anwesen*, coming-into-presence, a topic around which Heidegger's latest writings gravitate in dealing with the stakes of thinking *[l'affaire de la pensée]*. Whatever the reason for Arendt's discretion on that point, it is really another insistent motif of Heidegger's latest writings, *Gelassenheit*, which brings a final touch to her sketch of a phenomenology of the relationship between thought and time. With this motif Arendt is obviously in agreement at a distance, when without mentioning Heidegger she writes: "Speaking in terms of tonality—that is, in terms of the way the mind affects the soul and produces its *moods*, regardless of outside events, thus creating a kind of *life* of the mind—the predominant mood of the thinking ego is *serenity*" (2: 38). It is hard not to detect here a double echo: that of the general teaching of Heidegger on *Befindlichkeit* and *Stimmung* and that of his late insistence on letting-be.

The fact that Arendt is far from being inattentive to the "gap" in which thought is settled is ascertained by the English title she gave to a collection of essays, *Between Past and Future*.

It will be noted that the discreet affinities just pointed out with a phenomenology of the thinking activity only concern Heidegger's latest writings. By contrast, it is the Heidegger of fundamental ontology who seems to inspire at a distance—not without major reservations and corrections, as we shall see—Arendt's phenomenology of willing.

First, this phenomenology seeks its own way through great texts of the history of philosophy whose phenomenal pertinence she attempts to evaluate at every step, according to a gesture akin in its style to the Heideggerian reading of the philosophical classics at the time of the project of fundamental ontology. Next, the thinkers she privileges are those, without a doubt, that Heidegger privileged at that time in his way: the Aristotle of the *Nicomachean Ethics*, the Augustine of the *Confessions*, the Hegel of Jena. Finally, the phenomenology of willing that is sketched out in these lectures overlaps on many points—not without reservations, let me repeat—Heidegger's existential analytic, of which Arendt salutes the "perspicacity" with respect to willing in connection with temporality.

But before investigating those overlappings, let me recall briefly the deconstructive part of that historical inquiry. Generally speaking, the "professional thinker" rests upon one single experience which he privileges, that of the thinking ego, of which we just recalled the most salient phenomenological features. I pointed out earlier that one of the most frequent "professional deformations" to which according to Arendt he succumbs consists in metamorphosing that experience into knowing, thereby confusing knowing and thinking. In this resides a speculative fallacy. As soon as speculation is brought to bear on willing, the thinker is liable to be tempted either to negate it or stunt it, as the result of the initial privileging of the thinking activity. In either case, it is his initial attachment to the past that guides him. To negate the will is in one way or another tantamount to reducing it to an illusion of consciousness, to being blinded by the determining weight of the past—whether this weight is attributed to naturalistic determinism or a theological or ontological predetermination. Stunting the will occurs when its existence is recognized but limited to being one mere arbiter between possibilities antecedently given and therefore already past.

These elements define *a contrario* some of the phenomenal features specific to willing. Far from being attached to the past, willing is oriented toward the future. Far from being a repetition or the expression of a prior antecedent, it is absolute beginning. Far from being subjected to and by necessity, it is radically free. Far from having as its element the intelligible universality aimed at by thinking when it is metamorphosed into knowing, it only exists in the singular. Far from having as its tonality serenity with touches and fringes of melancholy, or even nostalgia, as in the case of thought, its tonality is fundamentally restlessness *[inquiétude]*.

There is, therefore, a fundamental contrast between the experiences of the thinking and willing egos. Let us consider the experiences of the willing ego with respect to temporality, the dominating theme of Arendt's phenomenology of the will. Two of the readings through which her phenomenology makes its way will hold our attention. I have in mind those pages devoted to Augustine and those in keeping with Hegel's writings of the Jena period.

Let us begin with Hegel, by following the very order proposed by Arendt since she treats Hegel at length in the first chapter of the volume on Willing. The beginning of her exposition clearly announces the central motif with respect to the deconstructive aim she maintains. As we just said, this aim consists first of all in tracing within the texts of the professional thinkers the very marks of a fundamental conflict between the experience of thinking and that of willing, in order to question in a second phase the "solution" purportedly given to it by those professional thinkers. She writes: "No philosopher has described the willing ego in its clash with the thinking ego with greater sympathy, insight, and consequence for the history of thought than Hegel" (2: 39). What is at stake in the analyses that follow? Not at all a claim of allegiance to Hegel, nor even less—it goes without saying—a contribution to the *Hegelforschung*, whose works however she was aware of at a distance. Instead, the issue was to highlight, in Hegel's text and thanks to those works, the typical fashion in which the speculative philosopher bears witness to the clash between thinking and willing; this testimony is a rigorously phenomenological account, which Hegel nevertheless never ceased covering over, especially with his claim to solve it for the benefit of thought alone. His solution, ingenious though it is, is tantamount to turning away from the phenomenon.

That Hegel should bear witness to a few specific phenomenological features of the thinking activity cannot obviously be very surprising. Moreover, the fact that this testimony should aim in particular the essential connection between this activity and the past is indicated with clarity by one of Hegel's most celebrated mottoes, "Minerva's owl takes flight at night." In this respect, all reserves made concerning its overall phenomenological pertinence, Hegel's philosophy of history has at least for Arendt an undeniable phenomenological pertinence, in spite of the many fallacies that it contains. It is through and though sustained by the experience of thinking and its relationship to the past "re-collected by the backward-directed glance of the thinking and remembering ego, . . . is 'internalized' *(er-innert)*, becomes part and parcel of the mind through the 'effort of the concept' *('die Anstrengung des Begriffs')*, and in this internalizing way achieves the 'reconciliation' of Mind and World" (2: 40). Thus we see that it satisfies the wish for meaning inherent, as we indicated, in the thinking activity.

The fact that Hegel, on the other hand, recognized the specific phenomenological features of the activity of willing is found by Arendt in the Hegelian descriptions of time, whose account and commentary she borrows from a 1934 essay, "Hegel à Iena" (Hegel at Jena) by Alexandre Koyré, with whom at that date—corresponding with her immigration to France—she had started a friendship. Koyré maintains not without reason that the Hegelian writings of Jena *(Jenenser Logik* and *Realphilosophie)* insist on the future in dealing with time and grant it a priority over the past. Indeed in the

Jenenser Logik Hegel insists that "the now is empty . . . It is filled in the future. The future is its reality" (Lasson ed., 204). This analysis is confirmed in the *Realphilosophie:* "The future is directly in the present, for it is contained there as its negation" (Hoffmeister ed., 2: 10). Neither Hegel nor Koyré, his commentator, evokes the will with respect to this priority of the future. But for Arendt, who is in agreement with Koyré insisting that the time thus described is strictly "human" (2: 40), there is no doubt that the so-called negation is made possible by the will and that "Hegel's description of experienced human time relates to the time sequence appropriate to the willing ego" (2: 41). The restlessness of temporality and the work of the negative are, therefore, what in Hegel is tantamount to a phenomenological testimony to the experience of willing. She stresses forcefully: "Man is not just temporal, he *is* Time" (2: 42).

The question is that of knowing how in Hegel the phenomenological testimony of willing is related to that of thinking. This relationship is determined with respect to death. After recalling that in Hegel man is not distinguished from other animals "by being an *animal naturale* but by being the only living creature that knows about its own death" (2: 43), she adds: "It is at this ultimate point of the willing ego's anticipation of death that the thinking ego constitutes itself. In the anticipation of death, the will's projects take on the appearance of an anticipated past and as such can become the object of reflection" *(ibid.)*. Hegel's Preface to the *Phenomenology* posits that only the mind that "does not ignore death" enables man "to dominate death," to "endure it and to maintain itself within it" *(ibid.)*. In the terms of Arendt's phenomenology, this means that "at the moment in which the mind confronts its own end," the future "'has lost its power over it' [in the words of Koyré] and has become ready for the enduring present of the thinking ego" (2: 43–44).

Arendt is therefore justified in summarizing as follows the relationship found in the Hegelian presentation between thinking and willing after granting that it presents matters in an oversimplified form: "That there exists such a thing as the *Life* of the mind is due to the mind's organ for the future and its resulting 'restlessness'; that there exists such a thing as the life of the *Mind* is due to death, which, foreseen as an absolute end, halts the will and transforms the future into an anticipated past, the will's projects into objects of thought, and the soul's expectation into an anticipated remembrance" (2: 44).

As such, this turn by means of the relation to death from restlessness with respect to time to the tranquillity of remembrance has nothing specious. What is simply the case is that one activity takes the relay of another. But fallacy begins when the activity of thinking far from being content with being the relay of willing deems itself justified in substituting for it, in depriving it of every consistency, and in acting as though willing did not take place. This coup enacted by the professional thinker is tantamount to eliminating the *life* of the *mind*, that is to say, to abolishing the conflict between willing and thinking which sustains that life. We see that it turns out once more that the basic phenomenological situation is a paradox and that the propensity of professional philosophers is to overlook it.

In Arendt's eyes it is such a coup that founds Hegel's philosophy of history and his system more generally speaking.

The ingeniousness with which speculation combines the peaceful motif of the circle with the linear restlessness of negativity, eternity and the temporal course of human affairs, rational necessity and freedom is aimed at bringing peace to the conflict between thinking and willing. But peace, conquered at such a price, is fallacious and was obtained to the detriment of the two fields of experience that it claims to reconcile by overlooking their phenomenal properties. Evoking the Odyssey of the *Phenomenology of the Spirit* Arendt writes:

> Such a movement, in which the cyclical and the rectilinear motions of time are reconciled or united by forming a *Spiral* is grounded on the experiences of neither the thinking ego nor the willing ego; it is the non-experienced movement of the World-Spirit that constitutes Hegel's *Geisterreich*, "the realm of spirits . . . assuming definite shape in existence, [by virtue of] a succession, where one detaches and sets loose the other and each takes over from the predecessor the empire of the spiritual world." No doubt, this is a most ingenious solution of the problem of the Will and its reconciliation with sheer thought, but it is won at the expense of both—the thinking ego's experience of an enduring present and the willing ego's insistence on the primacy of the future. In other words, it is no more than a hypothesis [whose plausibility] "depends entirely on the assumption of *one* World Mind ruling over the plurality of human wills and directing them toward a "meaningfulness" arising out of reason's need." (2: 48–49)

This presupposition is unfaithful to both the phenomena it pretends to integrate since in the case of willing it is tantamount to abolishing its singularity—and plurality as well as the openness to a future—and in the case of thinking it is tantamount to arresting it on enduring immobile eternity and to freezing its quest for meaning into a truth accomplished as absolute knowledge.

In what sense does this reading, it may be asked, concern Heidegger? In two ways. In the sense, first, that, generally speaking, the deconstruction that is at work unearths a schema, which Arendt—as we shall see later—finds repeated in Heidegger's text: a strictly phenomenological account, on the one hand, of the specific traits of willing as well as of thinking, *and* the speculative abolition conducted "outside of any experience" of their conflict. In the sense, second and more particularly, that the reading of which we outline the movement already causes the overlapping one over the other of the Hegelian and Heideggerian views. Arendt, indeed, evokes Heidegger concerning the primacy of the future in the Jena texts with a naiveté that seems to me somewhat affected because she could not but be privy to the fact that Koyré in his 1934 essay and Kojève in his wake—whose lectures she attended—were reading Hegel while keeping *Being and Time* in mind. Allusive though this indication is, it signifies that in Arendt's eyes the existential analytic, which stresses factors such as the primacy of the future, the existential nature of oriented temporalizing, the restlessness that characterizes it, and freedom, indeed counts among the most pertinent phenomenologies of the will. She insists that "Heidegger's insights into the nature of willing are incomparably more profound" than Hegel's (2: 49). Yet this does not mean that *Being and Time* escapes speculative fallacy, as in discreet yet firm contrast we shall note in considering Arendt's reading of Augustine. Equally significant seems to me the second evocation of Heidegger's name in the context of Arendt's reading of Hegel. She is aiming at the writings from after the famous *Kehre*, which she claims consisted "in fact" in turning away from willing for the benefit of thought, not without falling prey at the same time to a speculative fallacy analogous to the one she detected in Hegel. When Heidegger posits in his text on the "Overcoming of Metaphysics" in *Vorträge und Aufsätze* that it is "not human will that is the origin of the will to will," but that "man is willed by the will to will without experiencing what this will is about," Arendt does not hesitate to say that this amounts to a solution "similar" to the one the Hegelian philosophy claims to bring in the conflict between willing and thinking (2: 49). The fact that this solution is "similar" means that it is not less specious and not less removed from the description which their conflict calls forth.

As for the long section devoted to Augustine, the "first philosopher of the will," whose writings teem according to her with "phenomenological descriptions," Heidegger is mentioned there only
once and very allusively. But it is easy to realize that many of the
themes upon which Arendt insists overlap the thematic of fundamental ontology, which as we know is itself indebted to a long-time
practice of the Augustinian texts.

The first Augustinian theme that will hold Arendt's attention is
the way in which *De libero arbitrio* proves the freedom of the will
by drawing "exclusively on an inner power of affirmation or negation that has nothing to do with any actual *posse* or *potestas*" (2:
88), because if it is true on the one hand that willing must be present for there to be "power" to perform, "power" must be there so
that willing may draw from it, it also remains true that it is possible to will while being unable to perform (2: 87–88). She says that
this proof draws its plausibility from a comparison between willing
and the intellect on the one hand and between willing and the desires on the other. Neither intellect nor desire are free, the first because the truths it apprehends constrain it and the second because
appetites are borne automatically in the body or arise in the wake
of external bodies. And even when I resist those appetites and desires under the rulership of a reasoning, it is not the latter as such
that allows me to resist, for even when it is demonstrated to me
that I should resist an appetite or desire, this demonstration is in-
sufficient to cancel the wish of still indulging it. This capacity to
affirm or deny without a constraint is a free choice, a *liberum arbitrium*. In no way does it consist in selecting after deliberation the
means to an end, but exclusively in opting between *velle* and *nolle*,
between a will that wills and a will that refuses. To the question of
knowing what causes this choice between *velle* and *nolle*, or more
precisely what causes the will thus tensed between approval or refusal, Augustine answers peremptorily: "For either the will is its
own cause, or it is not a will" (2: 89). Thus Arendt comments that
"the Will is a fact which in its sheer contingent factuality cannot be
explained in terms of causality" *(ibid.).* It is at this juncture that
she alludes to Heidegger. He suggests, she says, that "since the will
experiences itself as *causing* things to happen which otherwise
would not have happened" perhaps it is the will and "neither the
intellect nor our thirst for knowledge (which could be stilled by
straightforward information)" that "lurks behind our quest for
causes" *(ibid.).* This is an allusion that in my view could aim *Vom
Wesen der Warheit* as well as *Vom Wesen des Grundes,* inasmuch

as these essays show that the essence of truth is freedom and that freedom is the foundation of the principle of reason.

But the allusion most probably goes even further. Since Augustine allows us to see freedom of the will at the very heart of its intrinsically conflictual character—between *velle* and *nolle*—the allusion suggests so to speak that the distinction held in place by the existential analytic between the affirmation of the ownmost and the dismissal of it is phenomenologically pertinent with respect to willing. But this, of course, does not mean that this distinction remains pertinent if it is broadened to encompass either the entirety of the life of the mind or the entirety of human activity.

A second overlapping with Heidegger looms in the treatment Arendt makes of what she calls "the severe limitation of the willing activity" (2: 91). For the will cannot say: "I'd rather not be" because such a proposition rests on the "firm ground of Being" and the "very existence" of the individual who says it is what prevents him "from either thinking or willing absolute non-existence" *(ibid.).* When Augustine writes: "Temporal things have no existence before they exist; while they exist, they are passing away; once they have passed away, they will never exist again," Arendt comments: "All men fear death, and this feeling is 'truer' than any opinion that may lead you 'to think that you ought to will not to exist'" *(ibid.).* It is not arbitrary to detect in these words a major theme of the existential analytic: the essence of *Dasein* once it came into existence, a fact over which it has no control, is to exist as a mortal.

Augustine does not limit himself to showing that willing is free in the very core of the conflict that limits its coming to being because the one who wants did not choose to be. His examination does not bear merely on willing considered as an isolated mental phenomenon. It also bears on the links that unite it to other mental faculties, so that after a certain point in the investigation "the leading question is: What function has the will in the life of the mind as a whole?" (2: 97). It is in Arendt's treatment of his answer that there looms a third overlapping with the existential analytic. In Augustine, she claims, the answer to the question of the function of the will in the life of the mind as a whole is inspired by the theological mystery of the Christian trinity. "For Augustine the mysterious three-in-one must be found somewhere in human nature since God created man in His own image; and since it is precisely man's mind that distinguishes him from all other creatures, the three-in-one is likely to be found in the structure of the mind" (2: 93–94). It is not a theological inspiration that brings Arendt's interest but the strictly phenomenological description of the life of the mind to which this inspiration gives rise in *De Trinitate*. This description highlights the nature—both triadic and unitary—of the mind. The triad in question is that of memory, intelligence, willing. While they are all distinct, they are inseparable and intimately connected with one another: "I remember that I have memory, understanding, and will; and I understand that I understand, will, and remember; and I will that I will, remember, and understand" (2: 99, quoted from *De Trinitate*, x: 11, sec. 18). But it is ultimately willing that maintains the union and cohesion of the three faculties of equal rank, which prompts this comment by Arendt:

> The Will tells the memory what to retain and what to forget; it tells the intellect what to choose for its understanding. Memory and Intellect are both contemplative and, as such, passive; it is the Will that makes them function and eventually "binds them together." And only when by virtue of one of them, namely the Will, the three are "forced into one do we speak of *thought*"—*cogitatio*, which Augustine, playing with etymology, derives from *cogere (coactum)*, to force together, to unite forcefully. (2: 99–100)

The study of the reappropriation by Heidegger of Augustine remains to be made, but it does not seem doubtful to me that the phenomenological pertinence greeted by Arendt in what she calls the Augustinian "voluntarism" overlaps the teaching of Heidegger's existential analytic. If we grant that this teaching can be concentrated in the formula, upon which Heidegger insisted on a number of occasions, "*Das Dasein existiert umwillen seiner*" (Dasein exists for the sake of itself), we must add following Heidegger's very terms that "a for-the-sake-of *[Umwillen]* is possible only where there is willing *[Willen]*."[2] To exist for the sake of oneself is, according to the existential analytic, to exist in the mode of care. The fact that care consists for *Dasein* in being ahead of itself while having already been and while holding oneself close to beings (*S.Z.*, sec. 41) points to a triadic structure, whose affinity with the one noted by Arendt in the Augustinian text is obvious. Is this tantamount to saying that in her phenomenology of willing she does no more than restore to the Heideggerian existential analytic what she implicitly was denouncing in her phenomenology of action? Is this tantamount to saying—to put it differently—that the contrast we highlighted above between speculative individuation and individuation in the midst of appearances and plurality must be revised? The answer is negative. This is what comes out in the final theme of her analysis, where the contrast between the two approaches overrides the affinity in a decisive fashion.

Before broaching this final theme, let us still note two corollaries of the voluntarism underscored by Augustine in his "phenomenological description" of the nature, both triadic and unitary, of the mind. Both of these corollaries punctuate the existential analytic. The first corollary concerns perception (2: 100–101). Arendt stresses that it is the force of cohesion of the will that according to *De Trinitate* makes it possible for perception not to be mere reception of sensory impressions but "attention" to an object. There is an obvious overlapping with those analyses by Heidegger in which he underscores that perception is never the mere reception of impressions but a relationship to things sustained by a project. Percipient are not the sensory senses, but percipient is someone, and those things that he or she perceives are as so many appeals to willing. The second corollary concerns time. In the same fashion as one of the essential functions of willing is to connect the sensorial equipment to external things, it is willing again which, according to Arendt's analysis of the famous eleventh book of the *Confessions*, is

the great unifier, which here, in what Augustine calls "distention of the mind," binds together the tenses of time [past, present, and future] into the mind's present. "Attention abides and through it what will be present proceeds to become something absent," namely the past. And "the same holds for the whole of man's life," which without the mind's distention would never be a whole; "the same [also] for the whole era of the children of men, of which all the lives of men are parts," namely, insofar as this era can be recounted as a coherent continuous story. (2: 107–8).

It cannot be said then that humans are in time, but that their mind by virtue of the unifying function of willing is involved in a "temporalizing action" (2: 107). Here too there is an obvious overlapping with Heidegger's analyses which connect ecstatic temporality and the project of existing that constitutes care.

But it is at this juncture and by means of a final theme that the contrast with Heidegger can be noted. This theme is beginning. Arendt insists that the will as such cannot as such be redeemed from its internal conflictual character or from the "fluctuation" which characterizes its freedom: "The Will's redemption cannot be mental

. . . ; redemption comes from the act which . . . interrupts the conflict between *velle* and *nolle*" (2: 101). In other words, "the Will is redeemed by ceasing to will and starting to act, and the cessation cannot originate in an act of the will-not-to-will because this would be another volition" (2: 102). Arendt maintains that this notion of redemption of the Will by action looms in certain passages of *De Trinitate*, which are prolonged by Duns Scotus whom she admired without reservations; but according to her, this notion is being mixed with another form of redemption, namely the transformation of the will into Love, notion that independently of its theological inspiration she suspects of resulting less from the experience of willing than from that of thinking and its quest for serenity for an enduring ego. In any case, it is in continuity with the motif of the redemption of the will by action that the theme of beginning is broached. Augustine is not without succumbing, as do all "professional thinkers," to the fallacy of fatalism, especially in the form of the theological doctrine of predestination, independently of the fact that we find in him—in his response to the theological problem of reconciling human freedom and divine omnipotence and omniscience—the classical argument that God knows in advance but does not constrain; yet, according to Arendt, Augustine brings an additional element to his analysis of the will when he confronts the temporality of humans with the non-temporality of God. It is in the context of this confrontation—theological in part, but strictly phenomenological in another—that the theme of the beginning appears. That confrontation is brought about in books eleven to thirteen of *The City of God*, whose gist Arendt presents as follows, with respect to a phenomenology of the will. God, who is not temporal and therefore without beginning, not only created time at the same time as the world, but created man as intrinsically temporal, not merely as a creature that is in time. One thing is the creation of the world, another is the creation of man. The former, the creation of the world, has its principle *(principium)* in God; the latter, the creation of man, consisting in setting up an *initium*, a power of innovation, which is not that of the kind or species, but is strictly indissociable from the individuation manifested by the will.

> In other words . . . man is put in this world of change and movement
> as a new beginning because he knows that he has a beginning and
> will have an end; he even knows that his beginning is the beginning
> of his end—"our whole life is nothing but a race toward death." In
> this sense, no animal, no species being, has a beginning or an end.

With man created in God's own image, a being came into the world that, because it was a beginning running toward an end, would be endowed with the capacity of willing and nilling. (2: 109)

The phenomenological tenor of that speculation consists in the fact that the primacy of the will, as capacity of willing and nilling, necessitates not only the primacy of the future but the individual's capacity for innovating in the singular, of being "a new beginning by virtue of his birth." Arendt can therefore add: "If Augustine had drawn the consequences of these speculations, he would have defined men, not, like the Greeks, as mortals, but as 'natals'" (2: 109). It is difficult for me to conceive that Arendt might have articulated the analysis of that last Augustinian theme without seeing in it a response to the phenomenology of *Dasein,* even though she makes no mention of Heidegger. In any case, the contrast between Arendt's "natal" and the Heideggerian "Being-toward-death" is patent.

Even before investigating the pages dealing expressly with Heidegger, this contrast invites us—since it is based on a deconstructive approach proceeding in two steps, one dealing with Hegel and the second with Augustine, which I have attempted to retrace—to delineate in light of this double reference what in *Being and Time* is faithful to the phenomena and what is speculative fallacy.

If it is true, as Arendt says in her interpretation of the Augustinian *initium,* that the will is the "mental organ" of "the freedom of spontaneity, [which] is part and parcel of the human condition" (2: 110) and if it is true also, as she insists elsewhere, that the individuated, strictly singular character of that spontaneity is indissociable from plurality and comes to be invested in innovations coming to fruition by means of acting, we can wonder, first of all and in this line, whether it was not precisely the privileging of the radical solitude of death that toppled the Heideggerian analytic from phenomenal faithfulness to speculative fallacy. Numerous though the signs are of the phenomenological pertinence of this analytic concerning the will—and I have noted them along the way—its privileging of death in loneliness and outside of any relations is tantamount to severing the will from any essential connection to action as well as to appearances and the plurality in which action is inscribed. This severance, it might be said, is not yet specious and affects the Heideggerian phenomenology of the will merely with incompleteness. We may answer that this is possibly the case. Let us recall, however, that it is by dint of the relation to death that Hegel operated the shift from restlessness in the face of time to the serenity of remembrance.

Concerning this shift, we noted that it was not yet specious, but became so when Hegel granted the activity of thinking the right of substituting for that of willing, thereby treating the latter as if it did not exist. This fallacy, I argued, is what sustains the Hegelian philosophy of history. To be sure, nothing of the sort is to be found in the existential analytic. In it no mention is made of a philosophy of history. Instead, Heidegger talks of historicity (or historicality). But from the fact that the Hegelian philosophy of history is a specious modality of the substitution of the thinking activity for that of willing, it could not result that it is the only possible form of this substitution. If it is true that *Dasein*'s mortal existence for the sake of itself involves the will as Heidegger insists and if it is indeed upon this will that the "meaning of Being" rests, do we not have here as well an equally specious modality of the amalgamation between willing and thinking? But there is more. If willing only lives by being the mental spring of action in the midst of plural appearances, is it not a specious gesture to close it up within its own circle as though its ultimate formula were *volo me velle*? Isn't this formula, which is given by Arendt concerning Heidegger precisely in the second section of book two of *The Life of the Mind*, just as specious as that other one, *cogito me cogitare*, if it is true that the thinking activity, at the very same time as it withdraws from appearances, still remains attached to them and is only alive by virtue of preparing a sensible return to them? If we remain limited to the will alone, we can indeed speak of the "abyss of freedom" and since the will is singularized and each time mine, it is indeed solipsistic. In this sense, to speak as Heidegger does in *Being and Time* of the "forsakenness in which existing is delivered to itself" (sec. 57) is to give the correct formula of the mode of being of the will. But the fallacy begins when under the guise of ontological voluntarism this abyss carries into itself the entire field of active life and the totality of mental life. Doesn't such an extrapolation take place when abyssal freedom is proclaimed as the essence of truth, the essence of the foundation and the horizon of intelligibility for the questioning on the meaning of the Being of beings in their totality? The existential analytic and, more generally, fundamental ontology proceed in reverse of the path of *Erinnerung* followed by the *Phenomenology of the Spirit* and, more generally speaking, the Hegelian philosophy of history. But a speculative fallacy is at work in both cases. In Hegel it is sustained by a double gesture: on the one hand, there is the annexation of willing to thinking; on the other hand, there is the substitution of the absolute knowing of the true for the indefinite quest for meaning which is inherent in thinking. In Heidegger it is sustained by an analogous, albeit reverse, gesture: there is annexation of thinking to willing, therefore the attribution of the quest for meaning inherent in thinking to willing; there is the metamorphosis, on the other hand, of this quest—now become an affair of the will—into a knowing of the true conceived as the uncovering of the Being of beings.

Perhaps these remarks now put us in a better position for dealing with the final section of book two of *The Life of the Mind*, which is expressly devoted to Heidegger. But let me stress beforehand that the concordance we observed between the existential analytic and the phenomenology of the will, which was sketched out in the wake of reading Hegel and Augustine, is not for the most part expressly underscored by Arendt, but only touched upon by her in fleeting fashion here and there. So much so that my remarks prolonged the gist of passing suggestions, which—oblique though they are and rarely directly aimed—nevertheless do allow a reader to think that they may apply to the Heideggerian text.

Section 15, which will occupy us now, is entitled "Heidegger's Will-not-to-will." It is the penultimate of the book. It deals essentially with the famous *Kehre*, turn or turning-about, which is known to have taken place in the midst of a long debate with Nietzsche. Its arguments are sinuous and launched amidst some incorrectness since she says that "Nietzsche's name is nowhere mentioned in *Being and Time*" (2: 172) while in fact section 76 of that treatise is devoted to him.[3] Moreover Arendt weakens perhaps the impact of that section when, with respect to the inquiry that precedes it, she suggests—most likely as a result of a scholarly caution and considering that the word "will" holds nothing more than a marginal presence in the texts of the existential analytic—that Heidegger only truly began to analyze the will in his lecture courses on Nietzsche; she weakens it too by seeming to grant a single, quasi-exclusive interest to an English-speaking interpreter, J. L. Mehta, when in fact she had been able to read alone for decades many a Heideggerian text. Finally, the very writing of that section and its loose articulation show that we are in the presence of a first draft, which Arendt never had—unfortunately—the opportunity to revise. Let us therefore attempt to figure out its tenor keeping in mind that her ambition in those pages is not, obviously, to contribute to Heideggerian studies, but once more to distinguish between phenomenological pertinence and speculative fallacy.

The core of the argumentation is relatively simple: it is necessary to distinguish between the *Kehre* as a "concrete autobiographical event" in Heidegger's itinerary and the interpretation, or "reinterpretation," he gave of it after the fact.

Arendt locates the reorientation as biographical event, i.e., the original *Kehre*, between the first and second volumes of the substantial work on Nietzsche published by Heidegger in 1961, the first volume of which collects lectures given between 1936 and 1939, and the second volume lectures given between 1939 and 1941. In the wake of Mehta she notes that in the 1936–39 lecture course Heidegger "explicates Nietzsche by going along with him" (2: 173) whereas the lecture courses of 1939–41 adopt a "subdued but unmistakable polemical tone" *(ibid.)*. Since the 1936–39 lecture courses bear on the will to power then interpreted by Heidegger in the very language of *Being and Time*, Arendt concludes that the autobiographical reversal—the original *Kehre* attested to by the change in mood of volume two of the *Nietzschebuch*—consists less in a polemic of Heidegger against Nietzsche as against himself. There is no reason to contradict her on that point. Heidegger himself in a note not included in the 1961 published book had written that his debate with Nietzsche was borne by the "most intimate affinity" (*GA*, 43: 277). What the original *Kehre* takes issue with, in Arendt's eyes, is less the properly Nietzschean will to power, about which she detects judiciously that it is held in place by the motif, absent in Heidegger, of the inventiveness of life and of its inextinguishable character, than a "will to rule and dominate . . . of which he found himself guilty when he tried to come to terms with his brief past in the Nazi movement" (2: 197). Even if we may be justified in objecting forcefully that this past was less brief than Heidegger claimed, we must agree with Arendt that his militantness was short in duration and that it consisted for the most part in reappropriating the Platonic figure of the philosopher-king crowned with a Promethean halo. It is in this sense that Arendt writes that the original *Kehre* was turned against "the self-affirmation of man (as proclaimed in the famous speech delivered when he became rector of Freiburg University in 1933), symbolically incarnated in Prometheus, 'the first philosopher,' a figure nowhere else mentioned in his work" (2: 173).

By contrast, when the *Kehre* is reinterpreted after the fact—as in *The Letter on Humanism*, which in 1946 bears witness for the first time to a reinterpretation—it consists in taking issue with "the alleged subjectivism of *Being and Time* and the book's primary concern with man's existence, his mode of being" (2: 173). Whereas in

Being and Time the questioning into the meaning of Being led to an analysis of the mode of being of man because it rebounded upon him, the only entity caring about that question, *The Letter on Humanism* maintains in essence—such is the reinterpreted reversal of which Arendt speaks—that the question "Who is man?" must be substituted for by a heeding of the requirements of Being, the call to think which Being intimates. From the requirement which this call to think imposes by addressing the "difference between the sheer isness of beings and the Being of this isness itself, the Being of Being" (2: 174) it results that thought is the thought of Being, in the sense that it comes about by way of Being, and it also results that it belongs to it, in the sense that, belonging to it, it may also heed it (see *ibid.*). The fallacy of this interpretation in Arendt's eyes consists especially in the fact that it abolishes not merely the willing ego, but also the thinking ego (since it attributes the source of thought to Being itself), and in addition the acting ego (since thought, now become the heeding of Being, is taken to be the only authentic action and since this heeding requires turning away from the common world of appearances, which is the only site for possible action according to Arendt, yet viewed as a site of insistent errancy in *The Letter on Humanism*).

But before returning to the reading she has of the reinterpreted *Kehre*, let us consider how she views the original *Kehre*, whose testimony she seeks in the contrast between volume one and two of the *Nietzschebuch*, a contrast that interests her less for the interpretation Heidegger gives of Nietzsche than for the light he projects upon his own itinerary.

First, she notes that the first volume contains "strictly phenomenological analyses of the Will" that "closely follow his early analyses of the self in *Being and Time*, except that the Will takes the place ascribed to care in the earlier work" (2: 176), as is confirmed by the few sentences she quotes:

> "Self-observation and self-examination never bring the self to light or show how we are ourselves. But by willing, and also by nilling, we do just that; we appear in a light that itself is lighted by the act of willing. To will always means: to bring oneself to oneself . . . Willing, we encounter ourselves as who we are authentically." Hence, "to will is essentially to will one's own self, but not merely a given self that is as it is, but the self that wants to become as it is . . . The will to get away from one's self is actually an act of nilling." *(ibid.)*

These excerpts quoted by Arendt, of which she stresses the strictly phenomenological character, confirm, if it were necessary, in the overlap they cause between the text of Nietzsche and that of *Being and Time*, that the 1928 work was for her an authentic phenomenology of the will, as we detected obliquely in her readings of Hegel and Augustine. But this in no way signifies that *Being and Time* was in her eyes devoid of speculative fallacy.

What Arendt detects by contrast in the second volume of the *Nietzschebuch* is no longer a faithfulness to the phenomena but a deliberate and exclusive insistence on the will to power understood by Heidegger—and not in the Nietzschean understanding of it as expression of the life instinct and its superabundance—exclusively in the sense of a "will to rule and dominate" (2: 173). Arendt hints that this insistence results from abandoning the phenomenal ground. This abandoning becomes patent, she claims, when for example Heidegger, who previously underscored phenomenologically in volume one that "every act of willing . . . generates a counter-will" (2: 177) in the form of a refusal, transposes and generalizes this polarity to every act of fabrication, conceived as violence exerted against the material it transforms. It is even more so the case when Heidegger generalizes this violence to the relationship to any "object," which is there to be overcome by a subject" *(ibid.)*. Likewise, finally, when Heidegger posits that, in the words of Arendt's presentation, "the will to power is the culmination of the modern age's subjectivization" and that "all of man's faculties stand under the Will's command" or in his own words that "the Will is will to be master . . . [It is] fundamentally and exclusively command" (*ibid.*, quoted from *Nietzschebuch*, 2: 265). As the result of such extrapolations, the last word of the second volume on the theme of the will is then that it is fundamentally destructive, that is to say— quoting Heidegger interpreting the celebrated word by Nietzsche about the will which "would rather will nothingness than not will"—that it is tantamount "to will . . . the negation, the destruction, the laying waste" (2: 177; from *Nietzschebuch*, 2: 267). This destructive character manifests itself in the obsession of being master of the future and in the constraint not only of forgetting the past but also of destroying it. Arendt quotes *What Is Called Thinking?* "The Will's revulsion against every 'it was' appears as *the will to make everything pass away*, hence to will that everything deserve passing away" (2: 178). It is against this destructive character of the will, now torn from its specific phenomenality and metamorphosed by means of successive extrapolations so as to encompass an entire epoch, that according to Arendt the first *Kehre* is directed. It consists, hence, in substituting a thinking that remembers and lets beings be for the destructive voluntarism. That there is a phenomenological tenor in this first *Kehre* is beyond doubt and is suggested by Arendt since she detects in it "the insight that thinking and willing are not just two different faculties of the enigmatic being called 'man,' but are opposites" (2: 179). Arendt does not say expressly that the phenomenological tenor of the first *Kehre* is accompanied by speculative fallacy, but it is really what she seems to suggest when she detects a certain number of extrapolations and when she claims that this "version" of the "mortal conflict" between thinking and willing is the way in which Heidegger was absolving himself from the "sin" of Prometheanism of which he felt guilty at the time.

At this juncture, at the risk perhaps of overinterpreting, I am tempted to project a supplementary light on what I called earlier the speculative fallacy of the existential analytic. I have attempted to show elsewhere that the Heideggerian Prometheanism evoked just above did not have for sole expression the famous "Rectorial Address," contrary to what Arendt claims with some precipitation. This feature can already be sensed in the first version of the essay on *The Origin of the Work of Art*, in *An Introduction to Metaphysics* and in the first lecture course on Hölderlin. I noted elsewhere[4] that this Prometheanism was expressed in the same technical language as that of *Being and Time*, which does not mean at all that it came out up and ready from the existential analytic since the analytic concerned only the *Dasein* of an individual and not the *Dasein* of a people. We detected earlier in the first chapter that this inflation of the notion of *Dasein* to encompass the notion of a people had required a certain number of metamorphoses in the key notions of the existential analytic, especially those of *technē* and *poiēsis*. It is my view that the Arendtian reading here under analysis is an invitation to ask anew what in the existential analytic was lending itself to a Promethean metamorphosis. We detected earlier that the reading by Arendt of the one she termed "the first philosopher of the will" allowed to overlap one over the other the texts of Augustine and of Heidegger's *Being and Time*, and thereby to grant that the modern treatise was tantamount to a phenomenology of the will—except on one capital point, I argued, which is the opposition between "natal" and "mortal." The notion of "natal" in the Arendtian sense aims at not merely the field of innovation opened up by the birth of someone, but also the pluralization of such fields by the emergence of newcomers. The notion aims, therefore, at a close solidarity between singularity and plurality. Recognizing the natal is, therefore, tantamount to welcoming novelty, the unforeseen, the unknown, and accepting them as such. Such a welcoming acceptance, Arendt says and repeats, is resisted by the professional thinker, so much so that he always aims at reducing the new to the old and at bracketing or atrophying the will. We can wonder, by prolonging the readings we analyzed so far, whether it is not expressly the relationship to death that plays an essential role in atrophying the phenomenology of the will conducted without express recognition in *Being and Time* and in introducing in it the germ of Prometheanism recognized by Heidegger a few years after the publication of the book. To be master of the future by willing that every merit should pass, such is, according to the first *Kehre*, the characteristic destructive feature of the will. Now isn't this mastery of the future and this negative and voluntarist totalization precisely what characterizes Heideggerian Being-toward-death? Isn't Being-toward-death expressly defined by *Being and Time* as allowing a "total potentiality for being" *(Ganzsein können)* of *Dasein?* Isn't it part of the mastery of the future to view death and "the ownmost possibility of *Dasein*" as something "certain" even in spite of the total indeterminacy of the event? Inasmuch as it totalizes Being and makes it certain, Being-toward-death is in no way the welcoming of an unknown as unknown, and we may wonder whether it is not upon this that the weight of the speculative fallacy, as far as the phenomenology of willing is concerned, rests in *Being and Time*.

Let us return to the reinterpreted *Kehre*, whose speculative fallacy we already evoked. It deprives the first *Kehre* of its edge by turning both the existential analytic and the thinking on Being into two sides of the same massif, and Arendt's deconstructive irony does not fail to detect in it the renewed play of speculative fallacy. What is, then, she asks, the History of Being if not "another, perhaps a bit more sophisticated, version of Hegel's ruse of reason, Kant's ruse of nature, Adam Smith's invisible hand, or divine Providence, all forces invisibly guiding the ups and downs of human affairs to a predetermined goal" (2: 179)? Doesn't the theme of an invisible manipulation loom as early as the invention of *bios theoretikos* in Plato, the first professional thinker, especially when in his *Laws* he treats the actions of mortals as though they were motions of puppets whose threads are pulled by the gods *(ibid.)?* The "stubborn resiliency" (2: 180) of this theme is not brought about by influences but is in keeping with the "déformation professionnelle," the professional bend and prejudice of thinkers and the tendency they have—the thinking activity being a quest for meaning—of eliminating from the history they remember everything that is merely an event and a fact, so as to bring them down to the level of inconsequential accidents when compared with the hidden meaning they claim to discover. The speculative fallacy in that recurring theme consists, in Arendt's eyes and her deconstruction, in hypostatizing a simple phenomenal truth into what Nietzsche used to call a "rainbow-bridge of concepts" and therefore in obliterating it: "No man can act alone even though his motives for action may be certain designs, desires, passions, and goals of his own. Nor can we achieve anything wholly according to plan (even when, as *archōn*, we successfully lead and initiate and hope that our helpers and followers will execute what we begin)" (2: 180). It is this phenomenological fact of experience, connected with the consciousness we have of "being *able* to cause an effect" *(ibid.)*, that is the phenomenal ground from which are borne—while they also obliterate that ground—all those equally specious versions of the invisible hand.

Arendt does not hide that, in her eyes, the Heideggerian version of this theme accentuates its speciousness. In order to detect its increased fallacy, we must confront the two versions given by Hegel and Heidegger of the theme of the invisible hand. In Hegel action is hypostatized into the chronological efficacy of the World Spirit, and the thinker remembering it is merely its witness. For if Hegel reportedly said one day, after seeing Napoleon at Jena, that he had seen the Spirit of the World riding a horse, he was far from considering that the Emperor, just by himself alone, was the agent of that Spirit, much less that he was its conscious agent. Neither did Hegel consider himself as such an agent, since he limited himself to the role of remembering. In Heidegger, by contrast, in the case of the reinterpreted *Kehre,* which gives rise, as we know, to the meditation on the History of Being—deemed to culminate today in the epochal tension between the *Gestell,* the realm of technology ruling over the acts of humans, and *Ereignis,* the advent of Being which only the solitary thinker heeds—what Hegel dissociated is now brought to coincide. The thinker is no longer here, as thinker, the witness of actions that unfold outside of him. He has become, as thinker, an agent of the History of Being, so that in him alone "*acting* and *thinking* coincide" (2: 180). With respect to this point, Arendt quotes a lecture given by Heidegger in 1949 on the reinterpreted *Kehre* (it was published in 1962):

If to act means to give a hand to the essence of Being, then thinking is
actually acting. That is preparing [building an abode] for the essence
of Being in the midst of entities by which Being transposes itself and
its essence into speech. Without speech, mere doing *[Tun]* lacks the
dimension in which it can become effective and follow directions.
Speech, however, is never a simple expression of thinking, feeling, or
willing. Speech is the original dimension in which the human being
is able to respond to Being's claim and, responding, belong to it.
Thinking is the actualization of that original correspondence. (2:
180–81)

In light of her deconstructive irony, we understand that Arendt is
not hesitant to express her surprise in front of this "notion that
solitary thinking in itself constitutes the only relevant action in the
factual record of history" (2: 181). Concerning this amalgamation of
acting and thinking, she specifies that what is at stake is not merely
the elimination of the gap between object and subject in order to de-
subjectivize the Cartesian ego, but at stake is the real melting of
the changes in the *Seinsgeschichte* into the thinking activity of
thinkers (2: 186). She adds with amusement, causticity, uncompro-
mising severity:

Here the personified concept whose ghostlike existence brought
about the last great enlivenment of philosophy in German Idealism
has become fully incarnated; there is a Somebody who *acts out* the
hidden meaning of Being and thus provides the disastrous course of
events with a counter-current of wholesomeness. *(Ibid.)*

A final salvo is fired:

With Heidegger, [the Spirit of the World, this ghostlike Nobody] allegedly acting behind the backs of acting men, has now found a flesh-
and-blood incarnation in the existence of the thinker, who acts while
he does nothing, a person, to be sure, and even identifiable as
"Thinker"—which, however, does not signify his return into the
world of appearances. *(Ibid.)*

In light of such words, it must be concluded that those readers
who claim that Arendt was a disciple of Heidegger and that her last
writings indicate a return to her first love must have decided not to
read what she says. Far from showing a return, or what God knows
what Arendtian *Kehre*, these words reveal in their very causticity

what the deconstructive irony of the last writings retains from the critique expressed as early as the 1946 article from the *Partisan Review* (see my Introduction). Arendt, indeed, does not limit herself to hunting after the speculative fallacy of the first and second *Kehre;* she stresses in addition that there is a continuity between the History of Being—the theme of the reinterpreted *Kehre*—and the existential analytic, to which she delivered the brunt of her attacks back in 1946.

I highlighted earlier the contrast between what I called speculative individuation in the context of fundamental ontology and the life of someone in the midst of plurality and the world of appearances. What Arendt detects in the *Kehre* such as Heidegger reinterprets it for the benefit of the History of Being is precisely the continued claim, in spite of the reversal, to solipsism inherent in speculative individuation. It is this continued claim that she detects in the very metamorphosis undergone by the notion of *Selbst,* which I have analyzed in chapter two. Wondering about the fortunes of this notion after the reinterpreted *Kehre,* Arendt invites us to bring an important phenomenological correction to the analysis that we conducted then with respect to the world of appearances in which the life of someone is inscribed by his or her action. With respected to this world, we were saying, the Heideggerian individuation of the *Selbst* has been purified to such a degree that it is no longer the individuation of someone. But the phenomenology of action is one thing, and the phenomenology of the life of the mind is another. Concerning the mental phenomenon of the will, it is phenomenologically pertinent to speak of *solus ipse.* This qualification, however, does not apply to the phenomenon of the activity of thinking. This activity could not emanate from a *solus ipse,* if only because the dialogue with oneself of which it consists reveals the echo of plurality at the core of thinking. Furthermore, in the phenomenology of thinking, Arendt was aiming at showing the correctness of a favorite motto, one owed to Cato "Nunquam minus solum esse quam cum solus esset," which for her meant that one is never less lonely than when one thinks. By contrast, it is exclusively by being alone that one is willing. In this regard, and in this regard only, Heidegger's "existential solipsism" is pertinent phenomenologically. It is "one of the existential functions of the Will," Arendt says, to bring about "the actualization of the *principium individuationis*" as *solus ipse* (2: 183).

This is tantamount to saying that, although Arendt refuses to grant the existence of neither a phenomenology of action nor of a phenomenology of thinking in *Being and Time*, she nonetheless sees in it a phenomenology of willing. This does not mean, let me repeat once more, that this phenomenology is not fraught with speculative fallacy. It is affected by it inasmuch as this phenomenology of the will aims at extrapolating itself by including thought, under the form of a quest for meaning (the quest for the meaning of Being), and also at extrapolating itself by including action, by means of the distinction between inauthentic, public, and speech-related action on the one hand and authentic, private, and silent one on the other. Although this distinction is phenomenologically erroneous with respect to action, it is perfectly pertinent according to Arendt with respect to the will. In this respect *Being and Time* can be read as a description that heeds faithfully some immediate data of consciousness *[les données immédiates de la conscience]* in a way akin to Bergson, another philosopher of the will, who indeed may be said to heed them when noting the coexistence of two egos, one social and the other deep-seated (see 2: 183).

What in all this pertains to the continuity between the existential analytic and the History of Being? The continuity does not concern the phenomenological part of the existential analytic, but rather its speculative part. Dealing with the *Selbst* of *Being and Time*, Arendt underscores in the Heideggerian analytic a description that seems particularly specious to her, that of *Gewissen* (conscience). She recalls that

> the Self in *Being and Time* becomes manifest in the "voice of conscience," which calls man back from his everyday entanglement in the *"man"* (German for "one" or "they") and what conscience, in its call, discloses as human "guilt," a word *(Schuld)* that in German means both being guilty of (responsible for) some deed and having debts in the sense of owing somebody something. (2: 184)

The Heideggerian analysis of *Gewissen* thus understood seems to her as lacking in "phenomenological evidence" (2: 185) and is affected by fallacy on three counts. First, to claim that each existing being is guilty—not because of something brought about "through omissions or commissions" (2: 184) but inasmuch as he or she is thrown into the world and exists there factually—is tantamount to severing guilt from any relationship to action and to plurality, and under cover of universalization the thus ontologized dereliction is tantamount to "actually proclaiming universal innocence" *(ibid.)*. To ontologize guilt is to deny it. To cut it from any relation to plural interaction is tantamount to depriving promise and forgiveness, the remedies to the fragility of *praxis*, of any meaning. Secondly, to claim that it is only to one's own *Selbst* that the call of *Gewissen* refers *Dasein* by making it perceive its fundamental guilt is tantamount to substituting for action in the midst of plurality another "type of acting" *(handeln)*, only deemed authentic acting, what she describes as "this entirely inner 'action' in which man opens himself to the authentic actuality of being thrown" (2: 185), in other words the "activity of thinking" *(ibid.)*. It is no doubt by virtue of a *metabasis eis allo genos*, Arendt suggests, that Heidegger was able to declare in section 60 of *Being and Time* that "throughout his whole work, [he had] 'on principle avoided' dealing with action" (2: 185; see *Being and Time*, 300). The third fallacy noted by Arendt in the description of *Gewissen* consists in the one-sidedness with which Heidegger, after extracting conscience from any relation to action and plurality so as to make it into a pure activity of thinking, subjects to a "violent denunciation" the idea that conscience might consist in a dialogue with oneself, a denunciation that she says is all the more surprising since Heidegger, to be sure in another context, speaks of "the voice of the friend that every Dasein carries with it" *(ibid.)*. In any case, she concludes from her reading of the Heideggerian interpretation of *Gewissen* that for him "what the call of conscience actually achieves is the recovery of the individualized *(vereinzeltes)* self from involvement in the events that determine men's everyday activities as well as the course of recorded history—*l'écume des choses*" (2: 185), of which Paul Valéry speaks.

Now it is this very distinction between a plural and event-related *praxis* on the one hand and an internal and solitary action on the other hand that the reinterpreted *Kehre*, i.e., the thematic of the History of Being, reproduces. The fact that the call of Being has been substituted for the call of *Gewissen* leaves that distinction untouched. To be sure, at the outcome of the *Kehre*, "the Self no longer acts in itself (what has been abandoned is the *In-sich-handeln-lassen des eigensten Selbst*) but, obedient to Being, enacts by sheer thinking the counter-current of Being underlying the 'foam' of beings—the mere appearances whose current is steered by the will-to-power" (2: 187). Here we see the reappearance of the "they" of which the *Selbst* of *Being and Time* had severed itself, the difference being that this "they" has for its main characteristic no longer idle talk, but the destructiveness of the will to power. In this case too the solitary thinker "remains the '*solus ipse*' in 'existential solipsism,' except that now the fate of the world, the History of Being, has come to depend on him" *(ibid.).*

But finally, it may be argued, isn't there anything in the thus reinterpreted *Kehre* that resists the phenomenological vigilance that sustains Arendt's irony? The answer is negative. We have already noted that underneath the speculative speciousness of the History of Being Arendt salutes in Heidegger's latest writings the strictly phenomenological acknowledgment by him of the specific features of the thinking activity. To those features that we noted along the way—memory, the settling within an enduring present, serenity, the endless repetition of a questioning aspiration for meaning—the penultimate section of *The Life of the Mind* adds another: to think is to thank, *Denken ist Danken.* It is of little consequence, in Arendt's eyes, that this link between *Denken* and *Danken* should in Heidegger find its first anticipation in the specious analysis of *Gewissen,* more precisely in *Schuld* interpreted as debt inherent in being-thrown. The historically repeated affirmation of this link—from Plato's surprised and admirative *thaumazein* to Nietzsche's *Amen!*—is sufficient to attest that it constitutes a phenomenological feature of the thinking activity, as we find confirmed, outside of any speculation, in the Singing of those poetic works that Arendt held as most powerful in the century, because such works were informed by the horror of domination.

Such was the case for Mandelstam in 1918:

> Earth for us has been worth a thousand heavens

or for the Rilke of the *Duino Elegies*:

> Erde, du liebe . . .
> Namenlos bin ich au dir entschlossen von weit her,
> Immer warst du im recht . . .

> [Earth, you darling. . . .
> I've now been unspeakingly yours for ages and ages
> You were always right]

or, much later, for W. H. Auden:

> Bless what there is for being.

Arendt often said that the poetic work was a work of thought. Without taking this as a pretext for glossing over *Dichten und*

Denken, it can be maintained that, on this point at least, she was in accord with the Heideggerian meditation on the work of art in spite of some forms of speculative fallacy one may be justified in detecting in it: the gathering of the Dasein of a people, the voluntaristic project, the contribution to the counter-current of the History of Being. The point of agreement is the recognition that in the end the work is, without any of those specious frames, the simple offering of a *"daß es sei"* (that it is) (*Holzwege*, 54).

NOTES

1. *La Condition de l'homme moderne*, trans. Georges Fradier, Paris: Calmann-Lévy.
2. Martin Heidegger, *The Metaphysical Foundations of Logics*, trans. Michael Heim, Bloomington: Indiana University Press, 1984, p. 185.
3. See my *Heidegger and the Project of Fundamental Ontology*, trans. Michael Gendre, Albany: State University of New York Press, 1990, chap. 6, "The Presence of Nietzsche in *Sein und Zeit*," pp. 175–89.
4. See Jacques Taminiaux, *Poetics, Speculation, and Judgment*, trans. Michael Gendre, Albany: State University of New York Press, 1993, pp. 153 ff.

SIX

Enduring *thaumazein* and Lacking Judgment

Everyone knows that *The Life of the Mind* was due for a final triptych, which would have analyzed the faculty of judging. Arendt died before being able to tackle the third part of her project. Only after her death was its first page found inserted in her typewriter. In addition to the title "Judging" it contains two epigraphs: the first is a verse by Lucan in *Pharsalis* (1: 128): "The victorious cause pleases the gods, but the defeated one pleases Cato." The second is a quotation from Goethe's *Faust:*

> Könnt'ich Magie von meinem Pfad entfernen
> Die Zaubersprüche ganz und gar verlernen,
> Stünd'ich, Natur! vor dir ein Mann allein,
> Da wär's der Mühe wert, ein Mensch zu sein. (1140–47)

> [Were I to remove magic from my path,
> Totally and absolutely unlearn the incantations,
> Were I to stand, Nature!, facing you a man alone,
> This would make worthy the effort of being human.]

In the Postscriptum of the book's first volume Arendt explained the meaning she attributed to the words of Lucan concerning Cato. They were in her eyes tantamount to an antidote to the famous verse of Schiller Hegel had reappropriated, *Die Weltgeschichte ist das Weltgerichte* (The history of the world is the judgment of the world). To what extent are these words an antidote to Hegelianism, and how does this antidote concern judgment? These questions may be answered very clearly (1) in light of the perspectives sketched out in this Postscriptum, which reveals the major axes of her deconstruction, as she was contemplating its continuation in line with the examination of the thinking activity and (2) in light also of the total glimpse this small text gives on the phenomenological teaching she intended to draw from the deconstruction as it is conducted in the extant parts of the book.

Concerning the will, Arendt declares in the Postscriptum that she follows the "experiences men have had with this . . . faculty" (1: 214) and that it is a mental activity that "always [deals] with particulars" and is "an organ of free spontaneity that interrupts all causal chains of motivation that would bind it" (1: 213); yet, as Bergson said, "it seldom happens that we are willing" (1: 214), and she argues that we are dealing with a "paradoxical and self-contradictory faculty" *(ibid.)*, in the sense that every will elicits a counter-will, that willing is oriented toward projects and the future, and finally that it is "the inner capacity by which men decide about 'whom' they are going to be, in what shape they wish to show themselves in the world of appearances" *(ibid.)*. But the Postscriptum also announces that among the moderns (Hegel, Schelling, Nietzsche, Marx, and "existentialism"[1]) we find the constant tendency to cover these phenomenal features over with metaphysical fallacies, first by granting the faculty of willing a primacy in the life of the mind, by turning it into the substitute for thinking, and finally by extrapolating it either to the process of History or to Being. Regarding the will, I have already attempted to probe the separation between phenomenon and fallacy.

Concerning thinking, the Postscriptum recalls elliptically some of the features upon which I insisted, such as the relationship between this activity and what remains invisible in experience, its tendency to move within generalities, its settling within an enduring present, its "purposeless quest for meaning," its conflict with common sense. To these features Arendt adds in the Postscriptum the inability of thinking when it returns from its withdrawal to the world of phenomena—which are always particular—to confront them in their particularity. It is then necessary, she says, to rely on another faculty of the mind, the ability to judge. But it so happens, she insists, that "not till Kant's *Critique of Judgment* did this faculty become a major topic of a major thinker" (1: 215). It is therefore in the wake of the third Critique that Arendt announces that she is going to treat the faculty of judgment. This treatment, she says, is "of some relevance to a whole set of problems by which modern thought is haunted, especially to the problem of theory and practice, and to all attempts to arrive at a halfway plausible theory of ethics" (1: 216). But she adds that since Hegel and Marx it is in the perspective of History that those questions have been treated "on the assumption that there is such a thing as Progress of the human race" *(ibid.)*. Hence "we shall be left with the only alternative there is in these matters—we either can say with Hegel, *Die*

Weltgeschichte ist das Weltgerichte, leaving the ultimate judgment to Success, or we can maintain with Kant the autonomy of the minds of men and their possible independence of things as they are or as they have come into being" *(ibid.).* According to the first part of the alternative, the acting plurality of human beings is merely the superficial foam of the real matters, and thus one version or another of the invisible hand holds the key to the meaning and inner core of action, which may be the setting-into-work either of Spirit, or of the productive forces, or of the History of Being. According to the second part of the alternative, it is plurality that matters, and the judgment of individuals is its measure.

It is in this context that Arendt mentions Cato leaving to the gods the criterion of success—which for the moderns is put under the heading of the philosophies of History—and entrusts humans taken in their singularity with the task of judging not processes but, instead, events.

One could be tempted, by the same token, to shed some light by contrast upon the meaning she attributed to the verses by Goethe inscribed at the beginning of her investigation of judgment. One thing is the solitude of which Faust speaks (*"ein Mann allein,"* one man on his own), another is the solitude of the one who judges. Faust's solitary stance consists in casting a disillusioned glance upon nature; the second consists in weighing human affairs. In the first case, it is after turning away from human affairs that one finds it worthy of being human; in the second, the one who is alone in judging human affairs withdraws from them only to open himself up to their future by inviting others along with him in his retreat. The contrast between these two epigrams would thus show the opposition between *bios theōrētikos* and *bios politikos.* In any case, it was indeed in light of this contrast that, well before the publication of *The Human Condition,* Arendt had treated judgment. To this point the conclusion of a series of 1954 lectures given at Notre Dame University bears witness (its latest version, after various drafts, was published in 1990 in *Social Research,* vol. 57, under the title "Philosophy and Politics"). For the most part the argument she develops in it concerns the "abyss between philosophy and politics" caused by the trial and condemnation of Socrates. In a gesture that her subsequent works would reproduce and prolong—and I have already attempted to show it—Arendt takes great care to contrast Socrates' teaching, as she sees it, with Plato's. The fact that Socrates was not successful in convincing his judges that he had behaved in the best interest of the City and, therefore, was innocent is undoubtedly what led Plato to question certain principles in the teaching of his master and to entertain no hope for *bios politikos*.

Socrates did not doubt the validity of *peithein*, i.e., persuasion, as "the specifically political form of speech" ("Philosophy and Politics," 73). In agreement with the City he considered rhetoric as the political art *par excellence* and his own *Apology*, as related by Plato, is a famous case in point. He was, however, not successful in persuading his jurors, and from his failure the result seems to have been that the City had nothing to do with philosophers who, in the City's view, were good for nothing. Neither was he more successful—and *Crito* is the case in point—in persuading his friends that, for political reasons, he should accept his condemnation. "In other words, the city had no use for a philosopher, and the friends had no use for political argumentation. This is part of the tragedy to which Plato's dialogues testify" (*ibid.*, 74).

But it is only one of its aspects, because when Plato concludes at the outcome of the trial that the validity of persuasion must be put into question, he supplements it with a denunciation of *doxa:* since the *doxa* of Socrates had been undone by the majority of the Athenians, *doxa* as such must be spurned, and truth, i.e., the search for absolute criteria, must be substituted for it. Arendt comments: "The opposition of truth and opinion was certainly *the most anti-Socratic conclusion* that Plato drew from Socrates' trial" (*ibid.*, 75, stress added).

This essay, which I will consider now, aims in summary at explaining how the Platonic conclusion is most anti-Socratic. It is in this context, four years before the publication of *The Human Condition*, that Arendt makes for the first time an allusion to the maid from Thrace. Commenting on the section of *Nicomachean Ethics* where the anecdote resurfaces, she says that Aristotle merely expresses the opinion of the City concerning the *sophoi:* "Anaxagoras and Thales were wise, but were lacking in *phronēsis*. They were not interested in what is good for human beings *[anthrēpina agatha]*" (1140a25–30; 1141b4–8). The corroboration of this criticism lies in the fact that Thales did not even know what was good for him, and thus eluded *a fortiori* what is required for political wisdom and for the good of the *polis*. But there is more to the criticism. Not only does the *sophos* ignore what is good for the *polis*, but his interest lies elsewhere. In the case of Thales we see a "wise man . . . concerned with matters outside the *polis*" and interested in "eternal, nonchanging, nonhuman matters" (*ibid.*, 76). From the perspective of the City, therefore, there is an opposition between *sophos* and *phronimos*. The former turns away from human affairs, and the latter displays perspicacity about them and, for this reason, can—as in the case of Pericles who was acclaimed by Aristotle—be a guide even without claiming to govern. The "enormity" of the Platonic demand that the *sophos* should govern consists (1) in returning to the existing City the irony that the citizens addressed to the *sophoi*—in the same vein as the reflection of the maid from Thrace—because of their lack of attention to human affairs and (2) in abolishing purely and simply the old opposition between *sophos* and *phronimos*, which is tantamount to disregarding the citizen's aptitude to judge. Whereas from the perspective of the City the concern the *sophos* has for truth, exclusive of consideration for the domain of human affairs, "drove its adherents out of the *polis* and made them unfit for it" (*ibid.*, 76), or "good-for-nothing," Plato by contrast claims that the philosopher has the right to govern precisely because, as a solitary individual, he is capable of contemplating the Idea of the Good, after first severing the *agathon* from any connection to human affairs, that is, after removing it from *anthrōpina agatha* and hypostatizing it into an eternal sphere (*ibid.*, 76–77). She writes:

> Plato's elevation of the idea of the good to the highest place in the realm of ideas, the idea of ideas, occurs in the cave allegory and must be understood in this political context . . . Plato, obviously, was guided by the Greek proverbial ideal, the *kalon k'agathon* (the beautiful and good), and it is therefore significant that he made up his mind for the good instead of the beautiful. Seen from the point of view of the ideas themselves, which are defined as that whose appearance illuminates, the beautiful, which cannot be used but only shines forth, had much more right to become the idea of ideas. The difference between the good and the beautiful, not only to us but only more so to the Greeks, is that the good can be applied and has an element of use in itself. Only if the realm of ideas is illuminated by the idea of the good could Plato use the ideas for political purposes and, in the *Laws*, erect his ideocracy, in which eternal ideas were translated into human laws.
>
> What appears in the *Republic* as a strictly philosophical argument has been prompted by an exclusively political arguement—the trial and death of Socrates. (*Ibid.*, 77)

In other words, the recourse to *agathon* means that one continues to be heard by the men of the City; but substituting an *agathon* without mixture for the *anthrōpina agatha*, hence substituting *sophia* for *phronēsis*, and also opposing *alētheia* and *doxa*, all these are gestures of severance from what constitutes the political. But of this substitution Arendt finds no trace in Socrates himself.

> The *polis* did not understand that Socrates did not claim to be a *sophos*, a wise man. Because he doubted that wisdom is for mortals, he saw the irony in the Delphic oracle that said he was the wisest of all men: the man who knows that men cannot be wise is the wisest of them all. The *polis* did not believe him, and demanded that he admit that he, like all *sophoi* was politically good-for-nothing. But as a philosopher he truly had nothing to teach his fellow citizens. (*Ibid.*, 77–78)

Let us consider in greater detail how the conclusions Plato drew from Socrates' trial are anti-Socratic. What is most anti-Socratic in him is not the irony of his dialogues, but instead the idea of "the tyranny of truth, in which it is not what is temporally good, of which men can be persuaded, but eternal truth, of which men cannot be persuaded, that is to rule the city" (*ibid.*).

Precisely because he was not claiming for himself the title of *sophos*, Socrates made new demands on philosophy. Dialectic is one of them, and Arendt thinks that "it is more than probable that Socrates was the first who had used [it] . . . systematically" (*ibid.*, 80). Unlike rhetoric, whose aim is to persuade a multitude, dialectic is only possible in a dialogue between two interlocutors. Whereas rhetoric aims at imposing a single opinion upon many opinion-holders, and thus contains an element of constraint or even violence, dialectic consists in discussing a subject through and through, yet without allowing the fecundity of that discussion to "be measured by the result of arriving at this or that general truth" (*ibid.*, 81). Socrates used to call "maieutic" this dialectic. It consisted in "the art of midwifery: he wanted to help others give birth to what they themselves thought anyhow, to find the truth in their *doxa*." In light of this activity, "the role of the philosopher, then, is not to rule the city but to be its 'gadfly,' not to tell philosophical truths, but to make citizens more truthful" (*ibid.*).

It is this type of dialectic—in direct connection with *bios politikos*—that is attested to by the early Platonic dialogues, which are never concluded on a result. It is attested to, also, by Aristotle when, in opposition to Plato's *Republic*, he views *philia*, not justice, as the bond of political communities. She writes:

If we use Aristotle's terminology in order to understand Socrates better—and great parts of Aristotle's political philosophy, especially those
in which he is in explicit opposition to Plato, go back to Socrates—we
may cite that part of the *Nicomachean Ethics* where Aristotle explains
that a community is not made out of equals, but on the contrary of people who are different and unequal. The community comes into being
through equalizing, *isasthēnai* (*Nicomachean Ethics*, 1133a14). This
equalization takes place in all exchanges, as between the physician and
the farmer, and it is based on money. The political, non-economic
equalization is friendship, *philia*. That Aristotle sees friendship in
analogy to want and exchange is related to the inherent materialism of
his political philosophy, that is, to his conviction that politics is necessary because of the necessities of life from which men strive to free
themselves. Just as eating is not life but the condition for living, so living together in the *polis* is not the good life, but its material condition.
He therefore ultimately sees friendship from the point of view of the
single citizen, not from that of the *polis:* the supreme justification of
friendship is that "nobody would choose to live without friends even
though he possessed all other goods" (*ibid.*, 1155a5). The equalization
in friendship does not of course mean that the friends become the
same or equal to each other, but rather that they become equal part-
ners in a common world—that they together constitute a community.
Community is what friendship achieves, and it is obvious that this
equalization has as its polemical point the ever-increasing differentia-
tion of citizens that is inherent in an agon[istic] life. Aristotle concludes that it is the friendship and not justice (as Plato maintained in
the *Republic*, the great dialogue about justice) that appears to be the
bond of communities. For Aristotle, friendship is higher than justice,
because justice is no longer necessary between friends. (*Ibid.*, 82–83)

It is at this juncture that Arendt seems to be in a position to
sketch her first analysis of judgment—by taking a stance against
the *Republic*, which to a degree or another has been the reference
book of all professional philosophers until Heidegger, including
Hegel. What is at stake in Aristotelian friendship is not emotional
life but the form of understanding to which Aristotle gives the
name *phronēsis*, for which *sophoi* such as Thales and Anaxagoras
had no concern. This friendship consists less in understanding "the
friend as a person" than in understanding in what particular articulation the common world appears to another or someone "who as a
person is forever different" (*ibid.*, 83–84). Arendt writes that "this
type of understanding—seeing the world (as we rather tritely say

today) from the other fellow's point of view—is the political kind of insight *par excellence" (ibid.)*. Here the Kantian theme of the en-larged mentality is foreshadowed, and it will permit Arendt to read the *Critique of Judgment* as a major document of political philoso-phy—to which we shall return later. Political perspicacity consists in "understanding the greatest possible number and variety of reali-ties" inasmuch as these are not subjective viewpoints but perspec-tives on the common world that "open themselves up to the vari-ous opinions of citizens" *(ibid., 84)*. She adds:

> If such an understanding—and action inspired by it—were to take place without the help of the statesman, then the prerequisite would be for each citizen to be articulate enough to show his opinion in its truthfulness and therefore to understand his fellow citizens. Socrates seems to have believed that the political function of the philosopher was to help establish this kind of common world, built on the under-standing of friendship, in which no rulership is needed. *(Ibid.)*

The echo of this Socratic conviction may be found in Aristotle's characterization of *phronēsis* as *doxastic* excellence. Such a convic-tion entails that *"doxa* was neither subjective illusion nor arbitrary distortion but, on the contrary, that to which truth invariably ad-hered" *(ibid., 85)*. When Socrates adopts the Delphic adage *gnōthi seauton*, the issue is not for him one of withdrawing within himself into a solitary *nous*, but of recognizing that "only through knowing what appears to me—only to me, and therefore remaining forever related to my own concrete existence—can I ever understand truth" *(ibid., 84)*, truth that consequently could not be something absolute, which would mean that it is the same for everybody, and is therefore independent of the existence of anyone, and has been extracted from the condition of being mortal. But to admit that there is a limitation to *doxa* is to admit at the same time that it is legitimate to recognize "in every *doxa* truth and to speak it in such a way that the truth of one's opinion reveals itself to oneself and to others" *(ibid., 84–85)*. In this sense,

> if the quintessence of the Sophists' teaching consisted in the *dyo logoi*, in the insistence that each matter can be talked about in two different ways, then Socrates was the greatest Sophist of them all. For he thought that there are, or should be, as many different *logoi* as there are men, and that all these *logoi* together form the human world, insofar as men live together in the manner of speech. *(Ibid., 85)*

It is this multiplication of *logoi*, each understood in its singular truthfulness, that holds together according to Arendt the properly Socratic dialectic, of which we see that it is indissociable from *doxa* and plurality making its way into each interlocutor, even when alone with himself. Indeed, to be truthful in the expression of one's *doxa* presupposes that one is in agreement with oneself and that in the dialogue with oneself—which is what thinking is—one should remain one's own friend. It is the search for this friendship that makes it possible for the Socratic *logos*, which even in its solitary exercise is equiprimordially thinking and speaking, to refuse extracting itself from appearances and plurality. This plurality is indicated by the fact that the solitary *logos* is already a one-in-two. This one-in-two affects the Self with "changeability" (*ibid.*, 88) and "equivocality" (*ibid.*), but that is precisely why it represents plurality at the time when I keep myself company. Such a plurality goes hand in hand with *doxa* because what I expect from others is determined by "ever-changing potentialities" (*ibid.*) of the Self with which I am living. This determination is what condemns the murderer not only to live in the company of his or her criminal Self, but also "to live in a world of potential murderers" (*ibid.*) and to have no other *doxa*, view on the world, and manifestation of it than that of crime. His *doxa*, "the way in which the world opens to him and is part and parcel of the political reality he lives in" (*ibid.*), obviously has a political meaning. The advice "Be as you want to appear to others" therefore means, Learn to choose your own *doxa*, learn to appear to yourself as you would like to appear in the eyes of others and as you would like them to appear to you (see p. 88).

In this way we can clarify the words lent to Socrates by the *Gorgias* alluded to earlier: "Better to be in disagreement with all than, being one, to be out of tune with myself" (482c). They signify that "only he who knows how to live with himself is fit to live with others" (*ibid.*, 86–87). The origin of the principle of non-contradiction, therefore, is ethical no less than logical. In Socrates, Arendt insists, the two orders are not dissociated. To him,

> who was firmly convinced that nobody can possibly want to live together with a murderer or in a world of potential murderers, the one who maintains that a man can be happy and be a murderer, if only nobody knows about it, is in twofold disagreement with himself: he makes a self-contradictory statement and shows himself willing to live together with one with whom he cannot agree. This twofold disagreement, the logical contradiction and the ethical bad conscience,

was for Socrates still one and the same phenomenon. That is the reason why he thought that virtue can be taught, or, to put it in a less trite way, the awareness that man is a thinking and an acting being in one, someone, namely whose thoughts invariably and unavoidably accompany his acts, is what improves men and citizens. (*Ibid.*, 88–89)

In other words, to the pre-Socratic identity of speech and thinking, Socrates adds

the dialogue of myself with myself as the primary condition of thought. The political relevance of Socrates' discovery is that it asserts that solitude, which before and after Socrates was thought to be the prerogative and *professional habitus* of the philosopher only, and which was naturally suspected by the *polis* of being antipolitical, is, on the contrary, the necessary condition for the good functioning of the *polis*, a better guarantee than rules of behavior enforced by laws and fear of punishment. (*Ibid.*, 89, stress added).

One might be tempted to conclude from this presentation that Arendt saw in the Socratic approach a sort of Golden Age in which thinking and acting were in harmony, in which philosophy was both fully philosophical (because it questioned radically) and fully political (because it was animated by *philia* and the recognition of plurality). I believe, on the contrary, that she credited Socrates for recognizing that the condition of humans is paradoxical inasmuch as human beings are both thinking and acting and for calling for the confrontation of the paradox of that condition. Upon closer inspection, indeed, all the themes she considers in her analysis of Socratism are intrinsically conflictual: *philia*, in Aristotle as well as in the myths of foundation, is agonistic by nature; plurality and the action it conditions are no less so (all individuals are similar, yet different); thinking is agonistic, also, because it is a two-in-one; likewise, every *doxa* is in a state of rivalry with other *doxai*; but truth likewise is agonistic—because it is indissociable from the frail openings on the world in which the *doxai* consist and because, in addition, the truth of a response (and every response is a provisional one) is able to address a determinate question only to the extent that every specific question (with solutions) is in fact sustained by a questioning mode of being itself fraught with questions without answers, i.e., with those famous "ultimate questions."

Politically speaking, therefore, Socratism such as Arendt understands it functions as a revealing agent of the essential fragility of the public world of action. This fragility is in keeping with the fact that the world is intrinsically paradoxical: its identity is held in place by the extreme variety of the perspectives being opened on it; the plurality necessary to its enduring is both friendly and agonistic; and the consensus—the common way of perceiving or "common sense"—which this world calls forth would be destructive of that plurality if each public actor did not have the possibility of withdrawing within himself, so as to articulate his own *doxa*, i.e., did not have the latitude to think on his own. Because he detects this fragility and its constitutive paradoxes, Socrates essentially invites us to take their measure, or—put differently—he teaches political excellence and virtue in which *phronēsis*, the aptitude to judge, consists.

In this sense, if Arendt speaks of a tragedy concerning the trial and the condemnation of Socrates, it is not only because the whole affair rested upon a misunderstanding (he was taken for one of the *sophoi* given over to the solitary contemplation of the eternal, while in fact he absolutely did not belong to that ilk), it is more profoundly because there was some *hubris* on the part of the City in refusing to recognize its intrinsic paradoxes and its essential fragility. In other words, the *hubris* in the case of the City consisted in refusing to acknowledge that striving for consensus and obedience to the laws, which are requisites for the City's enduring, should not be viewed as opposed to the freedom of thinking by oneself, because freedom of thinking, on the contrary, works as a counterweight to silent consensus and blind obedience to laws. Likewise, there had already been *hubris* on the part of the City since the death of Pericles in allowing the agonistic element of *eris* to overrun that of *philia* in its own midst and in relation to other cities.

Philosophically speaking, on the other hand, Socratism reveals a constitutive paradox of the human condition, namely both the belonging of human beings to appearances and the necessity to withdraw from them in order to think for themselves. But Arendt, it seems to me, suggests that there was perhaps in Socrates—at the same time as the recognition of this paradox—a tendency to cover it over, and therefore a sort of *hubris*. What Socrates "seems not to have realized" (*ibid.*, 90) (and this is suggested by the aporetic character of Plato's early dialogues and the fact that Socrates refused every public office in order to devote himself fully to the task of the "gad fly") is that, when this role takes itself as an end, it produces the "catastrophic result that all *doxa* is altogether destroyed" (*ibid.*). In this respect Socrates might be akin to another tragic character, King Oedipus, evoked by Arendt in this context: "Oedipus is left without any *doxa*, in its manifold meanings of opinion, splendor, fame, and a world of one's own" *(ibid.)*.

In any case, Plato appears to Arendt as anti-Socratic to the extent that he claims to solve the paradox that Socrates was calling others to assume and take upon themselves.

Someone may ask whether this presentation does not take us away from my objective, the debate between Arendt and Heidegger, the only "professional thinker" she came to know closely and whose brilliance she found seducing. I answer this suggestion in the negative. It does not seem doubtful to me that the extraordinary analysis—whose essential articulations I have attempted to re-create here, and I should underscore again that she produced this text a mere eight years after the rejection of Heidegger in the 1946 article "What Is *Existenz*-philosophy?" which spoke of his "selfishness" and irresponsible "romanticism," as I noted in the Introduction—is if not the very first document, at least among the first ones, in the debate for which I suggested the heading of the "irony of the maid from Thrace toward the professional thinker." Not only are these two emblematic characters present in her analysis reconstituted here only schematically, but its essential articulations already overlap the axes of fundamental ontology, i.e., of the reappropriation of Plato by means of what at Marburg Heidegger called "the Aristotelian ontology of *Dasein*."[2] The substitution of an unalloyed *agathon*, which is *epekeina tēs ousias*, for the *anthrōpina agatha*, of *sophia* for *phronēsis*, the opposition of *alētheia* to *doxa* are all themes that, according to Arendt, indicate Plato's rupture with *bios politikos* and the birth of the tyranny of *bios theōrētikos* in viewing human affairs. It is easy to find their equivalent in Heidegger as early as the lecture course on *The Sophist* and to note that they traverse fundamental ontology in its entirety. Everything happens as though, in those parts of *Nicomachean Ethics* which Heidegger investigates so as to reappropriate Plato to the ends of his existential analytic, Arendt seeks clues to reappropriate Socrates against Plato so as to produce analyses of the anthropological foundations of *bios politikos* and of the blindness of *bios theōrētikos* to the latter. That the shadow of Heidegger's text hovers over hers, that it is taken as target as much as Plato's, the central recourse made here to "the opening of the world" would already be sufficient to attest. That formula, to be sure, is never present as such in the texts of Plato and Aristotle, but it is—by contrast—everywhere in texts of Heidegger and it was thanks to it that Heidegger claimed to reappropriate the Greeks. When Arendt writes that *doxa* is "the world as it opens up to me" (*ibid.*, 80), "[someone's] own opening to the world" (*ibid.*, 81), or involves "realities [that] open themselves up" (*ibid.*, 84), and when she underscores that in Socrates this very opening is that to which truth is bound, her target is Heidegger as much as Plato because Heidegger claims that *Erschlossenheit*, the opening to the world by the existing being, consists in the ownmost being wrested away from *doxa* for the sake of truth.

That Heidegger as much as Plato is the target of that analysis is being confirmed by the insistence with which Arendt links the notion of conscience (which she discovered looming in Socrates in the words lent to him in the text of *Gorgias*) and that of friendship and, therefore, plurality, whereas Heidegger, as far as he is concerned, purifies the notion of *Gewissen* not only from any ethical connotation but even from any relation to others and makes it strictly monadological.

But it is undoubtedly in the pages of the 1954 essay, which are expressly focused on the Platonic rejection of plurality, that Arendt's critique of Plato turns out to be a challenge to Heidegger. Two themes mark the rejection of plurality by Plato: that of the cavern and that of *thaumazein*. Yet, already Plato's treatment of the relation between soul and body shows that he "rationalizes and generalizes" the conflict between the experience of thinking on the one hand and that of belonging to appearances on the other. With respect to the common world of appearances in which action unfolds, to think is to withdraw in order to take on a provisional double—in the dialogue of oneself with oneself—before being unified again in one's presentation to others in the midst of appearances, in the midst of a justified and assumed *doxa*. This paradox is indeed what Plato's rationalization obliterates by transposing the originary experience of withdrawal and return into a conflict between soul and body. Precisely because for him what, above all, the philosopher demands is to be alone in order to think, he separates himself from human affairs and moves into deliberate opposition to them. This is what the Platonic metaphor of the conflict between body and soul conveys. Arendt writes:

> The more a philosopher becomes a true philosopher, the more he will separate himself from his body; and since as long as he is alive such separation can never be achieved, he will try to do what every free citizen in Athens did in order to separate and free himself from the necessities of life: he will rule over his body as a master rules over his

slaves. If the philosopher attains rulership over the city, he will do no more to its inhabitants than he has already done to his body. His tyranny will be justified both in the sense of best government and in the sense of personal legitimacy, that is, by his prior obedience, as a mortal man, to the command of his soul, as a philosopher. (*Ibid.*, 93)

We saw above that what I called in Heidegger "speculative individuation" reproduced—by means of the whole purifying that supports it—a gesture of extraction from plurality, appearances, and the body. Was it not the old Platonic gesture of obedience to the commands of the soul and regulation of the body that governed the senseless project, reportedly entertained by Heidegger, of directing Spartan youth camps where he would have initiated his recruits not into Rosenberg's ideology, but instead into fundamental ontology?

Let us return to the theme of the cavern. The parable, Arendt insists, is at the center of Plato's political philosophy and "describes the relationship between philosophy and politics in terms of the attitude of the philosopher toward the *polis*" (*ibid.*, 94). It is, she says, a sort of "concentrated biography of the philosopher" which takes place in three stages, of which each one is a reversal of the preceding one, while all taken in their totality make the "*periagogē holēs tēs psychēs*, "that turning-about of the whole human being which for Plato is the very formation of the philosopher" (*ibid.*, 94). Arendt does not fail to underscore that the parable is a fallacy from the very first word because, at the very outset, it deprives the prisoners in the cavern (and for Plato this means the actors of *bios politikos*) of both *praxis*, since they are chained and motionless, and *lexis*, since they are all silent, in order to retain from this comportment only a gaze fascinated by shadows. The first turning-about of the gaze consists in substituting for the fascination, to which for Plato *doxa* may be summarized, the holding into view of those single things of which the various *doxai* are the shadows. The second turning-about consists in—upon exiting the cavern—taking into view "a clear sky, a landscape without things or men" (*ibid.*, 95), which is illuminated by the Sun, which the Idea of ideas is. But because he is mortal and is not the only one in the world, the one given over to that contemplation cannot maintain himself therein, he must turn away from it and return to the cavern, which is his human dwelling. It is with this final turning-about that "tragedy begins" (*ibid.*), which means of course the fate of Plato and all "professional thinkers." The tragedy resides in the *hubris* involved in destroying every *doxa*, because back in the cave he "can no longer

feel at home," he experiences loss of orientation, is in danger because "he has lost the common sense needed to orient himself in a
world common to all, and, moreover, because what he harbors in
his thought contradicts the common sense of the world" *(ibid.)*.[3] At
the end of the parable, Arendt writes, "Plato mentions in passing
the dangers which await the returning philosopher, and concludes
from these dangers that the philosopher—although he is not interested in human affairs—must assume rulership, if only out of fear
of being ruled by the ignorant" (*ibid.*, 96–97).

It does not seem doubtful to me that all this concerns Heidegger
as much as Plato, not merely because Heidegger would occasionally
express his own thought by means of a literal commentary on the
parable of the cavern—the essay "On Plato's Doctrine on Truth" is
the best case in point—but also because the movement of purifying
which takes the existential analytic to the core of what I called
speculative individuation goes very precisely through the same
steps as this "concentrated biography," to use Arendt's expression.
To the initial stage of attachment and fascination for shadows corresponds in Heidegger the position of the "they" which is bound to
what is in front of the hand *(vorhanden)* and which has no other
gaze than that of mere *Anschauung*. The first step of liberation
from this bondage consists in a reversal that allows to see that the
vorhanden is derived from *zuhanden* (for-the-hand) and in a position of fallenness with respect to it, and thus to see that *Anschauung* is a seeing that is derived from a higher seeing, that of *pratische
Umsicht*, or foreseeing circumspection. But this first step of liberation calls for another, which extracts itself from the cave of everydayness, and by means now of a second turn-about enables one to
see that the *Umwelt*, everyday environment, is itself derived and in
a position of fallenness with respect to what in the *Welt* is originary
and to realize at the same time that the internal seeing of circumspection is in a position of fallenness with respect to a higher gaze,
that of *Durchsichtigkeit*, or transparency, which relates Dasein not
to a mundane can-be but rather to its ownmost possibility, which it
itself alone is. In Heidegger as well as in Plato this extreme gaze
bears, indeed, on what Arendt calls "a landscape without things or
men," although now a metamorphosis has transformed the *agathon
epekeina tēs ousias* into *Dasein*'s *Umwillen*, while in Plato the
agathon epekeina tēs ousias was the Idea of ideas. In both cases, it
is indeed to the emptying-out of every *praxis* in the sense of appearing interaction in the midst of a plurality and of every *lexis* that
these biographical stages lead, since the Heideggerian *Dasein* is rad-

ically alone when it catches sight of its ownmost can-be in a seeing that overcomes every interlocution, even every monologue, as the analysis of *Gewissen* shows.

There remains the third stage, the return to the cave, with which "tragedy begins." To be sure, neither the trial nor the condemnation of Socrates has an equivalent in the genesis of fundamental ontology. Heidegger had no need to guarantee the security of *bios theōrētikos* since approval of it had been officially sealed ages ago in the Germanic world. In addition, nothing proves that he had any definite political opinion before 1933, and it seems established that in the 1932 *Reichstag* elections he still voted for the insignificant party of the Württemberg wine growers.[4] But then, why on earth did he join the Nazi madhouse? There is, to be sure, no peremptory answer to this question. But the way in which Arendt approaches it is perhaps the only one making some sense, because it is centered upon the relationship that *bios theōrētikos* maintains with human affairs. Indeed, reading Heidegger's Nazi declarations, we are forced to note two things: on the one hand, they displace some fetish words of Nazi vocabulary—such as *Kampf, Entscheidung, Aufbruch*—so as to define them with respect to fundamental ontology; on the other hand, these declarations superpose the themes of Plato's *Republic* over the main themes of fundamental ontology, which after being supplemented with a few novel lexical items is henceforth applied to the *Dasein* of a whole people. In either case, everything happens as though Heidegger had convinced himself that—to speak like Arendt on Plato—he had "to assume rulership for fear of being ruled by the ignorant," in this case by the Nazi riffraff deemed prisoner to the everydayness and *Vorhandenheit*. Quite obviously, the result is that the "biography" of which the existential analytic initiates a movement similar to that of the allegory of the cave made it possible for the philosopher (inasmuch as he might be tempted to return to the cave of everydayness and to the realm of human affairs in order to play a role in them) to approach these affairs from the perspective of tyranny, because his own dedication to *bios theōrētikos* sanctions a rupture with *doxa*, plurality, *lexis*, and amounts to a veritable dismissal of the faculty of judging.

This leaning toward tyranny and this dismissal of plurality is what Arendt highlights in her analysis of the second theme, for she maintains that the "biography" condensed in the parable of the cave would be incomplete if what Plato says regarding *thaumazein* were not brought into consideration. Concerning this incomplete biography, she writes: Plato "does not tell us why he cannot persuade his fellow citizens, who anyhow are already glued to the screen and thereby in a certain way ready to receive 'higher things' as Hegel called them, to follow his example and choose the way out of the cave" (ibid., 97). In this case, we have to understand that the speculative fallacy of the parable consisted in claiming that every man is naturally a philosopher in the sense given to the word by Plato. Which, of course, one may easily apply to the famous Heideggerian hermeneutic circle.

The complement that the parable presupposes without ever saying so expressly is that thaumazein "is the supreme pathos of the philosopher and the single origin of philosophy" (Theaetetus, 155d). What must be recalled, then, is the fact that Plato's Seventh Letter, which is after all focused on that pathos, claims that the eternal topic and goal of philosophy is "that about which it is impossible to speak as one speaks about other things one learns." All that can be said, after being practiced for a long time, is that thaumazein is "as a light lit on a flying fire" (341c).

In Plato thaumazein is both the beginning and the end of philosophy, so that the latter moves in a circle. At either point the philosopher breaks away from doxazein because in each case he is outside language and is extracted from anything particular. At the most wonder can be qualified—inasmuch as it consists in a "wonder at everything that is as it is [yet] never relates to anything particular" (ibid., 98)—in terms of "experience of no-thing, of nothingness" (ibid.). It is Kierkegaard that Arendt aims here, but it goes without saying that Heidegger is intended just as much; and Heidegger is also intended when she stresses that such an experience can only find expression in questions that remain without answer: "What is Being? Who is man? . . . What is death?" (ibid., 98); he is also intended when she evokes Hegel's famous assessment, "Philosophy is the world upside down" (ibid., 100).

Such an experience—as well as the questions without cognitive response the experience breeds—is not spurned by Arendt. Questioning arises out of the experience of not-knowing in which she recognizes "one of the basic aspects of the human condition" (ibid., 98) and, in her view, "were man to lose the faculty of asking ultimate questions, he would by the same token lose the faculty of asking answerable questions" (ibid., 99). But there is a significant difference between the questioning type of the philosopher of the Platonic kind and the interrogative questioning of the average person. It resides in the fact that the philosopher decides to dwell in *thaumazein,* whereas the majority of humans, and to be sure also a great number of philosophers, refuse to turn it into their residence although they may know the *pathos.* Now, it is precisely out of this difference that the attraction of the professional thinker for tyranny is borne. First, "since his ultimate experience is one of speechlessness, he has put himself outside of the political realm in which the highest faculty of man is, precisely, speech—*logon echon* is what makes man a *zōon politikon,* a political being" (*ibid.,* 99–100). Second, *thaumazein* affects the philosopher in his singularity "that is, neither in his equality with all others nor in his absolute distinctness" (*ibid.,* 100). In other words, he is the only one in the world "for one fleeting moment confronted with the totality of the universe, as he will be again only at the moment of his death" (*ibid.)*— a transparent allusion to Heidegger and one indicating a situation that alienates the philosopher from the City and the plurality from which the City draws its life, all citizens being peers and different. Moreover,

> since his own experience of speechlessness expresses itself only in the raising of unanswerable questions, he is indeed in one decisive disadvantage the moment he returns to the political realm. He is the only one who does not know, the only one who does not have a distinct and clearly defined *doxa* to compete with other opinions, the truth and untruth of which common sense wants to decide, that is, that sixth sense that we not only all have in common but which fits us into, and thereby makes possible, a common world. *(Ibid.)*

Hence the temptation he encounters of "speaking in terms of nonsense, or to use once more Hegel's phrase—to turn common sense upside down" *(ibid.).* Hence, finally, his propensity—in order to obviate those previous disadvantages and be capable of competing against what to him seems to be the "dogmatism of *doxazein*" (*ibid.,* 101)— to "prolong indefinitely the speechless wonder which is at the beginning and end of philosophy" *(ibid.).* In this fashion, Plato "tried to develop into a way of life (the *bios theōrētikos*) what can be only a fleeting moment, or, to take Plato's own metaphor, the flying spark of fire between two flint stones. In this attempt the philosopher establishes himself, bases his whole existence on that singularity which he experienced when he endured the *pathos* of *thaumazein*" *(ibid.).* And Arendt adds the following terrible commentary, which is the key to the entire affair: "And by this he destroys the plurality of the human condition within himself" (*ibid.,* 101).

Thus some fifteen years ahead of her 1969 text of homage to Heidegger we can clarify those (at first sight mysterious) words upon which she would conclude that later text: "The attraction to the tyrannical can be demonstrated theoretically in many of the great thinkers (Kant is the great exception). And if this tendency is not demonstrable in what they did, that is only because very few of them were prepared to go beyond 'the faculty of wondering at the simple' and to 'accept this wondering as their abode' [she makes here reference to *Vorträge und Aufsätze*, p. 259]" ("Heidegger at Eighty," p. 303). The fact that Heidegger was not named in her 1954 lectures at Notre Dame University is ultimately of little importance. The very terms in the conclusion of the 1969 homage are sufficient to confirm in hindsight that the 1954 text aimed at Heidegger as much as Plato, at the onto-cracy of the former as well as the ideo-cracy of the latter. In addition, it is patent that the transformation into a *bios*, into a constant way of existing, of the philosopher's *thaumazein*—who gets no other light than the one he receives from a frail spark when "confronted with the whole of the universe as he will at the moment of his death"—has its equivalent in Heidegger. We detected earlier that the very project of a fundamental ontology was held in place by the most extreme existential implication of the philosopher. In this implication, at issue is an "authentic and total can-be" whose light comes, as in Plato, from a frail spark, that of the *Augenblick*, the twinkling of an eye for resoluteness, by virtue of which the meaning of the Being of beings in their totality may be brought to light in one's relationship to death. To have established one's whole life on the renewed endurance of *thaumazein*, i.e., day after day, on the frail spark of the moment of vision, this for Arendt justified viewing Heidegger as a "professional thinker" *par excellence*—not the fact that he might have belonged to a corporation of professors or that he alone wrote more pages than all the German idealists combined. It was through this peculiar endurance that he had "destroyed in himself the plurality of the human condition" and, henceforth, was led to tyranny as his "*déformation professionnelle.*" That the homage of 1969 mostly refers to the writings postdating the *Kehre* in order to draw conclusions with respect to this professional deformation, only proves that in Arendt's eyes—as I attempted to show in the preceding chapter—the "turn" had left untouched the dismissal of plurality, in spite of the change affecting the moment of vision of the *Augenblick* now transformed into heeding and enduring the Parmenidean *eon emmenai*.

In light of this analysis, we shall be less surprised to note in Heidegger a glaring absence in dealing with the faculty of judging. The point may be made not only because he happened to characterize his Nazi engagement as *"Dummheit"* (stupidity), which is the very word Kant uses to designate the inaptitude to judge (*Critique of Pure Reason*, B173), but even more so because no sooner did it happen, at rare moments, to this indefatigable reader to hit upon the theme of judgment in philosophical texts than he eschewed it.

This can be sensed during the Marburg years in the treatment Heidegger reserves to *phronēsis*, because, as we saw, he superbly neglects its connection to *doxa*, plurality, event, the good life in the midst of agonistic *philia*, all characteristics present in the analysis of judgment extant in *Nicomachean Ethics*, and because he characterizes that Aristotelian work as an "ontology of *Dasein*." In the Heideggerian reading of Aristotle we would search in vain for the recognition of what anticipates the Kantian theme of the "enlarged mentality"; nor could one expect him to lend any attention to the theme of "the measure of excellence and the good man aimed at by everyone" (*Nicomachean Ethics*, 1176a17). This measure, which is aimed at in the midst of appearances and which Aristotle manifestly directs at the Platonic notion of a single *agathon* itself extracted from the *doxai*, is crystallized by Heidegger—in a very Platonic gesture against Aristotle—into the unique focus for the ontological intelligibility which *Dasein*'s *Umwillen* is, thereby allowing *phronēsis* to metamorphose into a new *sophia*, one that abolishes the faculty of judging for the benefit of *theōria*.

A similar avoidance is also sensible in those rare pages Heidegger ever devoted to *The Critique of Judgment*. But at this juncture it is essential to consider first the axes of Arendt's reading of the third Critique as it is conducted in the 1970 lecture course on Kant's political philosophy, who was as we recall the first philosopher to have directed irony at the "professional thinkers." Inquiring on these axes is merely to attempt answering the question of why, among them, Kant was the "great exception." When she contrasts Kant with Plato and Heidegger, Arendt does not limit herself to noting that, unlike what is the case with them, at no time do we see in him (and likewise in Socrates) any attraction whatsoever for tyranny. One might claim the same in the case of Spinoza, but this would not be sufficient to conclude that he was particularly attracted to plurality. Furthermore, we recall that, merely a few decades ago, a certain French reinterpretation of Marx in the light of Spinoza, was making no secret of favoring tyranny.[5] What should be our thread? In order to unravel the complex situation, Arendt presents us perhaps with a hint in the conclusion of her 1954 text, in which she calls for a *thaumazein* that should take plurality as its aim. We are, therefore I believe, invited to question the link that the thinking activity—not so much in the sense thematized by Kant as in the way he was practicing it and bore witness to its exercise—maintains with plurality. In Heidegger, I just underscored that the thinking activity starts from *thaumazein* and returns to it, so that it moves within its own circle, which is tantamount to saying that the thinking activity is, as Heidegger stressed in his last seminar, tautological. It results from this that the two-in-one, by which this activity is held in place, is merely a provisional medium and is effaced by a seeing that is strictly solitary, in excess of any speech, whether this thought might occur in the "speechlessness" of *Gewissen* and concern the mortal can-be or whether it bears on the withdrawal at the core of *alētheia*, the *Enteignis* in the heart of *Ereignis*. In both cases, this seeing, termed phenomenological not only in *Being and Time* but also in the last seminar, bears on the "inapparent" and is thus extracted from all *doxa*, from the world of appearances offered to a plurality of perspectives, and from every particular event. The two-in-one of thought, in this case, does not lead to its taking upon itself every *doxa* in which it would close itself up. And because this dialogue of thinking aims at a seeing that exceeds every sharing, it is far from being the echo of plurality and never ceases extracting itself from it.

Very different is the activity of thinking in the sense in which Kant aimed at exercising it. As early as the beginning of the 1970s lectures on Kant,[6] Arendt inscribes at the top of her manuscript a reflection of Kant which she insists is key to understanding the first part of the *Critique of Judgment*: "Company is indispensable for the *thinker*" (*Lectures on Kant's Political Philosophy*, 10). She is the one who underscores the word "thinker," thereby signaling that for Kant company is not peripheral to, but rather intrinsic in the thinking activity. This notion is opposed to the *bios theorētikos* of Plato as much as of Aristotle—inasmuch as, in spite of his rejection of the idea of the philosopher-king, Aristotle thought in line with Plato that such a *bios* enables those pursuing it "to enjoy themselves independently, without the help or presence of others" (*ibid.*, 21). Unlike Plato again, Kant expresses no opposition to belonging to the fleshy realm of appearances: the *Critique of Pure Reason* is according to Arendt an "apology of sensibility." Moreover, for Kant, the philosopher clarifies the experiences we all have; he does not claim that the philosopher can leave the Platonic Cave or join in Parmenides' journey to the heavens, nor does he think that he should become a member of a sect. For Kant, the philosopher remains a man like you and me, living among his fellow men, *not* among his fellow philosophers. Second, the task of evaluating life with respect to pleasure and displeasure—which Plato and the others claimed for the philosopher alone, holding that the many are quite satisfied with life as it is—Kant claims to be expected from every ordinary man of good sense who ever reflected on life at all. (*Ibid.*, 28)

In this connection Arendt quotes the Canon of the first Critique:

[In] matters which concern all men without distinction, nature is not guilty of any partial distribution of her gifts, and . . . in regard to the essential ends of human nature the highest philosophy cannot advance further than is possible under the guidance which nature has bestowed even upon the most ordinary understanding [*gemeinsten*]. (B 859)

There is, then, no opposition in Kant between the philosopher and *hoi polloi*, or the "they."

More importantly, what Arendt finds and celebrates in Kant is exactly what she used to find in Socrates, and she underscores the kinship between critical thinking and Socratic maieutic, some reservations being made for the Kantian project of a future system of metaphysics and certain metaphysical fallacies to which Kant on occasion would fall prey. With reference to the preface to the second edition of the *Critique of Pure Reason* she writes: "Kant is not unaware of this connection. He said explicitly that he wished to proceed 'in Socratic fashion' and to silence all objectors 'by the clearest proof of their ignorance'" (*ibid.*, 36). Similar to what happens in the case of Socratic maieutic, critical thought far from being segregated from the public sphere is on the contrary attached to it. Arendt underscores that Kant "believes that the very faculty of thinking depends on its public use; without the 'test of free and open examination' no thinking and no opinion-formation are possible. Reason is not made 'to isolate itself but to get into community with others'" (*ibid.*, 40; quoted from Kant's *Reflexionen zur Anthropologie*, sec. 897). Whereas the Platonic and Heideggerian notion of *bios theōrētikos* leads to destroying plurality, acknowledging it is at the core of the Kantian notion of thinking, as Kant's correspondence with Marcus Hertz shows in vivid fashion. In this correspondence Kant evokes "an impartiality" which is "not above the melee" but consists in considering its judgments "from the point of view of others" or in "so [enlarging] its point of view from a microscopic to a general outlook that it adopts in turn every conceivable standpoint, verifying the observations of each by means of all the others" (*ibid.*, 42). In a sense, *The Critique of Judgment* does nothing more than, in her words, "conceptualize these very personal remarks" and it is inasmuch as plurality resides for Kant at the core of thinking that, according to her, he was led to dealing with this faculty, whose exercise is possible only in the midst of plurality. Now, since plurality is the theme of politics in the Arendtian sense, we understand why she would have looked into the third *Critique* for the lineaments of the political philosophy Kant did not have the time to write. The fact that he did not write it is for Arendt tantamount to an evidence, because Kant's conjectural essays in the philosophy of history concern the human race, not plurality. As for the Kantian writings on right, they deal with institutions whose genesis is in keeping with the activity of *poiēsis*, not *praxis*. Moreover, supposing that he had the time to write it, it would have been impossible for it in the Prussia of Frederick William II to be centered on the link between plurality and action, of which, moreover, he could have no experience whatsoever (see p. 72). But without taking into account this limitation and in light of the adoption of the point of view of the spectator and not that of the actor, the third *Critique* presents us, according to Arendt, with those very features that are essential both to political judgment and to the aesthetic one.

To be sure, aesthetic judgment is treated only in the first part of Kant's book. Yet, well before giving attention to that part, Arendt underscores that the links that unite both parts of the book, although weak ones, "are more closely connected with the political than with anything in the other *Critiques*" (*ibid.*, 13). She dwells on two of those links.

The first one is negative. It resides in the fact that "in neither of the two parts does Kant speak of man as an intelligible or a cognitive being" (*ibid.*). Man as an intelligible being is the theme of the *Critique of Practical Reason* whose question "What must I do?" concerns not only every intelligible being but also "the conduct of the self independently of others" (*ibid.*, 19) in the sense that it makes no reference to the human condition of plurality—all are both similar and different—even though it is implicit in that question that "without other men there would be not much point in conducting myself" (*ibid.*, 20). Man as cognitive being is the theme of the *Critique of Pure Reason*, which answers the question "What can I know?" and shows what I may not know, although I do not escape thinking it, because this is of prime interest to me: God, freedom, the immortality of the soul. In either case, Arendt underscores—and the same thing obtains for the question "What may I hope?"—the fact that "the condition of plurality [is restricted] to a minimum" (*ibid.*, 20) and the notion underlying all three questions "is self-interest, not interest in the world." By contrast, it is indeed an interest in the world and in the plurality found in it that governs the third *Critique*.

The second link between both parts of the third *Critique* is connected with the fact that the faculty of judging concerns particular entities, either this thing or that work we judge beautiful, or this particular product of nature, which, in its particularity, it is impossible to derive from general causes and which, to this extent, may to a certain degree be integrated within the notion of natality. She writes:

> In other words, the topics of the *Critique of Judgment*—the particular, whether a fact of nature or an event in history; the faculty of judgment as the faculty of man's mind to deal with it; sociability of men as the condition of the functioning of this faculty, that is, the insight that men are dependent on their fellow men not only because of their having a body and physical needs but precisely for their mental faculties—these topics [are], all of them, of eminent political significance. (*Ibid.*, 14)

But, in addition to these topics, what then are the specific features of the activity of judging in the sense of the aesthetic reflecting judgment in the first part of the third *Critique*, whose pertinence to the political Arendt notes and by which she probably would have been inspired for the third volume of *The Life of the Mind*?

First, the faculty of reflecting judgment concerns a spectator, who at the outset is among others, "a spectator in the plural" as Arendt says, very different from the one that has given himself over to the *theōria* of the *bios theōrētikos* of Platonic origin, a solitary *theōria*, which Kant adopts on occasion when he considers history in light of the notion of progress (as Hegel would do after him), thereby falling prey to a speculative fallacy, which, nevertheless, he immediately relativizes because he underscores the conjectural character of such speculations. Arendt stresses that this spectator in the plural found in Kant is what establishes the link between genius, which is rare, and taste, in which no one is entirely lacking. Indeed, the task of a creator, if he wants to make communicable to all the *Geist* that inspires his genius, is to discipline it by means of taste, so that "a spectator in the plural," one able to judge, must be awakened in him (secs. 49 and 50 of the *Critique of Judgment*). This is what Arendt transposes to the political and the plural action sustaining it: "Without this critical, judging faculty the doer or maker would be so isolated from the spectator that he would not even be perceived" (*ibid.*, 63). In the same fashion as the originality of creators could not be perceived if they were unable to make themselves understood by means of judgment, likewise the "novelty" of the actors in the political realm depends on the aptitude each one has "of making himself understood by those who are not . . . actors" (*ibid.*).

Second, what Arendt retains, with respect to the political, of the Kantian analytic of aesthetic judgment is the role of the imagination (*ibid.*, 100–104). It is this role that allows Kant to speak of a judgment of taste, although, empirically speaking, taste—unlike the so-called objective senses, such as sight and hearing, which can be talked about with others—is a strictly subjective and idiosyncratic sense. "To everyone his taste" is the maxim of this subjective and radically singularized taste. This maxim is inapplicable, by contrast, to the aesthetic taste in the Kantian sense because this sense metamorphoses entirely the insularity of empirical taste. Similar to the empirical taste, the aesthetic one affects an individual and affects him or her immediately. But the pleasure that affects this individual is by virtue of the imagination "a pleasure of reflection." It is the imagination that allows the individual judging aesthetically—and this is always someone in relation to something specific—to overcome by means of "disinterestedness" his or her own idiosyncrasy and to grant to the object under judgment an "exemplary value," that is to say, a force of appeal to persons other than himself or herself. In the same fashion as, according to the *Critique of Pure Reason*, imagination makes possible cognitive judgment—by producing schemas that prepare the sensible given, which is always strictly *hic et nunc*, for apprehension by the concept, which is always general—similarly, according to the third *Critique*, it is again the imagination that makes aesthetic judgment possible by extracting that of which one judges from its contingency and by making it into an example fit for all. It is not doubtful that in Arendt's eyes this is also the way in which political judgment functions—whether it be that of a committed spectator (the historian for example, whose Greek appellation is *istōr*, the one who judges, inasmuch as this spectator is focused on significant events, not processes, because by nature processes make events insignificant) or whether it be the political actor, who must harbor a spectator to be awakened, if he or she wants to make understood the reaction demanded from his or her point of view by a given situation, because otherwise the action would have no political weight.

Finally, the third feature to attract Arendt's attention in the Kantian analysis of reflecting judgment is "sensus communis," which is treated in sections 39 and 40 of the *Critique of Judgment*. Judging a natural production or a work of art "beautiful" is, according to Kant, discriminating what its representation contains in terms of what is "generally communicable without the mediation of a concept" (sec. 40). The Latin word used by Kant, Arendt insists, aims precisely at distinguishing the apprehension of this communicability—in which the *sensus communis* consists—from the traditional common sense, which is a sixth sense that unifies the individual sources of sensory data and allows each of us to recognize that the object we see is also the one we can touch or cause to resonate. The *sensus communis*, she says, is "the specifically human sense because communication, i.e., speech, depends upon it" (*ibid.*, 70). She quotes in agreement Kant's words:

> Under *sensus communis* we must include the idea of a sense *common to all*, i.e., of a faculty of judgment, which, in its reflection, takes account *(a priori)* of the mode of presentation of all other men in thought, in order, *as it were*, to compare its judgment with the collective reason of humanity. . . . This is done by comparing our judgment with the possible rather than the actual judgments of others, and by putting ourselves in the place of any other man, by abstracting from the limitations which contingently attach to our own judgment. (Sec. 40)

It is, Arendt says, tantamount to the "community sense" (*ibid.*, 75) such that the third *Critique* allows us to "find that sociability is the very essence of men insofar as they are of this world only" (*ibid.*, 74). Which is something that she transposes in the following political terms:

> One judges always as a member of a community, guided by one's community sense, one's *sensus communis*. But in the last analysis, one is a member of a world community by the sheer fact of being human; this is one's "cosmopolitan existence." When one judges and when one acts in political matters, one is supposed to take one's bearings from the idea, not the actuality, of being a world citizen and therefore, also, a *Weltbetrachter*, a world spectator. (*Ibid.*, 75–76)

She also underscores that in Kant "bound up with judgment is our whole soul apparatus" (*ibid.*, 74).

From this assessment it is quite possible to surmise that she would have made this reading of Kant into the center of the last part of her own investigation on "our own soul apparatus" in *The Life of the Mind*, that she would have showed that judging comes at the outcome both of thinking and willing, and that she would have found in it the point of juncture with her inquiry on *vita activa*. At each step, I argued, her inquiry highlights a paradox. It is incumbent upon judgment not at all to solve the paradox—a solution that might amount to nothing but a fallacy—but rather to accept dealing with it in all lucidity.

It is easy to see that the teaching of the third *Critique* may prolong Arendt's phenomenology of active life. When Kant shows that the disinterested pleasure of reflection is distinct from the interested pleasure of mere satisfaction, when he extracts the beautiful from the register of attractiveness and emotions, we are perfectly allowed to translate all this in terms of the *vita activa* and say that, with respect to the first level of active life, an existence entirely absorbed in the cycle of labor to which leisure is the mere counterpart—i.e., an existence whose condition would be only mere biological life—would be unable to pass any judgment. When Kant underscores that the beautiful pleases without concepts and extracts it from the chain of means and ends and when he characterizes it as "finality without end," one may be also justified in translating it with respect to *poiēsis*, the second level of active life, and saying that, similarly, an existence entirely devoted to the utilitarian mentality of *homo faber* or the *banausos* spurned by the Greek city would be unable to pass judgment. Or, more precisely, this mentality would be restricted to those judgments Kant called "determinant," which are limited to applying pre-established models, norms, concepts, which can solve problems, but are inapt for "reflection," or are incapable of welcoming with imagination something unforeseen, whether a really innovative work of art or an unexpected event. As far as the relationship of reflecting judgment to action is concerned, the link is quite patent in Arendt's analysis, as we evoked it.

There still remains the question of the relation of judgment to the two other mental activities. Concerning the relation to thinking, the fact, first, that the 1970 lecture course on Kant superposes Kant and Socrates and also that she notes that in both cases this activity refuses to find satisfaction in the self-sufficiency of pure thinking and finally the fact that she underscores that the thematizing made by Kant of the activity of judging does nothing but conceptualize an experience of thinking animated by plurality—this is all sufficient proof that the thinking activity thus understood is favorable to the activity of judging and that the withdrawal necessary for the first one is nothing but the expectancy of the return of the second to the apparent and common world inhabited by plurality. Concerning the relationship to willing, I shall limit myself to noting that—after her stressing in the second volume of *The Life of the Mind* the apparent impasse with which we are presented when confronting the "abyss" of freedom, because that "bewildering spontaneity" (2: 210) of the will "seems to tell us no more than that we are doomed to be free by virtue of being born, no matter whether we like freedom or abhor its arbitrariness" (2: 217)—Arendt immediately adds that "this impasse, if such it is, cannot be opened or solved except by an appeal to another mental faculty, no less mysterious than the faculty of beginning, the faculty of Judgment" *(ibid.)*. This is a way of saying that there is an abyss only if the will remains enclosed in the circle of its radical singularity and refuses that judgment should open it up toward plurality.

This long detour is perhaps sufficient to cast a fresh look upon the few pages Heidegger devotes in his *Nietzsche* to the *Critique of Judgment*. If it is true, as Arendt claims, that in turning *thaumazein* into one's residence one might be led to dismissing both appearances in their particularity and also plurality, it is safe to surmise that none of the features detected by Arendt in her reading of Kant would find their way into the Heideggerian one. And such is, indeed, the case. In Heidegger's pages no mention at all is made of "the spectator in the plural" or of the constitution by the imagination of examplarity within events, or of *sensus communis*. What is at stake then?

We noted earlier that Arendt had traced in the first volume of Heidegger's book, *Nietzsche,* a surprising amalgamation between Nietzsche's language and that of the existential analytic. The pages on the third *Critique* to which I alluded belong to these lectures and, in essence, bear witness to this amalgamation.

The argument Heidegger develops is simple: When Nietzsche criticizes the Kantian notion of "disinterestedness" as it is developed in the third *Critique*, he does not understand that it is in reality Schopenhauer that is being criticized since Schopenhauer celebrated the Kantian disinterestedness and saw in this suspending of the will a first step toward renouncing the absurdity of willing. But, so goes the argument, allowances being made for this misunderstanding, what Kant says on the beautiful is closely akin to what Nietzsche says and what Heidegger adopts for his own benefit.

From the Kantian analytic of the beautiful Heidegger only retains one notion, which he finds central, that of favor *(Gunst)*. According to him this notion is akin to Nietzschean affirmation *(Bejahung)*, to which he subscribes. The teaching of the analytic may be summarized as follows: "The Beautiful is what we estimate and honor as the model for our essence, for which we grant a 'free favor'—to speak like Kant—from the ground of our essence and for its sake" *(GA, 43: 130–31)*. Consequently the "pleasure of reflection" in the Kantian sense is akin in its tenor to what Nietzsche calls the "thrill" of being in the world and "reaches to a fundamental state of being-human, in which man gains access to the founded fullness of his essence" *(ibid.)*. Or elsewhere: "The beautiful . . . is what determines us, as well as our comportment and our power, inasmuch as we aspire to what is highest in our essence, that is to say, inasmuch as we rise above ourselves" *(ibid., 132)*. In other words, what Heidegger retains from the Kantian analysis of aesthetic judgment is exactly what he calls the "aestheticization of transcendence" as the movement of *Dasein* which exists for the sake of extracting itself from the everyday. Neither the spectator in the plural nor the examplarity of a work or event with respect to *sensus communis* are deemed worthy of any mention. The gesture is analogous to the one that at Marburg metamorphosed the Aristotelian *phronēsis* into *Dasein*'s resoluteness: in both cases it is as if judgment were nonexistent.

The pages I just analyzed date from 1936 before the famous *Kehre*. We may surmise that the works testifying to the *Kehre*—whether it be the first or the second—as well as the works of fundamental ontology never sought any special accommodation for the activity of judging from the usage Heidegger makes of the word *Ereignis*. In German that word means event and designates that upon which the judging activity is called upon to pronounce itself.

In the use Heidegger makes of it, the word does not designate any-thing particular, nothing being, nothing plural, but merely the movement of appropriation that Being is and to which the thinker corresponds. That *Ereignis* thus understood as appropriating event—indicating that Being withdraws from all those ontic ap-pearances to which it gives rise—exceeds every plurality and ulti-mately every sharing of words is something that Heidegger himself suggests when he writes in one of the densest texts on that theme: "What remains to be said? Only this: Appropriation *(Ereignis)* ap-propriates" (*On Time and Being*, trans. Joan Stambaugh (New York: Harper and Row, p. 24). The fact that in the relationship to *Ereignis* thus understood what is at stake is less the dialogue of one with oneself (in which the thinking activity consists) than *thaumazein* (inasmuch as it extracts its speechless sight from every plurality) is something that Heidegger himself suggests when he connects *Ereignis* to what he calls *Eraugnis*, i.e., to a gaze that collects and gathers.

Ereignis, therefore, needs a seeing that corresponds to it inti-mately, just as in *Being and Time* Dasein's ownmost *(eigentlich)* can-be needed the twinkling of the eye, the *Augenblick*. Once more *bios theōrētikos*, or more precisely dwelling in *thaumazein*, leads the speculative thinker to devour worldly events.

About Heidegger Arendt could have said nothing but her bitterness of 1946, then go no further than the human failing, that is to say, judge the event alone, which she did with unsurpassed perspicacity: one would still remain dumbfounded by the fact that in Heidegger so much depth could be associated with such blindness in the face of tyranny, such insensibility in the face of massacres, thereby leav-ing us free to look for an explanation in the prejudices of the social milieu, even in those of his wife, or perhaps for the derisive conso-lation that, after all, other philosophers of the twentieth century were no less blind to totalitarianism—Stalinism, Maoism, Castro-ism, the label is indifferent. But this bitterness is the *Stimmung* that launched her long inquiry into the fallacies of the professional thinkers, starting with Plato, a *Stimmung* that she metamorphosed into irony. She spoke at length and gave her judgment—in terms showing vivaciousness and the everyday, without the concern for erudition and without having the time to read herself again—at-tempting at every step to distinguish between phenomenon and fal-lacy, experience and the "rainbows of concepts," the immemorial and the ridicule. We cannot go about as though she had not spoken.

NOTES

1. Arendt did not like applying the label "existentialism" to *Being and Time,* but inasmuch as her American students always did it, she conceded it.
2. Although Heidegger is not mentioned by Arendt in her essay on "Philosophy and Politics" (that is, her 1954 lectures at Notre Dame University), it seemed obvious to me when I wrote this chapter that there is an implicit overlapping in this essay between Plato and Heidegger. This overlapping is now confirmed explicitly in a letter written by Arendt to Heidegger on 8 May 1954, in which, replying to a question of Heidegger on her own work, she answered that among other topics she was then working on philosophy and politics "in your interpretation" (see E. Ettinger, p. 100). [Note added by the author to the American translation]
3. There is an obvious similarity between the "concentrated biography of the philosopher" and Arendt's Kafka-like picture of "Heidegger the Fox," in her *Denktagebuch* of 1953, in which she depicts Heidegger as a fox who "couldn't even tell the difference between a trap and a nontrap," and who, at some point, "built a trap into his burrow" (see *Essays in Understanding,* p. 361). [Note added by the author to the American translation]
4. See Frank H. W. Edler, "Philosophy, Language and Politics: Heidegger's Attempt to Steal the Language of the Revolution in 1933–1934," in *Social Research,* pp. 197–238.
5. Reference is here made to the work of Louis Althusser. [Note added by the author to the American translation]
6. *Lectures on Kant's Political Philosophy,* ed. Walter Beiner, Chicago: Chicago University Press, 1982.

Time and the Inner Conflicts of the Mind

Arendt certainly owes to the early teaching of Heidegger a peculiar phenomenological method. It combines a historical genealogy of many philosophical notions and a description of their relevance to specific experiences. This method aims at dismantling, or deconstructing, many theses or conceptual structures that belong to the legacy of the history of philosophy and that are often taken for granted because no attention is paid to the specific phenomena to which they correspond. Such a deconstruction, therefore, has two sides: on the one hand, it includes a criticism of many fallacious generalizations or amalgamations; on the other hand, it requires the introduction of many phenomenological distinctions covered over by those fallacies.

The Human Condition is a good example of the way Arendt's deconstructive method proceeds. The topic of the book is "active life." But active life, *vita activa,* is itself a notion coined by philosophers, i.e., individuals themselves not interested in it but primarily in theoretical life. As a result of this shift of interest, philosophers—from Plato onward—have envisioned active life *en bloc* as amounting to a foil for which they show condescension. Consequently, in one way or another they blurred the essential distinctions pertaining to active life, such as the distinction between labor and work and that between work and action. Also they had a continuous tendency to transfer characteristics relevant to one form of activity alone to another form, for example, to transpose to action certain features relevant to work alone.

Since Heidegger himself was often guilty of that transposition, it goes without saying that Arendt's indebtedness to his method of phenomenological deconstruction was in no way scholastic. Nothing in her writing suggests that she was a scholar subjected to an influence. However she owes to Heidegger—in addition to the method I alluded to—a peculiar attention to time as a topic central to her investigations. To be sure, her deep concern for time had nothing to do with the question on Being. But, as Paul Ricoeur points out in his preface to the French translation of *The Human Condition*,[1] there is no doubt that time played a decisive role in her analyses of the various levels of the active life. Indeed, she describes labor as an activity whose particular time is trapped within the *eternal return* of nature, of life in the biological sense of the word. Likewise, she describes the activity of work as a rupture with the temporal cycle of nature. By virtue of this rupture, work makes possible—beyond natural cycles—the emergence of an *enduring* world. The world is composed of artifacts. It has a thingly solidity whose *durability* allows each of the mortal beings who dwell in it to acquire the consistency of a unique identity and of an individual biography, which, as a linear sequence between birth and death, is not absorbed in the eternal return of the same, which is characteristic of the biological realm. But this durability, the full force of which is made manifest in the works of art, itself depends on the ability of the world to welcome in its midst a modality of active life distinct both from labor and work. That modality is action, in the sense of *praxis*, which is conditioned upon plurality or the fact that human beings are all alike, yet all different. At this highest level of active life, time plays once more a decisive role. Whereas the time of labor is defined by the necessity of the eternal return of the same, the time of action is *free* and *unexpected* in its very beginning as well as *unpredictable* in its course and effects. Whereas work considered in temporal terms is conditioned upon the solid durability of a world, action—closely connected with the sharing of words and deeds—is curiously non-tangible and utterly fragile. Unlike the producing activity, it has neither a solid blueprint for its beginning nor a solid product for its result. Moreover, whereas both labor and work are reversible (the former by necessity, the latter in case of failure or flaw in the production), action is by contrast *irreversible*.

As a result of the temporal tensions obtaining between the three basic modalities of the active life, the human condition, envisioned in terms of activity, is intrinsically paradoxical. Arendt's point, I believe, was not to provide a solution to the paradox; quite on the contrary, her purpose was to confront it, to keep it in view, as an insurmountable datum. The first edition of *The Human Condition* contained a subtitle: "A Study of the Central Dilemmas Facing Modern Man." All the so-called solutions to the human condition invented by modernity—the triumph of *homo faber* with Hobbes and the triumph of *homo laborans* with Marx—are doomed sooner or later to face dilemmas, inasmuch precisely as active life is intrinsically paradoxical, while these so-called solutions aim at getting rid of the paradox.

I believe that, in Arendt's view, a similar paradox is also at stake in our mental life. And in this Appendix I would like to pay attention to the temporal factor in *The Life of the Mind* in order to bring out the tensions, or conflicts, which obtain between the faculties under investigation—such as affectivity, common sense, intellect, thought, will, and judgment. But before following her analyses of these topics, let me recall that her entire investigation takes for its foundational principle that we are not merely in the world, but of the world. This means that we belong to a realm of appearances in which "Being and appearing coincide" and where nothing exists in the singular because everything is offered to a plurality of spectators. In short, in continuity with *The Human Condition*, she takes her clue in the fact that "plurality is the law of the earth" (1: 19). However, the paradox at stake in Arendt's investigation emerges as soon as we realize that those whose existence is ruled by this law are also beings whose mental life is invisible. Our condition is such that while on the one hand we belong essentially to appearances, on the other hand we no less essentially withdraw from them.

Let me start with our *psychic life*, the life of our *psychē*. In agreement with Aristotle, Arendt claims that the entire range of our affectivity—with all its passions, feelings, emotions—is intimately linked to somatic experiences, which can no more become part and parcel of the world of appearances than our inner organs. And just as there is "a sameness of our inner organs," there is a "monotonous sameness" in the psychic life of all human beings. To be sure, this sameness vanishes as soon as we express these passions, feelings and emotions in speech. But by doing so we add to them an element of reflection and thought, and even some form of decision, by which we individualize them and turn them into appearances deserving of being displayed among other appearances in a world that is common to a plurality of human beings. Arendt argues as though the life of the *psychē* were strictly the inner counterpart of the metabolism with nature, by which she characterizes labor as a level of active life. In terms of time, there is indeed in both cases an eternal return of the same and a predominance of the evanescence of the present. Precisely because each effect is linked to the intensity of a somatic experience, it is so to speak entirely trapped within the now, to such an extant that it is almost impossible to remember its peculiar intensity. As soon as we recollect it, we transform its specific time, we elaborate it in thought and will, in order to adjust it to a world of appearances ruled by plurality. In short, the psychic life of the soul is *per se* impervious to appearances, to plurality, and to past and future.

By contrast—and here a first conflict and tension come to the fore—the life of our mind, although just as invisible as the life of our soul, is in no way the hidden side of our body. Instead of being narrowly linked to somatic experiences, it is not specifically bound up with any somatic experience. Moreover, instead of being *per se* speechless as the life of the soul, the life of the mind needs expression in speech albeit silently. The mind is alive thanks to this very need. By the same token, it is related to the world of appearances. Its invisibility certainly entails a withdrawal from appearances, but such a withdrawal is not at all a breaking away from them. Indeed, expression in speech, which the mind pursues in order to be active, is a testimony to the bond relating it to the realm of appearances. Not only most of the words in ordinary language refer to the outlooks and aspects of entities appearing in the world, but even our most abstract way of speaking is full of metaphors transposing into the realm of the activity of the mind notions and words originally rooted in the realm of appearances. Originally, an idea is an outlook, a concept is a capture, a metaphor is a displacement, a reason is a ground, and so on. In short, contrasting with the life of the soul, our mental life is *per se* open to appearances, therefore to plurality. Moreover, it is not trapped in the now, as the passions are. As Aristotle says in *Nicomachean Ethics*, the one who sees is always the one who has seen before, the one who understands is always the one who has understood before, the one who speaks is always the one who has spoken before.

There is, then, a tension, or a latent conflict, between life of the soul and mental life in general.

But the conflict I am dealing with is not limited to the overall contrast I just outlined. For the faculties of the mind are in no way related in the same manner to appearances, to plurality, and to time. More precisely, a close description of those faculties envisioned in their specific functioning demonstrates that, in addition to the overall tension between mind and soul, there are many tensions between the faculties of the mind.

Let me start with *perception*. In agreement with Merleau-Ponty and with an Aristotelian tradition Merleau-Ponty was perhaps unaware of, Arendt describes perception in terms of a *sensus communis*, which although it is an inner sense is nonetheless pervaded by an unshakable faith in the realms of the world of appearances (Part

I, 1: 19–65). To put it negatively, the community at stake in this *sensus communis* means that none of our senses taken in isolation can produce a sense of realness, that no sense-datum taken in isolation can produce it either, and even that no sense-object isolated from a context can assure us of any realness whatsoever. To put it positively, *sensus communis*, i.e., the true name for perception, means that our five senses cooperate in our intentional openness to one and the same object. It also means—in addition to this common operation of our senses—that a *context* is what we have in common with other people, that it is a world we share with a plurality of fellows and that guarantees the real identity of the appearing objects. And finally, it means that we repeatedly experience a *consensus*, in the original sense of the word, with others concerning the identity of objects of the world.

As soon as we turn to the faculty of thinking, in order to describe its functioning, we come to realize that everything opposes thought and *sensus communis*. Left to itself, the activity of thinking is far from being pervaded by an unshakable faith in realness and has no trust whatsoever in any reality. For the thinking activity there is no possible criterion between real and unreal. Thinking is doubting, for all those who think—not only for Descartes, Hume, or Wittgenstein. Instead of amounting to the experience of a consensus with one's fellows, it is lived in the singular and always on the verge of solipsism. Instead of sticking to what appears, it is again and again concerned with invisible meanings, which are elusive. Instead of being concerned with truth, it is concerned with meaning. In short, there is an "intramural warfare between thought and common sense" (see sec. 10, 1: 80–92).

What about the temporal factor in this contrast between thought and *sensus communis*? Again, inasmuch as time is concerned, a sharp opposition is unmistakable. Whereas *sensus communis* is experienced as a presence to the present, the activity of thinking is absent-minded in all senses of the word. Absence or nothingness—as all the heroes of that activity (Parmenides, Plato, Hegel, Heidegger) have repeatedly claimed—is the name of its realm.

But before paying closer attention to the peculiar relation of thought to time, let me refine what I stated earlier about perception. Perception, Aristotle said, is the beginning of *science*. It is the primary modality of cognition and with this Arendt agrees. To be sure, the Aristotelian motto, "Save the phenomena," does not apply to modern science in the way it applied to Greek science. In Greek science there was a strong continuity between *aisthēsis* and *epistēmē*. By contrast, the scientific revolution that occurred at the beginning of modernity was set in motion by putting in doubt perception and *sensus communis*. This certainly means, according to Arendt, that the thinking activity played an enormous role in the modern scientific revolution. And it keeps playing a decisive role in all the scientific enterprises of modernity. This does not mean, however, according to Arendt, that the modern sciences break away from the world of appearances as sheer thinking does. In fact, the sciences combine thinking and *sensus communis*. For them thinking is merely a means to an end, i.e., knowledge "which, having being obtained, clearly belongs to the world of appearances" (1: 54). In other words, science withdraws from appearances in order to find new and better approaches to them. "Science in this respect is but an enormously refined prolongation of common-sense reasoning in which sense-illusion are constantly dissipated just as errors are corrected" *(ibid.)*. Moreover, the very notion of a never-ending progress in scientific discovery testifies to a persistent overlapping between thinking and *sensus communis*. On the one hand, it is quite possible, Arendt says, "that it was the relentlessness inherent in sheer thinking whose need can never be assuaged, that, once it had invaded the sciences, gave rise to that notion" (1: 55). On the other hand, the same notion preserves a link with the world of appearances, to which *sensus communis* is related. After all, perception itself, from a strictly phenomenological point of view, is an endless new process of revealing new profiles, adumbrations or *Abschattungen* in the same world of appearances. However, in its hunt for ever-new perspectives, science needed the help of technology. But technology itself, however artificial it may be, is a "world building activity," which again and again "introduces scientific findings into the everyday world of appearances and renders them accessible to common-sense experience" *(ibid.)*.

In short, if we argue in terms of the faculties of the mind as Arendt does, we ought to say that the scientific enterprise requires, in Kant's language, both *Vernunft*, i.e., thinking, as an impulse, and *Verstand*, or intellect, in order to articulate (1) what is given to intuition and (2) what she terms *sensus communis*.

As a result of this description, it turns out that the temporal definition of *sensus communis* in terms of presence to the present has to be qualified. Being present to the present does not mean being trapped in the now. It means, rather—in close kinship with Husserl's notion of the living present—an openness to a constant renewal of the encroachment of given retentions upon potential protentions. Precisely because the world of appearances, to which *sensus communis* is related, is given through perspectives that both announce and hide other perspectives, presence as the temporal domain of *sensus communis* cannot be punctual.

Let me now return to the peculiar relation of thought with time. As I said earlier, the realm of thought is absence. But this again has to be qualified. True, the activity of thinking withdraws from what is present to the senses. It starts by *de-sensing* the particulars given to *sensus communis*. It transforms their visible outlook "into an invisible image" (1: 77), or it remembers them when they are no longer present to the senses. And the mind goes even further, for, in those operations of imagining and recollecting, it prepares itself to deal with things "that are always absent, that cannot be remembered because they were never present to sense experiences" *(ibid.).* In other words, the thinking activity, which always has remembrance as a precondition and therefore emerges as an "afterthought" (1: 78), has the curious ability to dwell in what Arendt calls "some never-never land" (1: 85). The peculiar time of that presence is such that in it the relationships that articulate the time of ordinary experience, above all the distinction between the nearby and the distant, are not only reversed, but even abolished. Arendt writes:

> Since time and space in ordinary experience cannot even be thought of without a continuum that stretches from the nearby into the distant, from the *now* into past or future, from *here* to any point in the compass, left and right, forward and backward, above and below, I could with some justification say that not only distances, but also time and space themselves are abolished in the thinking process. . . . I am rather certain that the *nunc stans,* the "standing now," became the symbol of eternity . . . for medieval philosophy because it was a plausible description of what took place in meditation as well as in contemplation, the two modes of thought known to Christianity. (1: 85–86)

Hence we read introduced, in connection with the activity of thinking, the word contemplation. Those individuals in the Western tradition who decided to devote their existence to the activity of thinking claimed their way of life to be *theōrētikos* or contemplative. They claimed to be themselves the highest possible spectators. But as soon as we pay attention to this contemplative element we are led to confront another conflict between the faculties of the mind. For, prior to the philosophical *theōria* so constantly insisted

upon by Plato, there was another *theōria*, one institutionally celebrated by the City of Athens. The spectacle which prior *theōria* was
concerned with was a very concrete spectacle, either comic or
tragic, staged under the sponsorship of the City in the Greek theater. The spectators of those spectacles were the citizens of Athens.
For them the spectacle was not a matter of thinking, but a matter of
judging. To be sure, as spectators, they were no longer involved in
the ordinary interaction and sharing of words and deeds and, to the
extent of some similarity with the thinker, they underwent a peculiar withdrawal. But their withdrawal did not entail a de-sensing of
particulars. Quite on the contrary, they had to watch the particular
deeds and words of particular characters on the stage. Of course,
they had to do more than merely observe, for at the end of the Dionysian festival, they had to make a decision on the quality of the
plays performed and decide who was the best poet. In order to do so,
although their peculiar withdrawal did not abandon the particulars,
it nevertheless included dealing with invisible meanings such as
beauty, fairness, justice, virtue, and so on. But again, in their way of
dealing with invisible meanings, they did not dwell in any way in
some "never-never land" or in a *"nunc stans,"* which would overcome the relations of distance and proximity that articulate the
time-continuum. Instead of enduring the *"nunc stans"* of thought,
they were merely dwelling for a while in the interval between a
given or present *sensus communis* and a potential or future *sensus
communis* (see sec. 11, 1: 92–98). Obviously, there is no intramural
warfare between judgment and common sense, but since there is
intramural warfare between thinking and common sense, an intramural warfare between thinking and judging remains a persistent
threat. Of this threat the history of philosophy conveys many examples, and I do not simply mean examples of poor judgment in
human affairs—as in Plato and Heidegger—but rather examples of a
tension in the same thinker between two contrasting ways of approaching the same event. For instance, confronting the French
Revolution, Kant, on the one hand, displayed disapproval in connection with a disturbance for thinking, and, on the other hand, displayed also enthusiasm in connection with enacting judgment or
enhancing the activity of judging. What was at stake in his disapproval was the contradiction between any rebellion against the law
and the non-temporal *a priori* demands of practical reason, which
require the rule of law in public matters. What was at stake in
Kant's enthusiasm was the future of human plurality and the correlative future of *sensus communis*.

But this very contrast amounts to an invitation to refine further the description of the temporal features of thought.

I have recalled earlier in this Appendix that the life of the soul is *per se* impervious to appearances, to plurality, and to past and future. It turns out that there is also a tendency to imperviousness in the thinking activity, although it is not at all tied to somatic experiences. Thinking's persistent doubt or *epochē* makes it resistant to appearances. Its peculiar solitude makes it impervious to plurality. Its installation in a *"nunc stans"* makes it impervious to past and future. If this is so, a further question has to be raised with respect to the similarity at stake. As I suggested above, the life of the soul is the inner and invisible counterpart to the metabolism with nature, which Arendt describes in *The Human Condition* under the general title of labor, conceived as a specific modality of active life. As far as time is concerned, I also suggested that the adequate characterization both of the metabolism with nature and of the life of the soul is the eternal return of the same. Hence, the question entailed by the similarity I just evoked is the following: Are we allowed, temporally speaking, to characterize the activity of thinking in terms of the eternal return of the same? It seems to me that the answer is positive. After all, this is the meaning of Arendt's use of the metaphor of Penelope's weaving in order to characterize the activity of thinking. And this is why, contrasting once again the cognitive activity and the thinking activity, Arendt claims that the former has an end outside itself, i.e., truth, whereas the latter is pure *energeia* and has its end in itself. With respect to this pure *energeia*, she insists that

> thinking is out of order because the quest for meaning produces no end result that will survive the activity, that will make sense after the activity has come to its end . . . The only possible metaphor one may conceive of for it is the sensation of being alive. Without the breath of life the human body is a corpse; without thinking the human mind is dead. This in fact is the metaphor Aristotle tried out in the famous seventh chapter of book lambda of his *Metaphysics:* "The activity [*energeia* that has its end in itself] is life." (1: 123)

However, despite the unavoidable metaphor of life, the analogy between the life of the soul and the life of the mind should not be pushed too far. As far as time is concerned, it is one thing to be at the mercy of the present, to be submitted to its *pathos* as the life of the soul is; it is another thing to turn the *nunc stans* into the abode of thought. After all, the only *pathos* of thought is wonder, the

Greek *thaumazein,* and it is a *pathos* that can deliberately be renewed again and again. In the passions of the soul necessity prevails; in the *pathos* of thought, freedom seems to be the rule.

At any rate, it is significant, I believe, that Arendt devoted the concluding section of her study of thinking to a closer examination of the peculiar *now* in which the thinking activity dwells. Part IV of volume one of *The Life of the Mind* starts by dismissing as almost irrelevant the question "Where are we when we think?" because, she says, "by asking for the *topos* of this activity, we are exclusively spatially oriented" (1: 201). But if the question is wrong with respect to space, it is meaningful with respect to time. In the hopes of clarifying "where the thinking ego is located in time and whether its relentless activity can be temporally determined," she turns to one of Kafka's famous parables.

Let me recall the parable, which is entitled "He." It describes a nameless individual who gives battle to two antagonists, the first pressing him from behind and the second blocking the road ahead of him, each one supporting him in fighting against the other. His dream, says Kafka, "is that some time in an unguarded moment . . . he will jump out of the fighting line and be promoted, on account of his experience in fighting, to the position of umpire over his antagonists in their fight with each other" (1: 202). Arendt claims that the parable "describes the time sensation of the thinking ego," a "time sensation which arises when we are not entirely absorbed by the absent non-visibles we are thinking about to begin to direct our attention onto the activity itself" (1: 202–3).

She insists that the "parable does not apply to man in his everyday occupations but only to the thinking ego, to the extent that it has withdrawn from the business of everyday life" (1: 206). Indeed in everyday life, "the three tenses—past, present, future—smoothly follow upon each other" and we shape time into "a continuum" thanks to "the continuity of our business and our activities in the world in which *we continue* what we started yesterday and hope to finish tomorrow" (205). In everyday activity there is neither a "gap" between past and future nor a "clash" between them. The continuity of the appearances to which we belong prevents both the gap and the clash from emerging. By contrast, the very parsimony of Kafka's language in the parable suggests a situation in which the continuous appearances have entirely vanished. And it is because of thought's withdrawal from all appearances that both gap and clash emerge. "The gap between past and future opens only in reflection, whose subject-matter is what is absent—either what has already disappeared or what has not yet appeared. Reflection draws these absent 'regions' into the mind's presence" (1: 206). Likewise, it is only in reflection that a clash opens up between past and future. The reason is that "the activity of thinking can be understood as a fight against time itself" *(ibid.).* In short, it is because the thinking ego, instead of being a self appearing and moving in the world,

> is ageless and nowhere, that past and future can become manifest to
> it as such, emptied as it were, of their concrete content and liberated
> from all spatial categories. What the thinking ego senses as "his"
> dual antagonists are time itself and the constant change it implies . . .
> As such, time is the thinking ego's greatest enemy. (1: 206)

This antagonism between thought and time is what explains the dream alluded to at the end of the Kafka parable, the dream, that is, to jump out of the fighting line and being promoted to the position of umpire, outside the game of life, the dream of a timeless region of thought in which an exclusive concern with meaning would prevail and persist.

It is significant that Arendt wants to go a step further and correct the image of thought given by Kafka's parable. "The trouble with Kafka's metaphor is that by jumping out of the fighting line 'he' jumps out of this world altogether and judges from outside though not necessarily from above" (1: 207). In other words, precisely because there is indeed an antagonism between thought and time, there can be a fallacious tendency in the activity of thinking.

What is right in Kafka's parable is that without "him" and "his" ability to think and search for meanings, "there would be no difference between past and future, but only everlasting change" (1: 208). What is misleading and somewhat fallacious is that it conceives of the region of thought as "situated beyond and above the world and human time" *(ibid.).* Accordingly, Arendt proposes another image: a parallelogram of forces in which both the force of the past against which "he" can fight with the help of the future and the force of the future against which he can fight with the help of the past result in a diagonal force, which is the correct metaphor for the activity of thinking.

The advantage of the new image compared with Kafka's parable is that the thinking individual does not jump

> out of the fighting line to above and beyond the *mêlée.* For although
> this diagonal points to some infinity (the endless search for meaning),

it is limited and enclosed, as it were, by the forces of the past and future and thus protected against the void; it remains bound to, and
rooted in, the present—an entirely human present though it is only
actualized in the thinking process and lasts no longer than this process lasts. (1: 209)

In other words, in keeping with this new image, the gap between
past and future remains tied to the worldly appearances of human
affairs. Somehow, it is—as Arendt says using another image—"the
quiet in the center of the storm, which totally unlike the storm,
still belongs to it" *(ibid.)*. Whatever the image, the point is that, described in this way, the activity of thinking escapes the temptation
of an ultimate contemplation of a higher realm of pure meanings.
Rather, it consists in "assuming the position of 'umpire,' of arbiter
and judge over the manifold, never ending affairs of human existence in the world, never arriving at a final solution to their riddles
but ready for ever-new answers to the questions of what it may be
all about" (1: 209–10). Only in this way can the persisting threat of
an intramural warfare between thinking and judging be avoided, because, according to the corrected image proposed by Arendt, thinking is nothing but a preparation for judging.

We have not reached the end yet.

The entire second volume of *The Life of the Mind* is devoted to
the faculty of *willing*. Let me recall the basic phenomenological
features of this faculty in order to show that they testify to another
intramural warfare in our mental life. The conflict at stake is already pointed to in the very fact that authors who explicitly dealt
with the will were for the most part professional thinkers, who in
principle were primarily interested in thinking. It is a sort of refrain, in the works of those authors, that the will is sheer illusion.
Apart from a few exceptions—such as Augustine, Duns Scotus,
and Kant—it is often taken for granted by philosophers that the
very existence of the faculty of willing should be refuted. According to Arendt's deconstructive method, such a repeated denial of
the will—either for onto-theological or empirical reasons—gives
rise to the suspicion that there is indeed a conflict between the experiences of the thinking ego and those of the willing ego. Arendt's
point in her deconstruction of those philosophical refutations is to
transform the suspicion into a phenomenological demonstration.
Once again the burden of the phenomenological demonstration at
issue is upon the respective relation of both faculties to time. We
have noted that, from the outset, the activity of thinking depends

upon memory as the ability to attend to what is no longer present to the senses. Remembrance of the past is paradigmatic of thought's power to deal with invisibles. By contrast, the activity of willing is at the very outset focused on the future. Accordingly, the activity of willing cannot have as its specific temporal region the enduring present understood as a gap between past and future. Instead, it is lived as a denial of the present. Thanks to its focusing on the future, willing is also experienced as a spontaneous initiative, or in Kant's terminology as the "faculty of spontaneously beginning a series in time," which "occurring in the world can only have a relatively first beginning not in time but in causality" (2: 110). By contrast, there is a tendency in the retrospection characterizing the onset of the activity of thinking to pay tribute to repetitions, or emanations of the past, in short to necessity. Besides, in connection with its dealings with what is no longer present to the senses, the activity of thinking is related to invisible universals, whereas willing is related to particulars. This initiative, this decision, this phenomenon that I want to cause to appear in the world are among particulars. Finally, because the beginning to which the will is geared is contingent—it may or may not occur, and its future is indeterminate—the will is thoroughly restless and disquieted, whereas thought tends to be pervaded by serenity, *Gelassenheit*.

In all respects thinking and willing are at war.

Once again the so-called theoretical solutions to the conflict amount to disloyalty toward both thinking and willing. A good example is given by Hegel's Philosophy of History in which a claim is made to reconcile the retrospective attitude of the bird of Minerva with the restlessness of negativity, or to conflate the eternity of the circle with the linear disquiet of human affairs, in short to identify necessity and freedom. The alleged solution, Arendt claims, turns out to be disloyal both to willing and thinking. It is disloyal to willing because it deprives it of its openness to the future. It is disloyal to thinking because it transforms its specific time region—the gap between past and future—into eternity and its renewed search for meaning into the ultimate truth of absolute knowledge.

But on top of being at war with thought, the will is also at war on two other fronts. It is at war with cognition and it is at war with the life of the soul envisaged in its appetites and desires. Last, but not least, it is at war with itself.

In agreement with Augustine, Arendt insists that the will is a free power of affirming or negating. The will is free between willing and nilling, between *velle* and *nolle*. In order to manifest this freedom Augustine compares the will with the intellect, on the one hand, and appetite and desire, on the other hand. By contrast to the will, the intellect—either the medieval *intellectus* or the Kantian *Verstand*—is thoroughly compelled. As a cognitive faculty, the intellect is related to truth, unlike thought, which is related to meanings. Such a relation to truth is either empirical or logical. In both cases, the intellect is compelled either by factual or phenomenal evidences or by the rules of logical inference. Likewise, the life of the soul, considered in its desires—in the broad sense of appetites, wants, inclinations, attractions, and so forth—is also compelling. As far as the life of the soul is concerned, I am subjected to the desires that occur in me, as it were without me, and persist in me even when it is demonstrated to me that they are wrong and I should get rid of them. By contrast to both the cognitive and the psychic way of being compelled, the will affirms or negates without being compelled at all. Augustine writes: "Either the will is its own cause, or it is not a will." To which Arendt adds the following commentary: "The will is a fact which in its sheer contingent factuality cannot be explained in terms of causality" (2: 89). To that extent, the will is at war both with cognition and with the life of the *psychē*. Once again, time is at stake in those two conflicts. Indeed, as I recalled above, in the life of the soul, i.e., our libidinal life, we are at the mercy of the present, we undergo its *pathos*. The very conflict between the will and desire has obviously much more to do with the intrinsic character of future-orientation of the will. On the other hand, I recalled previously that our primary cognition—perception or *sensus communis*—is characterized by presence to the present. I also brought attention to the fact that the scientific cognition aimed at by the intellect is but a refined version of the *sensus communis*. To that extent, its temporal domain is the present as well. Yet, since scientific cognition requires the cooperation of the intellect along with the activity of thinking—whose precondition is recollection—the life of the intellect is a repeated search for past conditions or causes explaining present occurrences. Like *sensus communis*, the intellect is focused on the present, but it approaches the present in terms of its derivation from the past. The conflict between will and intellect has much to do with the tension between the strictly future-oriented character of the former and the focusing of the latter both upon past and present.

Regarding the inner war of the will with itself, let me quote Arendt's commentary of Augustine's meditations:

> The split occurs in the will itself; the conflict arises neither out of a split between mind and will nor out of a split between flesh and mind . . . It is in the Will's nature to double itself, and in this sense, wherever there is a will, there are already two wills neither of which is entire *[tota]*, and what is present to one of them is then absent from the other. For this reason you always need two antagonistic wills to will at all; . . . *non igitur monstrum partim velle, partim nolle* . . . It is the same willing ego that simultaneously wills and nills. (2: 94)

Far from excluding its opposite, the mental activity of willing is then essentially a controversy through its own counter-will.

The only way to overcome that internal conflict is to act, a conclusion that Duns Scotus drew from Augustine's conception of the will. "In other words, the Will is redeemed by ceasing to will and starting to act, and the cessation cannot originate in an act of the will-not-to-will because it would be another volition" (2: 102). But since action taken as the redemption of the inner war of the will is always a singular appearing in the world—more precisely the appearing of somebody, a singular "who" that is itself a new beginning, an *initium* by virtue of its birth—it can be said that the will, beyond the *liberum arbitrium* between willing and nilling, is the mental organ of the freedom of spontaneous beginning, *qua* individual. This new beginning is what Kant later called "a series in time," which series Arendt views as existence itself, between birth and death. In short, the will, which is itself groundless for it is *causa sui*, is the mental organ for what is abyssal, or miraculous, in human action.

The question I would like to address by way of conclusion is the following: Is there a redemption of all the various conflicts I have evoked so far? Arendt suggests that the only redemption of the inner conflict is praxeological: it is action. It would be an easy temptation, accordingly, to claim that action affords in addition a redemption of the other conflicts I have tried to describe: the conflict between the life of the soul and the life of the mind, the conflict in the mind between perceptual and intellectual cognition on the one hand and the activity of thinking on the other; and the intra-mental conflict between thinking and willing. But the trouble with a praxeological redemption of those three fundamental conflicts is that it may consist in purely and simply overlooking that those conflicts are part and parcel of the human condition. If action simply means "let us stop searching for meanings," or "let us limit our business to truth," or "let us forget that we are sentient beings," the so-called redemption through action would indeed take place at the cost of overlooking the intrinsic paradoxes of the human condition. Hence, the real question is, How is it possible for action to keep a link with the tensions I have mentioned rather than simply pass them over? Obviously, the action at stake is the appearing of an individual "who." Such an appearing is the very action taking place when the individual expresses himself. On the other hand, the tensions I have described are tensions within the mind. Hence, the problem is, Is there in addition to willing an activity of the mind that would be geared both to individual appearances and to expressing itself actively as an appearance—while simultaneously being able to acknowledge the tensions described and overcoming their habitual warfare? Is there, in other words, an activity which could be peacefully at the juncture of the search for meanings inherent in thought, of the relation to truth inherent in the perceptual and intellectual cognition, of the two-in-one of willing, and of the *pathos* inherent in the life of the soul in spite of all the conflicts that obtain between thinking, knowing, willing, and the soul? As a matter of fact, the notion of a peaceful place in the midst of conflict is what Arendt was alluding to when, as I recalled above, she proposed in volume one of *The Life of the Mind* to correct Kafka's parable. Her own metaphor of a parallelogram of forces, or of a quiet eye in the center of the storm, pointed toward the peaceful intersection, which is at stake in the problem I am raising. As I recalled, her metaphors were meant to suggest that only the activity of judging is able to confront fully, rather than overlook, the tension between the withdrawal from appearances required in order to think at all and the persisting insertion of the one who thinks within these appearances. In terms of the problem I am raising here Arendt's metaphors clearly suggest that the activity of judging is an activity of the mind which is geared simultaneously to dealing with individual appearances and to acknowledging the persistence of an intramural warfare in the mind, yet one that does not destroy it. In the context of the first volume of *The Life of the Mind*, the warfare Arendt considered was limited to the tension between thinking and knowing, between the search for meanings and the relatedness to truth, whether perceptual or scientific. But we know that she intended to devote the third volume of the book to the activity of judging. Hence, we may surmise that she intended to approach judgment not only in terms of the conflict between thinking and knowing, but in connection both with thinking and willing, and even in connection with the whole range of tensions I tried to outline. We also know that in her view "not till Kant's *Critique of Judgment* did this faculty become a major topic of a major thinker" (1: 215). Moreover, from her lecture courses on Kant's third *Critique* we know that she intended to draw primarily on Kant's analyses of aesthetic judgment, though without any aestheticism.

Accordingly, the problem I am raising leads to the following question, a conjectural one, of course. Is it the case that Kant's aesthetic judgment dwells peacefully at the intersection of all the tensions obtaining between thinking, knowing, willing, and the affections of the soul? This will be our first question. Moreover, since different and conflictual relations to time characterize these tensions, this question now leads to another one, which has to be phrased in temporal terms, Does reflective judgment in Kant's sense reside indeed at the intersection of the primacy of the past, of the primacy of the present, and of the primacy of the future? This will be our second question.

To the first question it is easy to answer that, indeed, the judgment of taste presupposes the cooperation of all the faculties mentioned. It involves the life of the soul, for the individual appearance or presentation on which it bears is referred to what Kant calls "the subject's feeling of life, under the name feeling of pleasure or displeasure" (see sec. 1 of the *Critique of Judgment*). It involves the cognitive faculties as well, in both their perceptual and intellectual modalities: Indeed, according to Kant, it involves the interplay of imagination—taken as the faculty that unifies the sensory data—and the understanding (see sec. 9 of the *Critique of Judgment*). Does it involve the will? At first sight it seems that it doesn't, if the will is defined in strictly Kantian terms as a faculty of desire compelled by reason. But, on closer inspection, it turns out that some will is in fact involved in Kant's definition of taste in terms of choice *(Wahl),* which, instead of being compelled either by reason or by sensuous inclinations, is a free *favor,* i.e., an approval (see sec. 5). Apart from Kant's systematic definition of the will, his notion of a free favor is close to the Augustinian notion of the will as *causa sui.* And since there is a choice at stake in the approval called "favor," the Augustinian tension between willing and nilling is also implicit here, since it amounts to a choice between approving and disapproving.

What about thinking? Is it also involved in the judgment of taste? The answer is positive. Kant's term for the faculty of thinking is reason. He himself suggests that the requirement for universal assent inherent in the reflective judgment of taste is a demand of reason and a regulative Idea (see sec. 22). Moreover, he underscores that the beautiful thing produced by artistic imagination "makes reason think more than what can be apprehended and made distinct in the presentation" (see sec. 49).

Hence, indeed, the reflective judgment takes place at the intersection of thinking, knowing, willing, and the life of the soul. Can that place be described as a peaceful dwelling in the midst of many tensions? Of course, the answer is again positive. The entire critical project presupposes the acknowledgment of several antinomies which point to basic conflicts—notably between knowing and thinking, between knowing and willing, not to mention between willing and the inclinations of the soul. Moreover, the reflective judgment of taste is itself intrinsically conflictual or dialectical. There is an antinomy at its very principle, and matters of taste are open to contention. But despite these conflicts, such a judgment is characterized by Kant as a "halt," a "beholding," a peaceful "contemplation."

What about our second question, the one about time and temporality? A close examination of the implication of this question would go beyond these concluding remarks. Allow me, then, to limit myself to what I take to be the crucial temporal tensions in Arendt's study of the mind.

The crucial tension pointed out in the first volume of *The Life of the Mind* is the warfare between thinking and knowing. Temporally speaking, thinking starts with retrospection. It is an afterthought. As afterthought, it is related to the past. But its peculiar dealing with absence leads it to oppose time itself and to aim at an abode in a "standing now" impervious to time. By contrast, knowing is adjusted to the present phenomena. When it is retrospective, it searches for the causes of what is presently the case.

On the other hand, the second volume of *The Life of the Mind* insists that by being focused on the future the activity of willing is at war both with thinking and knowing, i.e., either with the retrospective or timeless tendency of thinking or with privileging the present taken for granted by knowing. With regard to the senses of time, it is as though each faculty of the mind were operating in terms of an exclusion of the tenses focused upon by the two other faculties. Now, it is precisely this exclusion that is overcome by the activity of judging. Only in the activity of judging do the three tenses get an equal right. At any rate, it can be argued that such an equality underlies Kant's critique of the reflective judgment of taste.

Such a judgment bears on a present appearance here and now, thereby acknowledging the right of the present. But the acknowledgment takes into consideration as a presupposition a prior *sensus communis,* defined as an inherited way of sharing and inhabiting the world with a plurality of fellows. Hence, such a judgment fully acknowledges the right of the past. However, the consideration for a legacy is in no way compelling, in no way conservative, let alone nostalgic. Indeed, the legacy at stake is without testament. It is not at all a set of established rules to be repeated, applied, and implemented. If the reflective judgment—unlike the determining one—is free approval, its consideration of the past is without servility. The past doesn't function as an example to be imitated, but as inspiration or invitation "to exercise [one's] freedom from the constraint of rules" (see sec. 49 of the *Critique of Judgment*). In other words, it is the past itself that launches an appeal to the invention of the new, i.e., of a future way of inhabiting the world.

NOTES

1. See *Condition de l'homme moderne,* trans. Georges Fradier, Paris: Calmann-Levy, pp. 5–32.

BIBLIOGRAPHY

WORKS BY HANNAH ARENDT
CITED IN THIS BOOK

————, *Between Past and Future*, New York: Penguin Books, 1968.

————, *Eichmann in Jerusalem: A Report on the Banality of Evil*, New York: Penguin Books, 1977.

————, *Essays in Understanding*, ed. Jerome Kohn, New York: Harcourt Brace Jovanovich, 1994.

————, *La condition de l'homme moderne*, French translation of *The Human Condition*, by Georges Fradier, Paris: Calmann Lévy.

————, *Lectures on Kant's Political Philosophy*, ed. Ronald Beiner, Chicago: University of Chicago Press, 1982.

————, *Love and Saint Augustine*, ed. Joanna Vecchiarelli Scott and Judith Chelius Stark, Chicago: University of Chicago Press, 1996.

————, *On Revolution*, New York: Penguin Books, 1962.

————, *Qu'est-ce que la politique?* (*What Is Politics?*), ed. Ursula Ludz, French trans. Sylvie Courtine-Denamy, Paris: Le Seuil, 1995.

————, *The Human Condition*, Chicago: University of Chicago Press, 1958 (referred to throughout as *H.C.*).

————, *The Life of the Mind*, 2 vols., New York: Harcourt Brace Jovanovich, 1978 (referred to throughout as *L.M.*).

————, *The Origins of Totalitarianism*, New York: Harcourt Brace Jovanovich, 1966.

————, "Labor, Work, Action," in *Amor Mundi: Explorations in the Faith and Thought of Hannah Arendt*, ed. James W. Bernauer, Dordrecht: Martinus Nijhoff Publishers, 1987 (referred to as *L.W.A.*).

————, "Martin Heidegger at Eighty," in *Heidegger and Modern Philosophy*, ed. Michael Murray, New Haven: Yale University Press, 1978.

————, "Philosophy and Politics," *Social Research*, Vol. 57, No. 1 (1990): 73–103.

————, "Understanding and Politics," *Partisan Review,* Vol. 20, No. 4, (July-August 1953): 377–392.

————, "What Is *Existenz Philosophy*" *Partisan Review,* Vol. 13, No. 1, (Winter 1946): 34–56.

WORKS OF MARTIN HEIDEGGER
CITED IN THIS BOOK

————, *Gesamtausgabe,* Frankfurt am Main: Vittorio Klostermann, 1976 (referred to as *GA*).

————, *An Introduction to Metaphysics,* trans. Ralph Manheim, New Haven: Yale University Press, 1959.

————, *Being and Time,* trans. John Macquarrie and Edward Robinson, New York: Harper and Row, 1962 (referred to either as *S.Z.* with the pagination of the German text or as *B.T.* with the pagination of the English translation).

————, Correspondence Heidegger Komerell, Paris: Minuit.

————, "Deutsche Literaturzeitung, Heft, 1928 [review of Ernst Cassireri's book on *The Philosophy of the Symbolic Forms,* vol. 2: *Mythical Thought,* trans. Ralph Manheim, New Haven: Yale University Press, 1953].

————, *Holzwege,* Frankfurt am Main: Vittorio Klostermann, 1977.

————, Lecture course on Hölderlin (1934–35).

————, *Nietzsche,* 4 vols., ed. David Farrell Krell, New York: Harper and Row, 1979.

————, *On Time and Being,* trans. Joan Stambaugh, New York: Harper and Row, 1972.

————, "Overcoming of Metaphysics" (see "Überwindung der Metaphysik" in *Vorträge und Aufsätze,* Pfüllingen: Neske, 1954), in *The End of Philosophy,* trans. Joan Stambaugh, New York: Harper and Row, 1973.

————, "Plato's Doctrine of Truth" in *Philosophy in the Twentieth Century,* vol. 3, ed. William Barrett, New York: Random House, 1962.

————, *Platons Sophist: Gesamtausgabe 19,* Frankfurt: Vittorio Klostermann, 1992.

————, Seminar on Parmenides (1942–43), *GA, 54.*

————, *The Basic Problems of Phenomenology,* trans. Albert Hofstadter, Bloomington: Indiana University Press, 1982 (referred to as *B.P.*).

————, *The History of the Concept of Time,* trans. Theodore Kisiel, Bloomington: Indiana University Press, 1985 (referred to as *H.C.T.*).

————, "The Letter on Humanism" in *Basic Writings,* ed. David Farrell Krell, New York: Harper and Row, 1977.

————, *The Metaphysical Foundations of Logic,* trans. Michael Helm, Bloomington: Indiana University Press, 1984 (referred to as *M.F.L.*).

————, "The Origin of the Work of Art" in *Poetry, Language, Thought,* trans. Albert Hofstadter, New York: Harper and Row, 1971.

————, *The Principle of Reason,* trans. Reginald Lilly, Bloomington: Indiana University Press, 1991.

————, *The Question Concerning Technology and Other Essays,* trans. William Lovitt, New York: Harper and Row, 1977.

————, "The Self-Affirmation of the German University" in *Martin Heidegger and National Socialism,* trans. Karsten Harries, New York: Paragon House, 1990.

————, "Vom Wesen der Warheit" (The Essence of Truth) in *Basic Writings,* ed. David Farrell Krell, New York: Harper and Row, 1977.

————, *What Is a Thing?* trans. W. B. Barton, Jr., and Vera Deutsch, New York: University Press of America, 1967.

————, *What Is Called Thinking?,* trans. J. Glenn Gray, New York: Harper and Row, 1972.

OTHER WORKS AND AUTHORS CITED

Adorno, Theodor, *The Jargon of Authenticity,* trans. Knut Tarnnowski and Frederick Will, Evanston: Northwestern University Press, 1973.

Aubenque, Pierre, *La Prudence chez Aristote (Prudence in Aristotle),* Paris: P.U.F., 1963.

Augustine, *De libero arbitrio.*

————, *De Trinitate.*

————, *The City of God.*

————, *The Confessions.*

Burkert, Walter, *Homo necans,* trans. Peter Bing, Berkeley: University of California Press, 1983.

Cassirer, Ernst, *The Philosophy of the Symbolic Forms,* vol. 2: *Mythical Thought,* trans. Ralph Manheim, New Haven: Yale University Press, 1953.

Cicero, *De Republica.*

Dante, *De Monarchia.*

Derrida, Jacques, *La voix et le phénomène* (Paris: P.U.F., 1967); see *Speech and Phenomena,* trans. David B. Allison, Evanston: Northwestern University, 1973.

Edler, Frank H. W., "Philosophy, Language and Politics: Heidegger's Attempt to Steal the Language of the Revolution in 1933–1934," in *Social Research,* pp. 197–238.

Else, Gerald F., *Aristotle's Poetics—The Argument,* Cambridge: Harvard University Press, 1967.

Ettinger, Elzbieta, *Hannah Arendt/Martin Heidegger,* New Haven: Yale University Press, 1995.

Gadamer, H. G., "Erinnerungen an Martin Heideggers Anfange" (Remembrances of Martin Heidegger's beginnings), in *Dilthey Jahrbuch,* 1986–1987.

————, "Heideggers theologische Jugendschrift" in *Dilthey Jahrbuch,* 1988.

Goethe, W. van, Faust, Part I.

Hegel, G. W. F., *Hegel's Philosophy of Right,* trans. T. M. Knox, Oxford: Oxford University Press, 1967.

————, *The Phenomenology of Spirit,* trans. A. V. Miller, Oxford: Oxford University Press, 1977.

Husserl, Edmund, *Ideas: General Introduction to Pure Phenomenology,* trans. W. R. Boyce Gibson, New York: Collier Books, 1967.

————, *The Crisis of European Sciences and Transcendental Phenomenology,* trans. David Carr, Evanston: Northwestern University Press, 1970.

———, *Logical Investigations*, trans. J. N. Findlay, New York: Humanities Press, 1970.

Kant, Immanuel, "Reflexionen zur Anthropologie" in *Kants gesammelte Schriften*, Prussian Academy Edition, 29 vols., Berlin: Reimer und de Gruyter, 1902–83,15:333.

———, *Critique of Judgment*, trans. J. H. Bernard, New York: Hafner Press, 1951.

———, *Critique of Practical Reason*, trans. Lewis White Beck, Indianapolis: Bobbs-Merill Educational Publishing, 1978.

———, *Critique of Pure Reason*, trans. Norman Kemp Smith, New York: St. Martin's Press, 1965.

———, *Project for Perpetual Peace* in "Project for Perpetual Peace and other essays on politics, history, and morals," trans. Ted Humphrey, Indianapolis: Hackett Publishing Company, 1983.

Koyré, Alexandre, "Hegel à Iéna" (Hegel at Jena), in *Etudes d'histoire de la pensée philosophique*, Paris, 1961.

Lucan, *Pharsalis*.

Nietzsche, Friedrich, *The Birth of Tragedy*, trans. Walter Kaufmann, New York: Vintage Books, 1967.

———, *The Gay Science*, trans. Walter Kaufmann, New York: Random House, 1974.

———, *The Use and Abuse of History*, "Second Consideration Out-of-Season," trans. Adrian Collins, Indianapolis: Bobbs Merrill Educational Publishing, 1957.

———, *Thus Spoke Zarathustra*, trans. R. J. Hollingdale, Baltimore: Penguin Books, 1961.

Nussbaum, Martha, *The Fragility of Goodness*, Cambridge: Cambridge University Press, 1986.

Plato, *Collected Dialogues*, ed. Edith Hamilton and Huntington Cairns, Princeton: Princeton University Press, 1982.

Richardson, William J., *Heidegger: Through Phenomenology to Thought*, preface by Martin Heidegger, The Hague: Martinus Nijhoff, 1967.

Ricoeur, Paul, *Soi-même comme un autre*, Paris: Le Seuil, 1990; see *Oneself* as *Another*, trans. Kathleen Blamey, Chicago: University of Chicago Press, 1992.

Sartre, Jean-Paul, *Being and Nothingness*, trans. Hazel E. Barnes, New York: Philosophical Library, 1956.

——, *The Critique of Dialectical Reason*, trans. Alan Sheridan-Smith, New York: New Left Books, Verso, 1991.

Symposium on Hannah Arendt, *Ontologie et politique* (*Ontology and Politics*), Paris: Tierce (Papers given in Paris at the Collège international de philosophie, 14–16 April 1988).

Taminiaux, Jacques, *Heidegger and the Project of Fundamental Ontology*, trans. Michael Gendre, Albany: State University of New York Press, 1991.

——, *Poetics, Speculation and Judgment*, trans. Michael Gendre, Albany: State University of New York Press, 1993.

Young-Bruehl, Elizabeth, *Hannah Arendt: For Love of the World*, New Haven: Yale University Press, 1982.